THE
LOW-CARB
GOURMET

250 Delicious and Satisfying Recipes

KAREN BARNABY

Photographs by Maren Caruso

RODALE

Printed in the United States of America
Rodale Inc. makes every effort to use acid-free ∞, recycled paper ♻.

Photographs by Maren Caruso
Book design by Joanna Williams

Library of Congress Cataloging-in-Publication Data
Barnaby, Karen.
    The low-carb gourmet : 250 delicious and satisfying recipes / Karen Barnaby ;
  photographs by Maren Caruso.
         p.   cm.
  Includes index.
  ISBN 1–57954–990–X hardcover
  1. Low-carbohydrate diet—Recipes.   I. Title.
  RM237.73.B37   2004
  641.5'6383—dc22   2004016025

Distributed to the trade by Holtzbrinck Publishers
2   4   6   8   10   9   7   5   3   1   hardcover

RODALE
WE **INSPIRE** AND **ENABLE** PEOPLE TO IMPROVE
THEIR LIVES AND THE WORLD AROUND THEM

FOR MORE OF OUR PRODUCTS
WWW.**RODALESTORE**.COM
(800) 848-4735

TO MY MOTHER
No longer beside me, but always in my heart

CONTENTS

ACKNOWLEDGMENTS

I would like to give thanks to all of the moderators and members of lowcarb.ca who generously gave me permission to use their creations, writings, and inspiration in this book. Here you are, in alphabetical order:

To Colin, Donald, Doreen, Fern, Judi, Kristine, Lisa N., Lisa P., Michelle, Nat, Norma June, Ruth, and Wa'il. It's hard to remember what life was like before lowcarb.ca.

To Drew, the general manager at the Fish House in Stanley Park for supporting the Low-Carb Dinner Series long enough to make them a success; Daishinpan International, the owners of the Fish House in Stanley Park for *all* their support; Jackie for maintaining the database and for her never-ending low-carb enthusiasm; sous chefs Wayne and Josh for their help with the low-carb dinners at the Fish House; Wanda for low carbing along with me and assisting me in teaching low-carb cooking classes; everyone who has worked at the Fish House since 1999 for tolerating my "eat meat, not wheat!" ranting.

To my always supportive father, who knew that low carbing made sense even in the 1960s; my sister Jennifer for her wonderful shopping trips to clothe my new body and her husband, Jim, who approved of them; and my sister Patty and her daughter Nora for learning to live in the low-carb light.

To the Vancouver and Canadian media for making my low-carb journey public and in turn giving others the courage to follow the same path; Cindy Evetts, Dawn, Paul, and Connie McCalla, Maureen Goulet, and Ro-Anne Johnston for knowing that low-carb cooking classes were a good idea and offering the venues to have them in.

To Steven, Adrian, Richard, and Simone for being great friends with hearty appetites.

To Marlaine for typing all the nutritional information into a database so we could have carb counts at a glance.

And a very special thanks goes to my dogs, Io and Tobias, who happily ate my test runs and were a constant source of distraction and joy.

And to Susan Wels and my agent, Carole Bidnick—huge hugs, kisses, and indebtedness, always.

INTRODUCTION

ALTHOUGH MY LIFELONG PASSION FOR FOOD ULTIMATELY HAS LED to a successful career as a chef, author, and teacher, it was once my greatest handicap. I used to think it was a cruel trick of fate to be able to feed myself so well. I am surrounded by food all day—buckets of chocolate, great desserts, artisan bread, buttermilk mashed potatoes. Imagine being in a place where you can eat whatever you want at any time. Before I started eating low carb, I grazed all day on this stuff plus candy and Coke and ate meals on top of it! I never even gave a second thought to what I was feeding myself. Once I realized the effect my grazing was having on my health, I found that it was hard to keep my hand and head out of the food and change a habit and addiction of years. I wanted to change my eating habits more than anything else. More than eating chocolate, ice cream, or a piece of bread. What I wanted most of all was to be healthy, happy, and free. I was a prisoner of food and it was controlling every aspect of my life.

Early on, when the cravings were overwhelming, I would physically remove myself from the food. I've had wistful times when I realized that there would be certain foods that I could never eat again; I actually went through a period of mourning.

Now when I hear people talk about deprivation, I am puzzled. Not having a roof over your head is deprivation, or not having food or water. Not having a piece of cake is not deprivation—it's a mature choice, and I finally can make that choice.

When I was growing up, my family ate in a way I suppose was normal for the 1960s: three squares a day, no junk food, soda only as a treat with a spaghetti dinner, sitting down

to meals together in the dining room regularly—and never in front of the TV—and dessert only on weekends. My maternal grandmother lived with us and cooked for us during the week and my mother took over on weekends. It was under their expert and affectionate guidance that I started cooking when I was about 9 years old. I have especially fond memories of the grand flurry of cookie baking at Christmastime.

Unfortunately, when puberty hit, I sought solace in sugar, sneaking sweets at every opportunity and stashing them in my pockets, spending my allowance on soda and chocolate bars. I was an overweight preteen plagued by ear infections and allergies.

In 1972, Dr. Atkins released his first edition of *Diet Revolution* and high-protein diets were all the rage. Without a clue about what I was doing—and without even reading the book—I set about restricting my carbohydrates. I'd eat one extremely thin piece of bread, one tiny spoonful of potatoes, and a thin sliver of dessert. It worked! I lost about 30 pounds that summer, just in time for the beginning of high school. I felt energized! I felt great! But it was a short-term diet for me. It never occurred to me that this way of eating could be a lifestyle choice.

I managed to maintain that weight loss into my twenties, passing through a few years of vegetarianism and macrobiotics. But then I discovered alcohol and Italian food. All that pasta, risotto, polenta, and red wine put me back on the road to ruin.

I was about 30 when I finally put a stop to daily wine drinking. To my surprise, I lost no weight. What I didn't realize was that I had replaced my wine habit with a huge sugar habit. For 10 years I got fatter and fatter until I weighed 235 pounds at the age of 40.

So, I jumped on the low-fat bandwagon and ate lots of Scottish oatmeal with skim milk and bowls of brown rice with tuna, vegetables, and lemon juice. The bowls of complex carbohydrates left me banging my head against the wall with insane cravings for dessert, so I ate loads of chocolate sorbet and bananas before falling into bed. After 10 months, I had lost only 10 pounds and my mood had not improved either. Little did I realize that I was eating more carbohydrates than I ever had before.

Miraculously, the answer fell into my hands in the form of the book *Protein Power,* by Drs. Michael Eades and Mary Dan Eades. The book offered me a diet plan I could live with for the rest of my life. It allowed me to eat many of my favorite things and to eat them until I felt satisfied. There have been many benefits along the way: I lost 70 pounds and improved my blood pressure and cholesterol levels.

Of course, I'm brimming with advice and opinions, but I'll just leave you with this: Don't be in such a great hurry to make changes that you can't enjoy yourself on the journey. I'm not advising you to eat high-carb foods—far from it—but I am suggesting that you shouldn't become so rigid that you are paranoid about the food you eat. To me, not eating a tomato or a lobster because it contains carbohydrates is a form of insanity. If you take that approach, the enjoyment of food will continue to elude you.

I can't remember a time when I felt saner, happier, and healthier than I do now. And this book is filled with more than 250 fantastic recipes that will help you feel the same way.

LIVING LOW-CARB

So what is a low-carb diet, and how does it work? The premise of the various published programs is that by controlling or restricting your intake of carbohydrates, you will control the release of insulin. Controlling insulin is the key that helps your body burn fat instead of storing it and that helps control appetite and cravings.

There's a vast difference between low-fat, calorie-restricted diets and low-carbohydrate diets. The standard low-fat, low-calorie weight-loss diet basically starves the body, causing both fat and muscle to be burned for fuel. You do lose weight, but the loss of lean muscle tissue will reduce your metabolic rate, eventually slowing the fat-loss process. With a properly planned low-carb program, your body will burn fat and will preserve the lean muscle. If you exercise, you'll add lean muscle while losing fat, which will increase your metabolic rate and increase the fat-burning effect. Another difference between low-fat and low-carb

WHAT ABOUT CAFFEINE, ALCOHOL, AND WATER?

Some low-carb plans recommend avoiding caffeine because it may trigger the release of insulin, while other plans don't make a comment one way or the other. If you tolerate caffeine-containing beverages and foods without affecting your weight loss, then you might decide to continue to enjoy them. Other people may find it best to avoid caffeine because it stalls their weight loss or they experience effects such as jitters, nervousness, and insomnia. Caffeine is most commonly found in coffee, but it is also present in teas, chocolate, colas, and some other soft drinks, as well as some pain-reliever tablets and cough remedies. Read the label carefully if you're not sure.

Alcohol is generally considered low carb when in the form of unsweetened distilled spirits or dry wine. Moderation is the rule. One problem with drinking is that a few drinks may impair your craving judgment, leading to eating indiscretions and high-carb bingeing. Be aware, and be prepared.

Drinking lots of water is especially important when low carbing to flush out the metabolic wastes and byproducts of all that fat burning. If you're not used to drinking water, you may experience thirst as hunger and will eat solid food rather than drink a glass of water.

It is generally recommended that you drink 64 fluid ounces (1.9 liters) of pure, plain water, plus an additional 8 ounces (240 ml) for every 25 pounds (11.34 kilograms) you want to lose—every single day.

There are many tricks to help you consume your required amount of water. In addition to filtering, you might try adding a slice of fresh lemon or lime. This adds extra flavor with only a trace of carbohydrate. Some people find that drinking water from a plain bottle or sport bottle helps. If you don't like ice cold water, try drinking it room temperature. Conversely, add some ice if you prefer it really cold.

diets is that most low-carbohydrate plans allow you to eat when hungry and to eat as much as you need to ease your hunger.

Most food labels show grams of *total carbohydrates,* then list the various carbohydrate components, including fiber. Because fiber isn't absorbed and doesn't impact glucose or insulin levels, it should be subtracted from the total grams of carbohydrate to find the *effective,* or net, carbs, which will be absorbed and will impact glucose and insulin. This is why

it is good to choose high-fiber carbs, such as green vegetables. You'll be able to have a larger portion and still keep your effective carb intake low.

The nutritional information at the end of each recipe in this book shows the effective carbohydrate count and the grams of protein per serving. The fiber has already been subtracted so you don't have to do it.

Generally, plain meats, poultry, and fish contain no carbs. But watch out for hidden carbs in commercially processed meats. They can have carbs added that you may not suspect—sausages and meat loaves may contain bread crumbs, milk ingredients, and sugars; bacon, ham, pastrami, and other cured meats are made with sugar, corn syrup, or dextrose; and many canned fish products contain sugar or starchy sauces. Always read the label to be sure.

Other sources of carbs that often get overlooked are coffee, plus any cream and sweetener used. These can add up quickly if you drink a lot of coffee throughout the day. Coffee has 0.8 carb grams for a 6-fluid-ounce cup—that's a small cup. Avoid any processed low-fat food. It's almost always high in carbs. Salad dressings and condiments such as mustard can add up, too. Make sure you measure your portions accurately or even on things like vegetables: ½ cup of broccoli is not 2 cups of broccoli. (If you are being truly vigilant, don't forget to count the carbs in those breath mints and in sugar-free gum.) Spices, herbs, and flavoring extracts have carbs, although usually a small amount is used to season a whole recipe; be watchful of things like curry powders and pastes used in larger quantities. Cheese and cream are also often overlooked as a source of carbs.

FAT FACTS

All fats found in fresh whole foods are good, healthy, and sometimes vital. It is wise to include a full spectrum of fats in your diet, which will work hard to keep you healthy and young-looking. This, of course, is not the message we have been getting in the popular media, and because of this we have built up an unhealthy guilt complex and fear of fat.

Certain fats are indeed bad for us, but luckily it is easy to spot them. **Trans fatty acids** have been linked to raising "bad" cholesterol (LDL) and lowering "good" cholesterol (HDL); they are also suspected of being behind that "stubborn fat" that won't leave no matter what we do. They are the result of processing oils through hydrogenation. You can spot the presence of trans fats in a product because hydrogenated fats have to be listed in the ingredient panel of food. By adding up all the fats listed in the panel and then subtracting that number from the total listed, you will come up with the amount of trans fats in the product. However, the easiest thing to do is just avoid anything that has any hydrogenated oil in it.

Rancid fat is the other bad fat—fat that has been mutated by oxygen, heat, moisture, and light. This fat is full of free radicals and can contribute to all the health and aging problems associated with them. At first you might think that it would be easy to avoid this one. Just reading the word "rancid" tends to make our noses wrinkle in disgust; however, we have been conditioned to accept rancid fats. The reason that dollop of butter is salty is to help preserve it and to cover up the rancid taste. Yes, butter is good for us, but rancid butter is not. That flax oil in the refrigerator is liquid gold to some, but if it is rancid, it is worse than useless. We have to retrain our noses and taste buds to discern fresh good fats from rancid bad ones. This is one reason for using unsalted rather than salted butter.

This retraining can be done by finding stores that sell their stock quickly, store their products properly, and rotate their stock on the shelf so that no old products linger there. Also check the expiration dates on products to help you find the freshest product.

Remember that the best fats come from fresh whole foods, so try making your own butter from some fresh, pure whipping cream. Add a bit of salt to taste, if you prefer it salty, and memorize the taste to compare with commercially prepared butter. If that is a bit too much work, just find the freshest frozen unsalted butter you can, and taste that. When dealing with vegetable oils, try grinding the seeds up and then smelling the fresh aroma. Again, if this is too much of a bother, just get a good smell of the oil when you first open

the bottle or tin and memorize that fresh scent. As soon as you notice that the smell is off, get rid of it.

BEGINNING THE LIFESTYLE CHANGE

A life without all the bread or pasta you've been used to eating may seem daunting at first. But low carbing is an almost hedonistic way to eat. As low-carb eating becomes a way of life and you start feeling great, you'll wonder how you ever ate the way you did before. An important thing to remember is that it's not all about losing weight. Low carbing is also about regaining health and, for some people, their sanity.

You may want to look at what's coming up on your social calendar before you start changing your eating habits. If there are many birthdays, weddings, and other celebratory occasions, it may not be the best time to start. It's really important that you get a good few weeks of strict low carbing under your belt to know what it feels like. But if you like challenges and have great willpower, you may find that you can breeze through these events without any problem.

The first few weeks of low carbing can be an odd, confusing time. We've been so used to relying on carbohydrates to fill our plates and stomachs that it takes a while to switch that train of thought. It also takes our bodies a while to get comfortable with the process. We experience lethargy, headaches, and other symptoms as our bodies switch to using fat—our own fat.

In the long run, indulging a few times a year will not cause harm, but take heed! I have sadly seen too many people go back to bad carb eating after indulging on big holidays such as Thanksgiving, continue on to Christmas, and then wonder what happened come the end of January. For some people—myself included—carbohydrate consumption is an addiction and one bite can set you off on a downward spiral. The key is in knowing yourself and your limits.

With your new low-carb way of life, you will have many opportunities to make small

changes that will turn into daily habits. These habits will become part of your way of life and ensure you future success.

I know that many people use programs to calculate their nutritional intake for the day so there is a table on page 313, where all the recipes are sorted in their categories from the lowest to the highest carbohydrate counts so based on your personal, daily, carbohydrate level, you can easily see at a glance which recipes are the most suitable for you.

Label reading is a very important part of low carbing. It's shocking to find out that you have been indulging in foods that you believe to be zero carbohydrates when they actually contain more.

In the United States, but not in Canada, Australia, the European Union, and Great Britain, items that are less than 1 gram of carbohydrates per serving can be listed as 0 carbs. But if you're counting carbs and use more than one serving, the carbs add up. A serving of fluid whipping cream is usually listed as 1 Tbsp. (15 ml). If you only use that amount per day, it's fine. But if you use more, it adds up.

Remember that the only foods that do not contain carbohydrates are muscle proteins and pure fats.

LOW-CARB SHOPPING IN A GOURMET FOOD STORE . . .

Gourmet food stores offer lots of possibilities. Some deal with only groceries and dry goods, and others have meats, cheese, produce, cookware, and all sorts of other goodies. Let's start with the basics:

Salt and pepper. I use sea salt and a good-quality peppercorn in my peppermill. Sea salt is much milder and less caustic than the regular supermarket salt. It also contains trace minerals. I'm a bit of a salt hound and look for it wherever I travel.

Gourmet stores carry a variety of sea salts, kosher salt, and flavored salts. One of my

favorites for sprinkling on cooked food is Maldon Salt from Great Britain, which has beautifully crunchy flakes.

There may also be a few varieties of whole peppercorns to fill your grinder. Tellicherry and Malabar are two of the most common, and both are complex in flavor, more so than any ground black pepper available. Interestingly, they both come from the same plant. The peppercorns that form toward the tip of the vine get bigger and ripen first, turning a reddish color; those are called Tellicherry. The Malabar are peppercorns closer to where the stem joins the vine. They ripen less, are smaller, and remain green.

Mustard. Mustard is a great way to add oomph to your cooking in salad dressings, sauces, and marinades. There are Dijon and whole-grain mustards as well as flavored ones like tarragon, horseradish, green peppercorn, garlic, dill, and wasabi lime.

Nuts and seeds. The store I frequent has a great selection of very fresh nuts and seeds: macadamias, almonds—whole, sliced, and ground—walnuts, pecans, hazelnuts, and sesame, sunflower, and pumpkin seeds. Don't forget unsweetened coconut—it's a nut too!

Oils. Now on to my favorite area, the olive oil selection! Varietals, flavored oils, and extra-virgin.

Many stores will have bottles open for tasting. One of the flavored oils that I think is great in mayonnaise is lemon-flavored olive oil—replace one-quarter of the oil in the recipe with an equal amount of lemon-flavored oil. It's also wonderful drizzled on roasted chicken or added to salad dressings. Don't use these flavored oils for cooking with heat or their wonderful fragrance will be lost.

There will be an overwhelming variety of oils infused with herbs, garlic, and chiles. These are great for adding the final touch to food, from soup to nuts!

Nut oils can add a delicious accent to salads and vegetables. The most common are walnut, hazelnut, pumpkin seed, and almond. I've also used roasted peanut and avocado oil. These should be combined with a less robust oil and not used full strength or for salad dressings. They really shine as flavorings.

One of the things I enjoy with fresh berries is a few drops of nut oil and a few drops of aged balsamic vinegar. The next time you're cooking green beans, asparagus, or broccoli, try drizzling them with nut oil and then sprinkling on finely chopped nuts that match the oil. A little Parmesan cheese doesn't hurt either!

Olives. If you're an olive lover, you'll find many varietals as well as olives that are deliciously spiced. I love the green olives stuffed with anchovy and the ones stuffed with almonds.

Peppers. If you like roasted red peppers and don't want to go to the trouble of roasting and peeling them yourself, there are different brands packed in either liquid or olive oil. I'm partial to the oil-packed variety.

Pickles and artichokes. If you like pickles, you'll find many that are not cucumbers! Asparagus, beans, onions, and mixed pickles are very good with cold cuts and cold meats. I was never a fan of canned artichoke hearts until I found them packed in olive oil. Besides using them in salads or as a dip, you'll find they are great for pizza toppings or enclosed in a wrapping of prosciutto or salami.

Preserved lemons. Along the Middle Eastern vein are preserved lemons, which give indescribable flavor to stews, casseroles, and salads (see Roasted Red Pepper and Preserved Lemon Salad on page 79). To use, discard the pulp and chop the peel.

Sauces. These stores will carry a large variety of hot sauces, wing sauces, and salsas. Check the label for sugar content before you buy.

Spices. You can also find good spice mixtures. Some of the outstanding ones are ras al hanout (a robust Moroccan blend that can contain dozens of different spices) and dukkah (a combination of spices, seeds, and nuts). Dukkah is wonderful sprinkled on salads or meats. The way it's traditionally used is as a dip for bread with olive oil, but we can circumvent the bread and use vegetables as a dipping medium. Another great spice that has been available for a few years is smoked paprika from Spain. It adds a wonderfully smoky aroma to meats, soups, and stews when judiciously used.

Vinegars. You will find a great selection of vinegar in the same area as the oils. I like to keep several ages of balsamic vinegar around. The youngest I use in cooking, the middle-aged are for salads, and the oldest are respectfully used by the drop. Besides balsamic, there are sherry vinegar and vinegars made from wine varietals like Zinfandel, Champagne, and Cabernet Sauvignon, as well as plain red and white wine vinegar. Good-quality vinegar does make a difference. As with oils, there are many infused vinegars to choose from.

To make a dressing with lots of depth, try using a blend of different oils and vinegars.

AND IN A JAPANESE FOOD STORE . . .

Japanese food is simple and brilliant at the same time. It incorporates ingredients that are high in essential minerals, fatty acids, and antioxidants. If you're fortunate enough to have a good Japanese grocery where you live, here are some of the things to look for.

Fish. I find the fresh and frozen fish to be of excellent quality. You're also likely to find tuna, cooked octopus, salmon, mackerel, flying fish roe, sea urchin roe, sablefish, sardines, and sashimi sliced and ready to go. All you have to do is take it home and eat it!

Meat. Most of the meats are sliced very thin for hot-pot cooking. Short ribs, rib eye, pork loin, and fresh bacon are good to use for quick stir-fries.

Quail eggs. They're just the thing for when you just need a tiny bit of egg! They're good hard-cooked as an appetizer and served with mayonnaise that has been mixed with wasabi.

Vegetables. There's a dazzling array. Some of the highlights are:

➭ Daikon radish is an all-purpose low-carb vegetable. See more about daikon radish on page 117.

•ᢒ Edamame, the green soybeans in the pod, are great for nibbling. See the recipes on pages 38 to 39.

•ᢒ Enoki mushrooms with tiny caps and thin stems are good raw and thrown into clear soups at the last minute.

•ᢒ Fresh shiitake mushrooms are lighter in flavor and texture than their dried counterparts and are good used in stir-fries, mushroom soup, and sauces.

•ᢒ Japanese cucumbers are small, slender, and virtually seedless. One of them is a nice serving for one.

•ᢒ Japanese eggplants, which are smaller than their Italian cousins, are usually less bitter and creamier. They can be used in any eggplant recipe. They're good grilled whole, peeled, and served with a dash of soy sauce and lemon.

•ᢒ Japanese leeks can be used wherever you would use regular leeks.

•ᢒ Kim chee comes in many different varieties. The most common is very spicy pickled Napa cabbage that is great as a condiment. It's good in stir-fries and Asian soups or with cured meats like corned beef and pastrami. Try it in a breadless Reuben. Be sure to check the label for sugar.

•ᢒ Miso comes light, dark, and in between. Besides its most common use as soup, miso makes a great marinade for oily fish such as mackerel and salmon as well as for beef steaks, pork steaks, and duck breast.

•ᢒ Napa cabbage, also known as Chinese cabbage, is great in stir-fries, soups, and salads. The leaves provide the "mane" around Lion's Head (page 217) and make good "sandwich" greens.

•ᢒ Traditional farmhouse pickles, both daikon and Napa cabbage, are fermented in rice bran and salt. Rinse before using to remove some of the salt.

•ᢒ Green tea has so many types that I find constantly fascinating. Gyokuro is one of my favorites, but then so is the lowly Bancha. I drink a variety and have an assortment available so I can alternate.

When I was a budding cook, barely out of my teens, I would frequently find myself in one of the few Chinese food stores in my city, poring over the dry goods. None of the stores carried fresh products, save for a few pieces of tofu floating around in plastic tubs. I would pick up the packages and wonder what the heck you would do with these items. Since then, I've happily and gratefully found out.

Besides being a treasure trove of low-carb vegetables and meats, Chinese grocery stores can be one of the least expensive places to shop.

Vegetables. Starting off in the vegetable section, you'll find typical Chinese vegetables—gai lan (Chinese kale), sui choy (Chinese cabbage), bok choy, water spinach, mustard—and others that may be new to you, like pea sprouts or tips, daikon radish, fresh water chestnuts, and unusual types of squash. These range from the zucchini-shaped fuzzy or hairy melon to the giant winter melon—so called because its exterior resembles snow. Many of these stores also carry ingredients for Thai and Vietnamese cooking: lemongrass, galingale root, Thai basil, and kaffir lime leaves being the most common.

One seasoning vegetable that's worth noting is the pungent Chinese chive, which makes a great addition to stir-fries. There are two types: light yellow, which are mild, and darker green. The chives are especially good with pork.

There are two types of sprouts, too—soy and mung bean. The soy are larger, sturdier, and chewier than the mung bean.

You will find an excellent selection of tofu and soy products, including soy milk, tofu skin, noodles, and fermented tofu products. If you like very traditional Chinese ingredients, there are different sorts of pickled cabbage, pickled mustard greens, pickled turnip, dried shrimp, and dried meats.

Condiments. Of course, there's an amazingly extensive array of soy sauces, chili pastes, hot sauces, and vinegars. A delicious vinegar is the complex and earthy black vinegar that's

great mixed with soy sauce and chili paste as a dipping sauce. There's also the lighter red vinegar that's good when combined with julienned threads of ginger.

Toasted sesame oil and chili-infused oil are two ways to add flavor with a minimum of fuss. Mayonnaise mixed with sesame oil and toasted sesame seeds is a great dip for cooked asparagus or broccoli.

Meat. In the meat section, you'll find a large selection of pork cuts. I must confess that I am a pork-belly lover. Roasted, braised, Chinese, or French-style, I can't get enough of its succulent texture.

There's more than pork, though. Beef, chicken—a great place to get wings—lamb for Mongolian hot pot, and sometimes even goat meat.

Fish. The fish section can be a most interesting place, with tanks of live crab, lobster, fish, prawns, and sometimes even turtles and frogs. It's a good place to get squid, clams, mussels, and oysters as well as fresh seasonal specialties like salmon and halibut. (Salmon is in season from May to October; halibut, from March to October.) Depending on what side of the continent you live on, there will be a trend toward fish from either the Atlantic Ocean or the Pacific Ocean. See page 146 for Basic Steamed Fish, a recipe that works with many types of fish.

There are many interesting types of canned fish. One that I've enjoyed is canned mackerel fillets with ginger that goes along nicely with a few drops of red vinegar and sesame oil.

To make your Chinese meal complete, check out the selection of tableware. Chopsticks, bowls, plates, ceramic spoons, steamers—you're sure to find something you can't live without.

AND IN THE ITALIAN DELI

Some Italian delis have fresh meat that's generally of a good quality. Try big steaks—bistecca alla Fiorentina—to grill and serve with olive oil, coarse sea salt, and a squeeze of lemon. High-quality veal for roasts and stews and fresh lamb are usually available to grace your table.

You haven't had a really good anchovy until you've had a good-quality, salt-cured one. Soak them in cold water for a few minutes to remove some of the salt and then strip the fillets from the bones. More Italian delights include the following.

Antipasto. This is usually a combination—such as cauliflower, celery, olives, and tuna—in a tomato base, but there are some available without tuna.

Artichoke hearts in olive oil or water

Balsamic pickled onions. Crunchy and slightly sweet, these are great with cold cuts.

Balsamic vinegar. As with olive oil, tomes have been written on balsamic vinegar. Modena is the home of traditional balsamic vinegar, and those from the region produced in the traditional manner have the CABM (Consortium for the Protection of Balsamic Vinegar of Modena) seal on the bottle. Balsamic vinegars can range in age up to 100 years old. Because the vinegar is aged in barrels, as it gets older, the flavor intensifies and becomes more complex, like a good wine. Some aficionados drink a small, neat glass of it, like an aperitif.

Canned Italian plum tomatoes. Use them for sauces and stews. They're much better than the domestic variety of canned tomatoes because of their taste, texture, and yield.

Dried porcini ("little pigs" in Italian) mushrooms. These delicious mushrooms need to be soaked in a scant amount of hot water before using. The soaking liquid is incorporated into the dish you are making to provide more intense flavor.

Eggplant in olive oil comes in either slices or strips and can be spicy or mild.

Hard and soft cheeses—like Parmigiano-Reggiano, Grana Padano, Pecorino Romano, Pepato, and Crotonese—are good for grating and sprinkling and add a real punch to your food. Many delis have a grater for these types of cheese that turns them into a fine powder and saves you the work.

For melting, there's full-fat mozzarella, fontina, Friulano, and young Asiago. All of these cheeses are lovely in casseroles and on pizza. Try fontina or Friulano on your next Meat-

Lover's Pizza (page 202) or Donald's Deep-Dish Pizza Quiche (page 213). They're so deliciously creamy. Full-fat mozzarella has better melting qualities than its leaner cousin.

In the soft, unripened cheeses, try the following:

◦§ **Bocconcini,** which means "little mouthful," became very popular as part of the salad Insalata Caprese—bocconcini with sliced ripe tomato, fresh basil, and extra-virgin olive oil. Its tiny shape makes it ideal for either wrapping with prosciutto or broiled eggplant, smearing with pesto, or marinating in herbs, garlic, and olive oil. (Or you can go all out and treat the bocconcini with all three!)

◦§ **Mozzarella di bufala,** made from water buffalo milk, takes over where bocconcini leaves off. It's milky, creamy, and subtle in the best of ways. I've occasionally—although I blush to tell—eaten a whole one as a lunch on the run. It's pricey, but if you like bocconcini, you'll love this.

◦§ **Mascarpone** is primarily used for desserts like Tiramisu (page 294) and can be used as a pan sauce, added to the frying pan for the last minutes of cooking something like chicken breasts. It's wonderful on fresh berries.

◦§ **Ricotta** is slightly grainy but smoother than cottage cheese. It's white, moist, and slightly sweet. Most Italian ricottas are made from the whey drained off while making cheeses such as mozzarella and provolone.

Italian cold cuts are distinct and delicious. If you like deli meats, it's worth your while to buy small amounts to see what you like. Check for sugars and starches before you buy.

There are many different types of salami, and good ones for snacking are the dried varieties that provide a satisfying chew. One of my favorites is Genoa salami—a delicious, garlicky salami that is great with a bit of cheese. Try it in Antipasto Skewers (page 33). Prosciutto and pancetta are great to use as a "seasoning," in the same way that you would

use bacon. Some delis have the shank end of prosciutto, unsliced and available at a bargain. This is what I use for dicing and adding to salads, sauces, and stews.

Italian olive oil-packed tuna, sardines, mackerel, and octopus. These are the ultimate in canned seafood. Some brands of tuna come in small tins and are perfect for a snack. I always have a few tins in my glove compartment.

Olivada. The Italian equivalent of tapenade is made from either black or green olives. It's lovely mixed with butter or olive oil and spread on grilled meaty fish such as swordfish, marlin, or tuna.

Peperonata. These rings of spicy peppers are great on pizza or with cold cuts.

Pesto. It's available in different flavors. You will usually find sun-dried tomato, olive, cilantro, and the classic basil. Pesto can also be found in tubes as well as fresh in the cold case. The tubes are good to have in your fridge when you need a little perk for a salad dressing or sauce. Also in tubes are various seasoning pastes such as porcini, sun-dried tomato, and basil.

Sugar-free syrups. Use them for coffee, Italian sodas, or baking. To make an Italian soda, pour a small amount of syrup over ice in a tall glass. Add soda water and then gently pour whipping cream on top. Stir or not, as you prefer.

Tomato sauce. There are many different varieties to choose from. The spicy arrabbiata, woodsy porcini, and the classic tomato and basil are but a few. You can often find smaller jars that are great to use in a single dish with no leftovers.

White asparagus. Try rolling it in prosciutto or salami or adding it to a salad. It's also delicious browned in butter, drizzled with a little balsamic vinegar, and sprinkled with coarse salt.

WHAT'S FOR BREAKFAST?

ONE OF THE QUESTIONS I HEAR MOST OFTEN IS: "WHAT CAN I EAT FOR BREAKFAST? I'M SICK OF EGGS AND BACON!"

I would like to see the commandment that says, "Thou shalt have eggs and pork products for breakfast!" You know, you can eat *anything* for breakfast, because it's just another meal. I would go a little crazy eating just bacon and eggs, too, so I don't. I like leftovers. *You* are allowed to eat anything you want for breakfast.

When you're pressed for time—or even when you're not—it's good to have a few breakfast tricks up your sleeve. Think outside of that breakfast box!

Can of tuna or salmon with mayonnaise

Gra(no)la (page 11)

Ham wrapped around a slice of cheese

Hard-cooked eggs or egg salad

Egg and Sausage Muffins (page 14)

Donald's Deep-Dish Pizza Quiche (page 213)

Meat-Lover's Pizza (pages 202 to 203)

Turkey Snackin' Cake (page 190)

Leftovers, leftovers, leftovers . . .

ALMOND PUFF PANCAKES

Makes 8 pancakes

These are really good and have passed in my cooking classes with flying colors! Some people like to use sugar-free syrup on theirs, but I like mine with melted butter, sweetener, and cinnamon.

This recipe calls for almond meal. In various recipes, you'll see it called almond flour or ground almonds. They're all the same thing: finely ground almonds!

When cooking these pancakes, don't fiddle around with them before ready to turn or they will break! Give them about 3 minutes to brown the first side before you attempt to turn them.

2		large eggs, separated
¼ cup	(60 ml)	whipping cream
¼ tsp.	(1.2 ml)	*each* Splenda and Canadian Sugar Twin or 1 tsp. (5 ml) Splenda
		Pinch of sea salt
½ cup	(120 ml)	almond meal (finely ground almonds)
¼ tsp.	(1.2 ml)	baking powder
1 tsp.	(5 ml)	unsalted butter

◆§ In a large bowl, mix the egg yolks, cream, sweetener, and salt until smooth. In a small bowl, whisk the almond meal and baking powder together; whisk into the yolk mixture until smooth.

◆§ Place the egg whites in a medium bowl and beat with an electric mixer until soft peaks form. Stir one-quarter of the whites into the yolk mixture to loosen it up and then fold in the remaining whites.

◆§ Heat a seasoned griddle or large heavy frying pan over medium heat. Add the butter and, when it melts, wipe it out of the pan. Form pancakes using a level ¼ cup (60 ml) of the batter for each pancake. Cook for about 3 minutes, or until lightly browned, and then gently turn over and cook for 2 minutes on the other side.

Per pancake. Effective carbohydrates: 0.9 g; Carbohydrates: 1.6 g; Fiber: 0.7 g; Protein: 2.9 g; Fat: 0.9 g; Calories: 84
Made with Splenda only: Add 0.15 g carbohydrates

UPSIDE-DOWN GOAT CHEESE SOUFFLÉ

Makes 2 servings

Here's a great way to use leftover whites if you make your own mayonnaise (you'll need the whites from 4 or 5 eggs)—or you can use the egg whites that come in a carton. A cheese of your choice can be used instead of goat cheese. For best results, use a frying pan that's about 9 inches (22.5 cm) in diameter.

½ cup	(120 ml)	egg whites
		Sea salt and freshly ground black pepper
3 Tbsp.	(45 ml)	unsalted butter
½ cup	(120 ml)	thinly sliced mushrooms
½		medium tomato, thinly sliced
½ cup	(120 ml)	crumbled fresh goat cheese

◆ Preheat the oven to 400°F (200°C).

◆ Place the egg whites in a medium bowl and season with salt and pepper. Beat with an electric mixer until soft peaks form. Melt the butter in a large ovenproof frying pan (preferably nonstick) over high heat. Add the mushrooms, season lightly with salt and pepper, and cook for about 5 minutes, or until the mushrooms become soft but not brown. Arrange the tomato slices over the mushrooms.

◆ Quickly fold the cheese into the beaten egg whites and spread evenly over the mushroom mixture.

◆ Transfer the pan to the oven and bake for 8 minutes, or until golden on top. Remove from the oven and run a heatproof rubber spatula around the sides to loosen. Flip over onto a plate and serve.

Per serving. Effective carbohydrates: 6.8 g; Carbohydrates: 5.9 g; Fiber: 0.9 g; Protein: 18.8 g; Fat: 32.1 g; Calories: 387

CHEESECAKE PANCAKES

Makes 8 pancakes

Serve with fresh strawberries and you will have something very similar in taste to a cheese blintz.

4		large eggs, separated
8 oz.	(227 g)	cream cheese, at room temperature
1½ tsp.	(7.5 ml)	*each* Splenda and Canadian Sugar Twin or 2 Tbsp. (30 ml) Splenda
½ tsp.	(2.5 ml)	ground cinnamon
		Pinch of salt
2 Tbsp.	(30 ml)	flaxseed meal
		Unsalted butter

➳ Place the egg whites in a medium bowl and beat with an electric mixer until stiff peaks form.

➳ Place the cream cheese in a large bowl and beat with the mixer until smooth. Beat in the egg yolks and then the sweetener, cinnamon, salt, and flaxseed meal. Fold in the egg whites.

➳ Heat a seasoned griddle or large heavy frying pan over medium-low heat. Grease lightly with the butter. Form pancakes using a scant ¼ cup (60 ml) of the batter for each pancake. Cook until golden brown, about 2 to 3 minutes on each side.

Per pancake. Effective carbohydrates: 1.5 g; Carbohydrates: 2.1 g; Fiber: 0.6 g; Protein: 5.5 g; Fat: 13.3 g; Calories: 149
Made with Splenda only: Add 0.4 g carbohydrates

NAT'S COTTAGE CAKES

Makes 6 cakes

Nat (an early member of lowcarber.org) says of her cakes: "While these are technically a breakfast food, I rarely have them for breakfast. Serve them with low-carb syrup, peanut butter, low-carb jam, or ricotta cheese. They make a great ricotta delivery device!"

2		large eggs
1 cup	(240 ml)	full-fat cottage cheese
3 Tbsp.	(45 ml)	oat flour
3 Tbsp.	(45 ml)	soy flour
3 Tbsp.	(45 ml)	almond meal (finely ground almonds)
¾ tsp.	(3.7 ml)	*each* Splenda and Canadian Sugar Twin or 2 Tbsp. (30 ml) Splenda
¼ tsp.	(1.2 ml)	baking powder
2 Tbsp.	(30 ml)	whipping cream
		Unsalted butter

◦§ Place the eggs in a large bowl and whisk to combine. Add the cottage cheese, oat flour, soy flour, almond meal, sweetener, baking powder, and cream. Mix well.

◦§ Heat a seasoned griddle or large frying pan over medium heat. Grease lightly with the butter. Form pancakes using a level ¼ cup (60 ml) of the batter for each pancake. Cook for about 3 minutes, or until bubbles appear on the surface and the bottom is golden brown. Gently turn and cook for 2 minutes on the other side, or until golden brown.

Per cake. Effective carbohydrates: 3.9 g; Carbohydrates: 5.1 g; Fiber: 1.2 g; Protein: 9.4 g; Fat: 7 g; Calories: 120
Made with Splenda only: Add 0.6 g carbohydrates

COLIN'S OMEGA WAFFLES

Makes 6 4 × 4-inch (10 × 10-cm) waffles

Besides being an all-around wonderful person, Colin—my friend and creative-cooking coconspir-ator—comes up with some wonderful recipes. These waffles are but one example of his genius.

I like to add a teaspoon of pure maple extract to the batter and slather the waffles with plenty of butter. The soy milk makes them very light in texture. The soy milk I use (Belsoy) has only 1.1 grams of carbohydrates per cup, which makes it excellent for low-carb cooking.

½ cup	(120 ml)	flaxseed meal
½ cup	(120 ml)	walnut pieces
½ cup	(120 ml)	almond meal (finely ground almonds)
2 tsp.	(10 ml)	ground cinnamon
¼ tsp.	(1.2 ml)	sea salt
1 Tbsp.	(15 ml)	*each* Splenda and Canadian Sugar Twin or ¼ cup (60 ml) Splenda
4		large eggs
1 cup	(240 ml)	unsweetened soy milk
1 tsp.	(5 ml)	baking powder

◦§ In a blender or food processor, combine the flaxseed meal, walnuts, almond meal, cinnamon, salt, and sweetener. Blend until the walnuts are finely ground.

◦§ In a large bowl, whisk together the eggs and ½ cup (120 ml) of the soy milk. Add the walnut mixture and combine well. Cover and refrigerate for at least 1 hour or up to overnight.

◦§ When you are ready to make the waffles, stir in the baking powder and the remaining ½ cup (120 ml) soy milk; beat well.

◦§ Set your waffle maker to high and, following the manufacturer's directions, cook the waffles until light brown.

Per waffle. Effective carbohydrates: 3.2 g; Carbohydrates: 8.7 g; Fiber: 5.5 g; Protein: 8.5 g; Fat: 16.7 g; Calories: 207
Made with Splenda only: Add 0.5 g carbohydrates

JUST THE FLAX MUFFINS

Makes 6 muffins

Before I started using flax, I was very surprised to find a Yahoo Group on the Internet that was solely devoted to low-carbers addicted to flaxseed muffins (http://health.groups.yahoo.com/ group/LCMuffinMania). Now I'm not so surprised anymore! Flax adds great flavor and an extra dose of fatty acids.

For fruity flax muffins, you can add blueberries, cranberries, raspberries, strawberries, or chopped rhubarb. Some people like to use flavored whey protein—chocolate or other flavors.

Note: *If your oven has a convection feature, turn it off when making these muffins or they'll end up looking like strange creatures. They will taste just fine but look a little odd.*

1 cup	(240 ml)	flaxseed meal
½ cup	(120 ml)	whey protein isolate
2 tsp.	(10 ml)	baking powder
2 tsp.	(10 ml)	ground cinnamon
½ tsp.	(2.5 ml)	sea salt
1 cup	(240 ml)	plain soy milk
2		large eggs
¼ cup	(60 ml)	vegetable oil
1 Tbsp.	(15 ml)	*each* Splenda and Canadian Sugar Twin or ¼ cup (60 ml) Splenda
1 tsp.	(5 ml)	pure maple or vanilla extract

◦§ Preheat the oven to 350°F (175°C). Coat a 6-cup muffin tin with nonstick cooking spray.

◦§ In a medium bowl, whisk together the flaxseed meal, whey protein, baking powder, cinnamon, and salt.

◦§ In a small bowl, whisk together the soy milk, eggs, oil, sweetener, and extract. Add to the dry ingredients and mix well. Let sit for a minute or two and then divide the mixture evenly among the prepared muffin cups.

⊷ Bake for 30 to 40 minutes, or until the muffins are nicely browned. Let sit in the pan for a minute or two before removing.

Per muffin. Effective carbohydrates: 2.5 g; Carbohydrates: 10.6 g; Fiber: 8.1 g; Protein: 9.2 g; Fat: 7.4 g; Calories: 183
Made with Splenda only: Add 0.6 g carbohydrates

FLAX PORRIDGE

Makes 10 servings

This porridge sticks to your ribs and contains an extreme amount of fiber—10.8 grams per serving!
    Below is the basic dry mix, which you can store in a plastic bag and use as needed.

1½ cups	**(360 ml)**	**flaxseed meal**
1½ cups	**(360 ml)**	**wheat bran**
1¾ cups	**(420 ml)**	**textured vegetable protein (TVP)**
2 Tbsp.	**(30 ml)**	**soy protein isolate**
¾ tsp.	**(3.7 ml)**	**sea salt**

⊷ In a gallon-size resealable plastic bag, combine the flaxseed meal, bran, TVP, soy protein, and salt. Seal and shake until well mixed. Shake well before every use.

⊷ To make the porridge: Place ½ cup (120 ml) of the flaxseed mix in a cereal bowl and stir in ⅔ cup (160 ml) hot (not boiling) water. Cover and let sit for a minute or so. Sweeten to taste and add cream or yogurt as desired.

Per serving (without sweetener and cream or yogurt). Effective carbohydrates: 2.8 g; Carbohydrates: 13.6 g; Fiber: 10.8 g; Protein: 1.8 g; Fat: 7.4 g; Calories: 147

FLAX AND YOGURT

Makes 1 serving

Flaxseed will not have the same texture as grain-based cereal. Flax has a unique texture and flavor, and I hope you'll find it as delicious as I do.

For flavoring, you can use cinnamon, pumpkin pie spice, a spoonful of cocoa powder, or extracts such as maple, banana, orange, or strawberry. Low-carb yogurt (already sweetened and flavored) is now available, so you can use it in place of the plain yogurt.

2 Tbsp.	**(30 ml)**	**flaxseed meal**
½ cup	**(120 ml)**	**plain full-fat yogurt**
		Sweetener
		Flavoring

➺ In a cereal bowl, mix the flaxseed meal and yogurt. Add the sweetener and flavoring to taste.

Per serving (without sweetener). Effective carbohydrates: 6.7 g; Carbohydrates: 11.2 g; Fiber: 4.5 g; Protein: 7.4 g; Fat: 9.5 g; Calories: 154

FLAX FACTS

Flax is good food! Besides being chock-full of essential fatty acids, it also, um, helps regulate bowel function.

Flaxseed is made up of 41 percent oil, and more than 70 percent of that is polyunsaturated fat. One of the unique features of flaxseed is the high ratio of alpha-linolenic acid (an omega-3 fatty acid) to linoleic acid (an omega-6 fatty acid). These two polyunsaturated fatty acids are called essential because the body cannot manufacture them from any other substances.

Flaxseeds can be purchased at natural food stores or well-stocked grocery stores. You can grind them yourself in a canister-type coffee mill or spice grinder. The seeds are too small and hard to grind properly in a blender or food processor. Ready-ground flaxseed meal is available, but it's usually a bit more expensive.

Air, light, and heat will make flax go rancid quickly. Fresh flax should have a "grassy" aroma. If it smells like linseed oil, it's gone off. Do not boil or microwave flaxseeds either. Use hot water, not boiling. Temperatures over 180°F (82°C) destroy the essential fatty acids.

GRA(NO)LA

Makes 8 servings

No grain here, just lots of soy and nuts. You can get the albumen powder—dried egg whites—in a natural food store, along with the soy flakes and TVP.

Soy flakes are soybeans that have been skinned, split, steamed, rolled, and dried. Textured vegetable protein (TVP) is made from soy protein concentrate, or spun soy fiber.

½ cup	(120 ml)	soy flakes
½ cup	(120 ml)	textured vegetable protein (TVP)
¼ cup	(60 ml)	soy protein isolate
2 Tbsp.	(30 ml)	whey protein isolate
½ cup	(120 ml)	sliced almonds
½ cup	(120 ml)	unsweetened shredded coconut
¼ cup	(60 ml)	almond meal (finely ground almonds)
1 Tbsp.	(15 ml)	albumen powder
¼ tsp.	(1.2 ml)	sea salt
¼ tsp.	(1.2 ml)	baking powder
1 tsp.	(5 ml)	ground cinnamon
1 Tbsp.	(15 ml)	*each* Splenda and Canadian Sugar Twin or ½ cup (120 ml) Splenda
¼ cup	(60 ml)	water
¼ cup	(60 ml)	vegetable oil
1 tsp.	(5 ml)	pure vanilla extract

◦§ Preheat the oven to 325°F (165°C).

◦§ In a large bowl, mix the soy flakes, TVP, soy protein, whey protein, almonds, coconut, almond meal, albumen powder, salt, baking powder, cinnamon, and sweetener.

◦§ In a small bowl, beat the water, oil, and vanilla with a fork until loosely combined. Pour over the dry ingredients and mix well. Spread evenly in a large rimmed baking sheet.

◦§ Bake, stirring every 10 minutes, for about 25 minutes, or until lightly browned and crisp.

Per serving. Effective carbohydrates: 4.1 g; Carbohydrates: 9.3 g; Fiber: 5.2 g; Protein: 14.6 g; Fat: 14.5 g; Calories: 206
Made with Splenda only: Add 1 g carbohydrates

PROTEIN SHAKES IN NO TIME

Protein shakes are a quick and easy breakfast alternative when you're pressed for time. I use plain whey protein isolate and add my own sweetener and flavorings to taste.

Frozen berries and extracts such as orange, coconut, and banana will give you a month's worth of flavor combinations. Or try cocoa powder or Chocolate Sauce (page 261).

I sometimes make what I call "instant breakfast," which is ¾ cup (180 ml) water, ¼ cup (60 ml) whipping cream, a scoop of plain whey protein isolate, stevia, a scant ½ tsp. (2.5 ml) xanthan gum, a shot of espresso, and a large handful of ice cubes.

If you're a flaxseed lover, you can add 2 Tbsp. (30 ml) of the flaxseed meal to any shake to make it a little thicker.

Xanthan gum has marvelous thickening properties and works very well in protein shakes. It will keep the ice crystals suspended in the liquid if you put ice cubes in the shake. To thicken 1 cup (240 ml) of liquid, use ¼ to ½ tsp. (1.2 to 2.5 ml) xanthan gum. Sprinkle the gum over the liquid and blend until thickened. Add the remaining ingredients and continue blending.

Another way to thicken shakes is by dropping in half of a peeled and pitted avocado and blending until smooth. Or try adding cream cheese to a berry shake. Soft tofu also adds a creamy texture. Here's another shake that's hard to resist.

STRAWBERRY CHEESECAKE SHAKE
Makes 1 serving

You can use ¼ cup (60 ml) frozen blueberries or raspberries instead of strawberries. A few drops of orange extract is delicious with the strawberries.

Note: The protein and carbohydrate counts will vary depending on the type of protein powder and sweetener used.

1	cup (240 ml)	water
1	scoop	whey protein isolate
¼	cup (60 ml)	cream cheese
		Sweetener
6		ice cubes
6		frozen strawberries

Place the water, whey protein, cream cheese, and sweetener to taste in a blender. Blend until smooth. Add the ice cubes and strawberries. Blend again.

Per serving (without sweetener). Effective carbohydrates: 7.3 g; Carbohydrates: 8.8 g; Fiber: 1.5 g; Protein: 26.6 g; Fat: 20 g; Calories: 326

NORMA JUNE'S SPAGHETTI SQUASH BREAKFAST CASSEROLE

Makes 6 servings

A great dish that can be eaten at lunch and dinner, too. This is what Norma June—a longtime member of lowcarber.org, affectionately known as N.J.—has to say about her casserole: "We used this for breakfast alongside eggs and bacon. Then the next night, we had it alongside our meat and vegetables in lieu of potatoes. There was enough left over to freeze and get another two or three meals."

Use Dottie's Cream of Mushroom Soup (page 53), not canned mushroom soup!

2 Tbsp.	(30 ml)	unsalted butter
½ cup	(120 ml)	finely chopped onion
½ cup	(120 ml)	Dottie's Cream of Mushroom Soup (page 53)
1 cup	(240 ml)	shredded aged cheddar cheese
1 cup	(240 ml)	sour cream
		Pinch of garlic powder
		Sea salt and freshly ground black pepper
3 cups	(720 ml)	Basic Spaghetti Squash (page 130)

◦§ Preheat the oven to 350°F (175°C). Butter a 9 × 9-inch (22.5 × 22.5-cm) baking dish.

◦§ Melt the butter in a large frying pan over medium heat. Add the onion and sauté for 5 minutes, or until translucent. Transfer to a large bowl and stir in the soup, cheese, sour cream, garlic powder, and salt and pepper to taste. Mix well.

◦§ Spread the mixture evenly in the prepared baking dish. Bake for 35 to 45 minutes, or until browned.

Per serving. Effective carbohydrates: 5.6 g; Carbohydrates: 6.7 g; Fiber: 1.1 g; Protein: 5.4 g; Fat: 19.1 g; Calories: 216

EGG AND SAUSAGE MUFFINS

Makes 12 muffins

These are great for a breakfast on the go. Use any type of sausage you enjoy and feel free to change the cheese. You can also add sautéed mushrooms or onions to the mix.

These muffins can be frozen and reheated in the microwave.

Note: *Flexible baking pans have been on the market for a few years and are great for preparing low-carb muffins, mini quiches, and more. They don't have to be buttered or oiled, and the food pops right out. They're also dishwasher-safe.*

1 lb.	(454 g)	sausage
12		large eggs
½ cup	(120 ml)	whipping cream
½ cup	(120 ml)	water
¼ tsp.	(1.2 ml)	sea salt
1½ cups	(360 ml)	shredded cheddar cheese

⊷ Preheat the oven to 350°F (175°C). Coat a 12-cup muffin tin with nonstick cooking spray.

⊷ Remove the sausage from its casing and crumble the meat into a large frying pan. Cook over medium heat, stirring to break up the pieces, for 5 minutes, or until browned. Divide the meat evenly among the prepared muffin cups.

⊷ In a large bowl, whisk together the eggs, cream, water, and salt. Pour over the sausage and top with the cheese.

⊷ Bake for 20 to 30 minutes, or until the eggs are cooked through. Cool slightly and remove from the tins.

Per muffin. Effective carbohydrates: 1 g; Carbohydrates: 1 g; Fiber: 0 g; Protein: 15 g; Fat: 15 g; Calories: 256

KRISTINE'S ASPARAGUS AND BRIE FRITTATA

Makes 4 servings

This is a Low-Carb Breakfast cooking class favorite. Thanks to Kristine, a lowcarber.org moderator, for sharing it!

¾ lb.	(340 g)	asparagus spears
¼ cup	(60 ml)	extra-virgin olive oil
1		garlic clove, minced
8		large eggs
¼ tsp.	(1.2 ml)	sea salt
		Freshly ground black pepper
4 oz.	(112 g)	Brie cheese, rind removed and cut into small cubes

◦§ Preheat the oven to 450°F (225°C).

◦§ Trim the woody ends from the asparagus and discard. Cut the asparagus on the diagonal into ¼ -inch (0.6-cm) slices, leaving the tips whole.

◦§ Heat the oil in a large ovenproof frying pan (preferably nonstick) over medium heat. Add the asparagus and cook, stirring, until bright green and tender-crisp, about 3 to 4 minutes. Add the garlic and cook for 1 minute, or until it sizzles.

◦§ In a large bowl, whisk together the eggs, salt, and pepper to taste. Add to the pan and cook over low heat until the edges start to set. With a heatproof rubber spatula, lift all around the sides of the frittata while tilting the pan, to allow the uncooked egg to flow underneath. Let cook for 1 to 2 minutes, then repeat. Scatter the cheese over the top and poke the pieces into the eggs with the spatula.

◦§ Transfer the pan to the oven and bake for 7 to 10 minutes, or until the eggs are set.

◦§ Remove from the oven and let sit for a few minutes. Run the spatula around the edges of the pan to loosen the frittata. Transfer to a plate or serve from the pan. Cut into wedges.

Per serving. Effective carbohydrates: 3.6 g; Carbohydrates: 5.4 g; Fiber: 1.8 g; Protein: 20.3 g; Fat: 32.1 g; Calories: 389

ROASTED RED PEPPER
AND SAUSAGE FRITTATA

Makes 4 servings

You can serve this cut into smaller pieces as an appetizer at an Italian-inspired dinner. Sprinkle this with mozzarella, Asiago, or Parmesan cheese a minute before it comes out of the oven if you like.

Note: *In classic frittata fashion, this starts on the stovetop and finishes in the oven. You could, however, make it entirely on the stove. Instead of transferring the pan to the oven, cover it with a lid, turn the heat to low, and let cook for 8 to 10 minutes to set the eggs. Sprinkle with the cheese and let it melt for a minute.*

1 Tbsp.	(15 ml)	extra-virgin olive oil
½ lb.	(227 g)	hot or sweet Italian sausage or chorizo
2		medium red bell peppers, roasted, peeled, seeded, and coarsely chopped
8		large eggs
¼ tsp.	(1.2 ml)	sea salt
		Freshly ground black pepper

❧ Preheat the oven to 450°F (225°C).

❧ Heat the oil in a 10-inch (22 cm) ovenproof frying pan (preferably nonstick) over medium heat. Remove the sausage from its casing and crumble into the pan. Cook, stirring to break up the pieces, for 5 minutes, or until lightly browned. Add the red peppers and stir for 1 minute, or until softened.

❧ In a large bowl, whisk together the eggs, salt, and black pepper to taste. Add to the pan and cook over low heat until the edges start to set. With a heatproof rubber spatula, lift all around the sides of the frittata while tilting the pan, to allow the uncooked egg to flow underneath. Let cook for 1 minute, then repeat.

❧ Transfer the pan to the oven and bake for 6 to 8 minutes, or until the eggs are set.

❧ Remove from the oven and let sit for a few minutes. Run the spatula around the edges of the pan to loosen the frittata. Transfer to a plate or serve from the pan. Cut into wedges.

Per serving. Effective carbohydrates: 3.5 g; Carbohydrates: 4.5 g; Fiber: 1 g; Protein: 27 g; Fat: 35.8 g; Calories: 455

THE FAITHFUL FRITTATA

Your fridge is almost empty, and you're wondering what to make for dinner. But you have a few staples around: some eggs, some cheese, a few vegetables. This sounds like a frittata to me. Easier than an omelet as far as technique goes and somehow more substantial, a frittata is a marvelous quick fix to have in your repertoire.

So, what is a frittata? It's a combination of eggs and other tasty ingredients cooked, without stirring, in a frying pan to make a large, flat cake. The name is Italian in origin, but many cultures have a similar egg dish. In Spain, it's known as *tortilla,* and what we know as egg foo yong could loosely be described as an Asian version. A frittata also means leftovers that are great for breakfast or a quick snack.

One of the best things is that there are no rules about what actually goes into a frittata. If you don't like a certain ingredient, you are absolved to use another one you do like. Just keep the texture in mind. It's good to have some juicy ingredients—like roasted red peppers, cooked zucchini, or asparagus—to complement the eggs and a flavorful cheese for contrast.

The choices are endless. Here are a few to get you started.

Broccoli and bacon	Smoked cheddar and tomato
Chicken and jalapeño Jack cheese	Zucchini and feta cheese
Cream cheese and salmon	

CURRIED TOFU, MUSHROOM, AND PEPPER SCRAMBLE

Makes 4 servings

A nice alternative to scrambled eggs.

2 Tbsp.	(30 ml)	vegetable oil
½ cup	(120 ml)	large red bell pepper cut into short, narrow strips
¼ lb.	(112 g)	mushrooms, sliced
2 12-oz.	(350-g)	containers firm tofu, drained and crumbled
3 Tbsp.	(45 ml)	thinly sliced green onion
1 tsp.	(5 ml)	curry powder
		Sea salt and freshly ground black pepper
½ cup	(120 ml)	finely diced tomato
1 Tbsp.	(15 ml)	coarsely chopped fresh parsley or cilantro

❧ Heat the oil in a large frying pan over medium heat. Add the red pepper and mushrooms and cook, stirring occasionally, until tender, about 5 minutes. Increase the heat and cook, stirring, until any liquid in the pan evaporates.

❧ Add the tofu, green onion, curry powder, and salt and pepper to taste. Reduce the heat and stir until heated through. Stir in the tomato and parsley or cilantro.

Per serving. Effective carbohydrates: 6.4 g; Carbohydrates: 11.9 g; Fiber: 5.5 g; Protein: 28.2 g; Fat: 22 g; Calories: 329

OVEN-FRIED BACON

If you like to eat bacon but don't like the messy splatters, you can cook a lot of bacon in advance with this oven method and simply reheat it as needed.

It's best to use a large pan that is not too deep, such as a jelly-roll pan or rimmed baking sheet. You need to have enough surface area to brown the bacon and the pan must be deep enough to hold the fat. You may want to cover the pan with foil for easy cleanup.

Position an oven rack in the middle of the oven and preheat the oven to 400°F (200°C). Lay the bacon slices in rows on the pan. The pieces can touch but not overlap. Bake for 5 to 6 minutes, then rotate the pan from front to back and continue baking for 5 to 6 minutes longer. If you use thick-cut bacon, increase the time.

Transfer the cooked slices to paper towels to drain. When they're cool, you can lay the strips between sheets of wax paper or parchment paper, place in a covered container, and refrigerate for up to 4 days, or freeze up to 6 months.

LITTLE NIBBLES
AND DIPS

IT'S A GRACIOUS TOUCH TO HAVE A FEW APPETIZERS SET OUT BEFORE DINNER WHEN YOU ARE ENTERTAINING, and it's always good to have something "snackable" in the fridge. The beauty of the dips in this chapter is that they have other applications—as fillings for omelets, as condiments for meats, or as last-minute stir-ins to sauces.

You can make a lot of impromptu "snappy appys" with just a few ingredients. Try roast beef rolled with cream cheese, blue cheese, and asparagus; prosciutto wrapped around mascarpone, pine nuts, and a sliver of melon; ham rolled with herbed cheese and a pickle spear.

There are other good potential starters, snacks, and appetizers dotted throughout this book. Pared-down versions of main-course salads are always good (see Salads and Dressings, page 67). Or try items like these.

Small pieces of frittata (page 16)
Stuffed eggs (pages 41 and 42)
Tofu-lafels (page 138) or To-frites (page 140)
Quick Prawns, Scampi-Style (page 166)
Turkey Tenderloin with Pesto and Smoked Mozzarella (page 189), served cold
Turkey Snackin' Cake (pages 190 to 91)

MUSHROOM TAPENADE

Makes about 1½ cups (360 ml)

This is more than just a great appetizer (serve it with sliced cucumbers, cheese, or hard-cooked egg)—it's also a fantastic omelet filling, steak condiment, or seasoning for sauces and salad dressings. The tapenade keeps, tightly covered in the refrigerator, for up to 1 week.

You can use different mushrooms, such as oyster, shiitake, or portobello. Just make sure to remove the woody stems.

1 lb.	(454 g)	fresh cultivated mushrooms
¾ to 1 cup	(180 to 240 ml)	extra-virgin olive oil
2 tsp.	(10 ml)	chopped fresh rosemary leaves
¼ tsp.	(1.2 ml)	sea salt
2		garlic cloves, minced
4		anchovy fillets
1 Tbsp.	(15 ml)	drained capers
		Freshly ground black pepper

•ᗢ Preheat the oven to 425°F (220°C).

•ᗢ In a large bowl, toss the mushrooms with 3 Tbsp. (45 ml) of the oil. Sprinkle with the rosemary and ¼ tsp. (1.2 ml) salt; toss to season evenly. Spread out in a baking pan large enough to hold the mushrooms in a single layer. Bake for 20 minutes, giving the mushrooms a stir after 10 minutes. Some of the mushrooms will look dried out, and this is fine.

•ᗢ Let the mushrooms cool and then coarsely chop them. Transfer to a food processor along with the garlic, anchovies, and capers. Process to a coarse puree. With the motor running, slowly add enough of the remaining oil—about ½ to ¾ cup (120 to 180 ml)—to form a juicy paste. Season to taste with pepper and additional salt.

Per 1 Tbsp. (15 ml). Effective carbohydrates: 0.6 g; Carbohydrates: 0.9 g; Fiber: 0.3 g; Protein: 0.8 g; Fat: 6.9 g; Calories: 66

HUMMUS

Makes about 2 cups (480 ml)

Hummus is a great dip for radishes and cucumbers as well as a good sauce for lamb. When serving it as a dip, drizzle it with a bit of extra-virgin olive oil and sprinkle with paprika.

12 oz.	(350 g)	medium-firm tofu
2		garlic cloves, minced
1 tsp.	(5 ml)	sea salt
½ cup	(120 ml)	tahini
6 Tbsp.	(90 ml)	freshly squeezed lemon juice

◦§ Process the tofu in a food processor until smooth. Add the garlic, salt, tahini, and lemon juice. Process until combined. Chill until ready to serve.

Per 1 Tbsp. (15 ml). Effective carbohydrates: 1 g; Carbohydrates: 1.4 g; Fiber: 0.4 g; Protein: 1.4 g; Fat: 2.3 g; Calories: 30

WHAT TO DIP?

Here are some munching alternatives to chips, pretzels, and breadsticks:

Cooked or raw asparagus

Cooked green or yellow beans

Cooked or raw broccoli or
  cauliflower florets

Cooked brussels sprouts

Cabbage leaves

Celery sticks

Cucumber sticks

Green onions

Small romaine lettuce leaves

Snow peas

Red, green, or yellow pepper strips

Red and daikon radishes

Sticks of salami or other deli meats

Cherry tomatoes

Turnip sticks

Wedges of hard-cooked egg

Strips of beef jerky

Strips of cooked chicken breast

Pork rinds

ENTERTAINING LOW-CARB STYLE

There comes a time in every low carber's life when you want to entertain guests. It can be worrisome to start because you're not sure how people will react. So a lot of Basic Cauliflower Mash (see page 112) is in order and you can always wow a crowd with a delicious German's Chocolate Cheesecake (see pages 270 to 272) or Zucchini Cake (see page 303). Cooking something absolutely delicious is a great way to introduce people to this way of eating.

In the first year of my low-carb life, I would cook a low-carb meal but have some potatoes, bread, and crackers around for the carbers. After a while, I realized that I was being almost apologetic and that there was nothing wrong with feeding anyone a complete, low-carb meal—and I've held parties for up to 30 people. I've never had a complaint.

Here are a few menu ideas to get your confidence up and your creative juices flowing. If you feel adventurous, turn to pages 62 and 207 for even more menu ideas.

Elegant Japanese

Edamame, page 38

Shirataki, Sukiyaki-Style, page 59

Salmon with Miso Glaze, page 157

Cucumber Salad with Umeboshi and Bonito Flakes, page 77

Soy, Sake, and Butter Glazed Mushrooms, page 127

Green Tea Ice Cream, page 263

Warm and Cozy

Warm Spinach Dip, page 30

One-Pot Chicken with Mushrooms and Sour Cream, page 170

Broccoli Dijon, page 104

Rutabaga with Balsamic Vinegar and Browned Butter, page 128

Silken Chocolate Pudding, page 292

Tapas

Prawns with Peppery Garlic Vinaigrette, page 26

Antipasto Skewers, page 33

Garlic, Olive Oil, and Parsley Stuffed Eggs, page 42

Unplugged Coriander Lamb Kebabs with Tomato Vinaigrette, page 222

Roasted Mushrooms with Garlic and Thyme, page 126

Clams Steamed with Bacon, Green Olives, and Tomatoes, page 164

Fresh Berries with Cool Champagne Sabayon, page 91

Cocktail Party

Pork and Shiitake Mushroom Meatballs, page 214

Kristine's Asparagus and Brie Frittata, page 15

Parmesan-Stuffed Eggs with Toasted Almonds, page 41

To-frites, page 140

Buffalo-Style Wings, page 176

Quick Prawns, Scampi-Style, page 166

My Brownies, page 312

Cream Cheese, Coconut, and Lemon Mounds, page 288

Italian Buffet

Antipasto Skewers, page 33

Tuna-Stuffed Eggs, page 42

Flat Roasted Chicken with Prosciutto and Green Olives, page 172

Broccoli Italianissimo, page 105

Eggplant Salad with Sour Cream Dressing, page 118

Tiramisu, page 294

PRAWNS WITH PEPPERY GARLIC VINAIGRETTE

Makes 10 servings

This dish can also be served as a main course. Choose some recipes from the Vegetables chapter (page 99) for a complete meal.

Note: *Whether you call them prawns or shrimp depends on where you live—with "prawns" being more prevalent on the West Coast. Either way, look for large ones, at least 26 to 30 per pound.*

½ cup	(120 ml)	extra-virgin olive oil
10		garlic cloves, thinly sliced
¼ cup	(60 ml)	red wine vinegar
¼ cup	(60 ml)	finely chopped fresh parsley
1 tsp.	(5 ml)	freshly ground black pepper
½ tsp.	(2.5 ml)	sea salt
3 lb.	(1.3 kg)	large prawns, peeled and deveined

◦§ Heat the oil in a small frying pan over medium heat. Add the garlic and cook until it starts to turn golden, about 3 minutes. Remove from the heat and cool.

◦§ In a small bowl, whisk together the vinegar, parsley, pepper, and ½ tsp. (2.5 ml) salt. Slowly whisk in the oil mixture.

◦§ Bring a large pot of water to a boil and season liberally with salt. (It should taste like sea water.) Add the prawns and stir to separate them. Cook until the prawns are opaque at the thick end about 3 to 4 minutes. Drain immediately and spread on a platter. Pour the vinaigrette over the prawns, toss lightly to coat, and serve.

Per serving. Effective carbohydrates: 2.2 g; Carbohydrates: 2.3 g; Fiber: 0.1 g; Protein: 27.8 g; Fat: 13.2 g; Calories: 244

GUACAMOLE

Makes about 2½ cups (600 ml)

I am pretty fanatic about the making of guacamole, which is why I've included a recipe. Lime juice—not lemon—must be used; no food processor should be involved; and no garlic, cumin, or other shocking seasonings should distract your tongue from guacamole's smooth, creamy greenness. The other ingredients are present to discreetly enhance by contrast, not overwhelm.

3		medium fully ripe Haas avocados
⅜ tsp.	(2 ml)	sea salt
2 Tbsp.	(30 ml)	freshly squeezed lime juice
1		ripe plum tomato, seeded and finely diced
1 Tbsp.	(15 ml)	coarsely chopped fresh cilantro
2 Tbsp.	(30 ml)	finely chopped white onion
1		hot chile pepper, finely chopped

➛ Pit and peel the avocados. Place in a bowl and coarsely mash with a fork. (Chunks of avocado are just fine—it shouldn't be completely smooth.) Stir in the salt and lime juice. Stir in the tomato, cilantro, and onion. Add chile pepper to taste. Cover and refrigerate. Serve within 1 hour.

Per 1 Tbsp. (15 ml). Effective carbohydrates: 0.4 g; Carbohydrates: 1.1 g; Fiber: 0.7 g; Protein: 0.3 g; Fat: 2.3 g; Calories: 24

CONSIDER THE AVOCADO

It's a natural in salads and chilled soups and as a garnish for hot soups and spicy dishes. The avocado can even star in desserts and protein shakes.

Packed full of healthy monounsaturated fat, the avocado should be included in your diet. It's also a great contributor of potassium and beta-carotene. Avocados are the highest fruit source of lutein, a phytochemical that helps protect against cataracts and macular degeneration.

The UCLA Center for Human Nutrition has presented new findings showing that avocados contain nearly twice as much vitamin E as previously reported, making them the highest fruit source of this powerful antioxidant known to slow the aging process and help protect against heart disease.

FIVE-SPICE SESAME WALNUTS

Makes 3½ cups (840 ml)

These spicy walnuts are nice to serve as a nibble before a Chinese meal. They keep for 2 weeks at room temperature if tightly covered—and if you can resist them for that long.

1½ tsp.	(7.5 ml)	*each* **Splenda and Canadian Sugar Twin or 2 Tbsp. (30 ml) Splenda**
½ tsp.	(2.5 ml)	**cayenne pepper**
½ tsp.	(2.5 ml)	**sea salt**
1½ tsp.	(7.5 ml)	**five-spice powder**
1		**large egg white**
1 tsp.	(5 ml)	**pure caramel extract**
3 cups	(720 ml)	**raw walnut halves**
½ cup	(120 ml)	**sesame seeds**

◦§ Preheat the oven to 350°F (175°C). Line a baking sheet with parchment paper.

◦§ In a small cup, combine the sweetener, cayenne, salt, and five-spice powder.

◦§ In a medium bowl, beat the egg white with a whisk until foamy but not stiff. Add the caramel extract, walnuts, and sesame seeds. Stir to coat with the egg white. Add the spice mixture and stir until evenly blended.

◦§ Spread out in a single layer on the prepared baking sheet. Bake for 10 minutes. Stir the nuts with a spoon and bake for 5 to 10 minutes longer, until lightly browned. Cool completely.

Per ½ cup (120 ml). Effective carbohydrates: 3.4 g; Carbohydrates: 5.5 g; Fiber: 2.1 g; Protein: 6.6 g; Fat: 23.7 g; Calories: 243; Made with Splenda only: Add 0.3 g carbohydrates

WARM SPINACH DIP

Makes 3 cups (720 ml)

This warm dip is much tastier than the cold variety. You can even use it as creamed spinach!

2 Tbsp.	**(30 ml)**	**unsalted butter**
½ cup	**(120 ml)**	**finely chopped onion**
6		**garlic cloves, minced**
¼ cup	**(60 ml)**	**chicken stock**
½ cup	**(120 ml)**	**cream cheese**
1 10-oz.	**(285-g)**	**bag ready-to-use spinach**
1 cup	**(240 ml)**	**packed freshly grated Parmesan cheese**
½ tsp.	**(2.5 ml)**	**cayenne pepper, or to taste**
		Sea salt and freshly ground black pepper

◆§ Melt the butter in a large pot over medium heat. Add the onion and garlic and sauté for 5 minutes, or until the onion is soft but not browned. Whisk in the stock and cream cheese. Bring to a boil, whisking constantly. Cook, stirring frequently, until the mixture thickens, about 4 or 5 minutes.

◆§ Remove from the heat and add the spinach, cheese, and cayenne. Stir until the spinach wilts. Season to taste with salt and pepper and serve.

Per 2 Tbsp. (30 ml). Effective carbohydrates: 0.9 g; Carbohydrates: 1.3 g; Fiber: 0.4 g; Protein: 2.2 g; Fat: 3.6 g; Calories: 45

FRENCH ONION DIP

Makes about 1¼ cups (300 ml)

I've often wondered what was "French" about the packaged soup mix. Doesn't matter—this low-carb version tastes much better!

¼ cup	(60 ml)	vegetable oil
3 cups	(720 ml)	very thinly sliced onions
1 cup	(240 ml)	finely chopped red bell pepper
⅓ cup	(80 ml)	sour cream
⅓ cup	(80 ml)	cream cheese
½ tsp.	(2.5 ml)	garlic powder
		Sea salt and freshly ground black pepper

◦§ Heat the oil in a large heavy frying pan over medium heat. Add the onions and red pepper. Stir for a minute until glistening with the oil, then cover and cook, stirring occasionally, for 10 minutes, or until the vegetables release their juice and become tender. Uncover and cook until the juice evaporates. Continue cooking, stirring occasionally, until the onions turn a deep, rich brown, about 30 to 40 minutes. As they start turning brown, you will have to stir more frequently. Cool completely.

◦§ Transfer the onion mixture to a food processor. Add the sour cream, cream cheese, and garlic powder. Process until coarsely pureed. Season to taste with salt and pepper. Transfer to a bowl and refrigerate for at least 1 hour to blend the flavors.

Per 1 Tbsp. (15 ml). Effective carbohydrates: 1.8 g; Carbohydrates: 2.3 g; Fiber: 0.5 g; Protein: 0.6 g; Fat: 4.4 g; Calories: 49

BLACK SOYBEAN DIP

Makes 2½ cups (600 ml)

This dip is great with salsa and pork rinds! Make sure you are buying black soybeans.

1 15-oz.	(440-g)	can black soybeans, rinsed and drained
¼ cup	(60 ml)	water
¼ cup	(60 ml)	mayonnaise
2 tsp.	(10 ml)	chili powder
1 tsp.	(5 ml)	sea salt
1 cup	(240 ml)	shredded aged cheddar cheese
1 Tbsp.	(15 ml)	finely chopped jalapeño pepper
2 Tbsp.	(30 ml)	grated onion
1 Tbsp.	(15 ml)	chopped fresh cilantro

In a food processor, combine the soybeans, water, mayonnaise, chili powder, and salt. Process until smooth. Scrape into a medium saucepan and, stirring frequently, bring to a boil over medium heat. Add the cheese, pepper, onion, and cilantro and stir until the cheese melts.

Per 1 Tbsp. (15 ml). Effective carbohydrates: 0.4 g; Carbohydrates: 0.7 g; Fiber: 0.3 g; Protein: 1.3 g; Fat: 2.3 g; Calories: 27

BUTTERY TUNA AND CAPER MOUSSE

Makes about 1½ cups (360 ml)

This can be the centerpiece of an antipasto plate or a dinner on its own.

2 6½-oz.	(185-g)	cans Italian tuna packed in olive oil
3 Tbsp.	(45 ml)	drained capers
½ cup	(120 ml)	unsalted butter, at room temperature
2 Tbsp.	(30 ml)	coarsely chopped fresh basil

Drain the tuna, discarding the oil. Place in a food processor with the capers and butter. Process until smooth. Transfer to a bowl and stir in the basil.

Per 1 Tbsp. (15 ml). Effective carbohydrates: 0.1 g; Carbohydrates: 0.2 g; Fiber: 0.1 g; Protein: 4.3 g; Fat: 8.4 g; Calories: 93

ANTIPASTO SKEWERS

Makes 8 skewers

You can serve these with Aioli (page 248) as a dip. While good off the grill, these can also be served ungrilled and just chilled.

8		thin prosciutto slices
8		small pickled hot cherry peppers, stems and seeds removed
16		Kalamata olives, pitted
16		cherry tomatoes
8		zucchini, cut into 1-inch (2.5-cm) cubes
8		small mushrooms, stems cut flush with the caps
8		Genoa salami cubes, about 1 inch (2.5 cm)
¼ cup	(60 ml)	extra-virgin olive oil
1 Tbsp.	(15 ml)	freshly squeezed lemon juice
1 Tbsp.	(15 ml)	balsamic vinegar
1		garlic clove, minced
½ tsp.	(2.5 ml)	dried oregano
¼ tsp.	(1.2 ml)	sea salt
¼ tsp.	(1.2 ml)	freshly ground black pepper

◆ Soak 8 bamboo skewers in cold water for 15 minutes and drain.

◆ Wrap a slice of prosciutto around each cherry pepper. Thread each skewer with the ingredients in this order: 1 olive, 1 tomato, 1 zucchini cube, 1 prosciutto-wrapped pepper, 1 mushroom, 1 salami cube, 1 olive, and 1 tomato. Place the skewers in a shallow baking dish.

◆ In a small bowl, mix the oil, lemon juice, vinegar, garlic, oregano, salt, and black pepper. Pour over the skewers and turn them in the marinade to coat them all over.

◆ Preheat the grill or broiler. Grill or broil the skewers until the vegetables are tender, about 4 to 5 minutes.

Per skewer. Effective carbohydrates: 3.4 g; Carbohydrates: 5.1 g; Fiber: 1.7 g; Protein: 5.1 g; Fat: 9.5 g; Calories: 129

SHRIMP AND NORI ROLLS

Makes 4 servings

Ahh . . . tastes like sushi! This should be made right before serving. You can add some avocado to this, too. If you use frozen shrimp, thaw them and lightly squeeze them dry. Fresh or frozen, they should be small.

1 cup	(240 ml)	small cooked salad shrimp
1 Tbsp.	(15 ml)	mayonnaise
1		green onion, thinly sliced
2		nori sheets
¼		English cucumber, seeded and julienned
1 Tbsp.	(15 ml)	toasted sesame seeds

◦§ Make sure that the shrimp are well drained. Place in a small bowl and mix in the mayonnaise and green onion.

◦§ Lay 1 nori sheet on a flat surface. Place half of the shrimp mixture 1 inch (2.5 cm) from the edge nearest you. Lay half of the cucumber pieces evenly beside the shrimp. Sprinkle with half of the sesame seeds. Roll up tightly to enclose the filling. Repeat with the remaining ingredients to make a second roll.

◦§ Let the rolls sit for a minute to soften. With a very sharp knife, cut each roll into 6 pieces.

Per serving. Effective carbohydrates: 0.4 g; Carbohydrates: 0.8 g; Fiber: 0.4 g; Protein: 0.3 g; Fat: 5.7 g; Calories: 54

A DYNAMIC DUO: GINGER AND SEAWEED

Kizami shoga ginger are short, red threads of pickled ginger that are distinctly gingery and salty. They're great with fish or any soy-marinated meat, in Asian-style soups, and sprinkled on top of stir-fries.

Fresh wakame seaweed is highly edible and can be used in soups—it's great in miso soup— or as a salad with a few drops of sesame oil, shaved cucumber, soy sauce, and toasted sesame seeds. One ounce of fresh wakame—a scant half-cup—has 2.6 grams of carbohydrate and 0.1 gram of fiber.

Sea vegetables are a "wonder" food. If you've eaten sushi, you've probably eaten nori wrapped around one of the rolls. Wakame is used in soups and salads. Kombu can be fried until crisp or is used in making traditional Japanese stocks. And hiziki is used in soup and salads, too.

The dried seaweeds—except for nori—need to be soaked in water until softened before further cooking. Nori is better-tasting if it's given a wee toasting over an open flame or run quickly under the broiler. The sheets make a good wrap for tuna or salmon salad, but you have to eat it fairly quickly.

Nori also comes seasoned in what I call "snack packs." Wasabi and chili flavors are two of my favorites. One sheet of nori contains 0.1 gram of carbohydrate.

NORI AND SESAME CRISPS WITH MISO CREAM CHEESE

Makes 8 servings

If you're a fan of sesame, you'll love this cracker-ish crisp. You can add different seasonings to the sesame seeds—even replace part of them with freshly grated Parmesan cheese.

Although cream cheese and Japan seem miles apart from each other, this hits that right, mouthwatering, salty note and is reminiscent of—dare I say it—Velveeta cheese. Cream cheese mixed with prepared wasabi is tasty too and tastes nothing like Velveeta!

2		nori sheets
½ cup	(120 ml)	lightly toasted sesame seeds
1		large egg white
		Sea salt
4 oz.	(112 g)	cream cheese, at room temperature
1 Tbsp.	(15 ml)	dark miso

•§ Preheat the oven to 350°F (175°C). Line a baking sheet with parchment paper.

•§ With scissors, cut each nori sheet into 4 squares. Spread the sesame seeds evenly on another baking sheet, keeping in mind that you want the seeds to cover the nori but not too thickly.

•§ Place the egg white in a large shallow bowl and beat until foamy but not stiff. Dip 1 side of each nori square into the egg white, dragging it over the lip of the bowl to create only a thin layer of egg white on the nori. Dip the square, egg side down, into the sesame seeds so the seeds adhere to the square. Place on the baking sheet with the sesame-coated side facing up. Sprinkle lightly with salt. Bake for 10 minutes and transfer to a rack to cool. Store tightly covered.

☙ Mix the cream cheese and miso together until smooth. Cover and refrigerate until needed. To eat, spread the cream cheese on the nori squares.

Per crisp. Effective carbohydrates: 0.8 g; Carbohydrates: 2.1 g; Fiber: 1.3 g; Protein: 1.8 g; Fat: 3.8 g; Calories: 47

Per 1 Tbsp. miso cream cheese. Effective carbohydrates: 0.8 g; Carbohydrates: 0.8 g; Fiber: 0 g; Protein: 1.2 g; Fat: 5.1 g; Calories: 53

MADE IN JAPAN: USEFUL KITCHEN GADGETS

There are a few miscellaneous items in Japanese food stores that will enhance your kitchen.

☙ One is a ginger grater. I prefer the aluminum ones. The tiny teeth grate ginger in no time, leaving behind the strings. The graters can also be used to grate whole nutmeg and daikon radish to a paste.

☙ A *suribachi* is a Japanese mortar and pestle. The ceramic bowl is grooved and is great for grinding sesame seeds and making dressings. It comes with a wooden pestle.

☙ Evert-Fresh Bags are light green produce-storage bags that keep produce fresh for a long time. They are originally from Japan but now are more widely available in supermarkets.

☙ Little green plastic grass "fences"—usually used to garnish sushi and sashimi—can spiff up your own food!

EDAMAME

Makes 6 servings

Edamame (pronounced ed-a-MOM-ay) are blanched young soybeans still in the pod. They are light green and about the size of baby lima beans, with a sweet, nutty taste. Serve them as a snack or appetizer or toss them into salads and stir-fries. Look for edamame in the frozen foods section of Japanese grocery stores or well-stocked supermarkets. Do not eat the pods. The beans will pop easily out of them.

1 lb.	**(454 g)**	**frozen or fresh unshelled edamame**
2 tsp.	**(10 ml)**	**sea salt**

Bring about 8 cups (1,920 ml) of water to a boil in a large saucepan. Add the edamame and salt. Allow the water to return to a boil, about 3 to 5 minutes. Cook for an additional 5 minutes. Drain and serve either warm or at room temperature.

Per serving. Effective carbohydrates: 3.7 g; Carbohydrates: 5.9 g; Fiber: 2.2 g; Protein: 6.9 g; Fat: 6.6 g; Calories: 78

UNPLUGGED SUSHI

Miss sushi? This is what I do to get all of the wonderful flavors without the rice or sugar.

On a plate, I arrange diced avocado, thin strips of cucumber, chopped raw tuna, cooked baby shrimp, strips of plain omelet, cooked or raw salmon, chopped green onion, and mayonnaise. Make sure that any raw fish you use has been frozen first.

You can make your choices as elaborate or as simple as you want. Cut pieces of nori into quarters. Don't forget to give it a light toasting over an open flame or under the broiler. Wrap the bits of filling in the nori, then dip into a mixture of soy and wasabi. Eat!

Bonito flakes are flakes of dried, shaved tuna that are used to make dashi—the ubiquitous Japanese stock—or sprinkled on cooked food. Large flakes are used for dashi, and smaller ones (purchased in smaller packages) are used on food. It's quite an experience to see them on top of hot food for the first time. The heat makes them wave back and forth like they're alive!

They are pleasantly briny, not overtly fishy, and have a subtle smokiness. You can try them sprinkled on salads or on dishes with Japanese overtones like sweet-and-sour cucumber salads or seaweed salads.

STIR-FRIED EDAMAME
WITH GARLIC, CHILES, AND SOY

Makes 6 servings

This is what I call "finger lickin' good." Pull the pods through your teeth to extract the beans and the flavor coating the pods.

2 Tbsp.	(30 ml)	**vegetable oil**
½ tsp.	(2.5 ml)	**dried chile flakes**
3		**garlic cloves, thinly sliced**
		Edamame (opposite), still warm
3 Tbsp.	(45 ml)	**soy sauce**

~§ In a large frying pan, heat the oil over high heat. Add the chile flakes and garlic and stir-fry until the garlic starts to turn golden but does not burn, about 30 seconds. Add the edamame and stir-fry until glistening with the oil. Add the soy sauce and stir-fry until it sizzles and reduces slightly. Serve immediately.

Per serving. Effective carbohydrates: 4.9 g; Carbohydrates: 7.2 g; Fiber: 2.3 g; Protein: 7.5 g; Fat: 8.2 g; Calories: 126

PARMESAN-STUFFED EGGS WITH TOASTED ALMONDS

Makes 8 halves

This dish would be great served with a platter of Italian cold cuts.

4		hard-cooked large eggs, peeled
2 Tbsp.	(30 ml)	mayonnaise
¼ cup	(60 ml)	extra-virgin olive oil
¼ cup	(60 ml)	freshly grated Parmesan cheese
2 Tbsp.	(30 ml)	finely chopped toasted almonds
		Sea salt and freshly ground black pepper
8		toasted almonds (garnish)

◦§ Cut the eggs in half lengthwise and use a thin, sharp knife to take a tiny slice from the bottom of each half so it will sit firmly in place after stuffing. Scoop out the yolks with a small spoon and place in a small bowl. Set the whites on a platter.

◦§ Mash the yolks with a fork until smooth (or press them through a sieve). Mash in the mayonnaise.

◦§ Stir in the oil, a drizzle at a time, until it is completely incorporated and the mixture is soft and fluffy. You may not need all the oil. Stir in the Parmesan and chopped almonds. Season to taste with salt and pepper.

◦§ Using a small spoon, stuff the whites with the yolk mixture. Top each half with an almond. Serve immediately or chill.

Per egg half. Effective carbohydrates: 0.7 g; Carbohydrates: 1.0 g; Fiber: 0.3 g; Protein: 4.8 g; Fat: 14.5 g; Calories: 153

TUNA-STUFFED EGGS

Makes 8 halves

I love the combination of tuna with anchovies and capers, but you can make one or both optional.

4		hard-cooked large eggs, peeled
1 3½-oz.	(100-g)	can olive oil–packed tuna, well-drained and mashed
2 Tbsp.	(30 ml)	mayonnaise
		Sea salt and freshly ground black pepper
4		anchovy fillets, cut in half lengthwise
16		capers

⋅§ Cut the eggs in half lengthwise and use a thin, sharp knife to take a tiny slice from the bottom of each half so it will sit firmly in place after stuffing. Scoop out the yolks with a small spoon and place in a small bowl. Set the whites on a platter.

⋅§ Mash the yolks with a fork until smooth (or press them through a sieve). Stir in the tuna and mayonnaise. Season to taste with salt and pepper.

⋅§ Using a small spoon, stuff the whites with the yolk mixture. Cut each strip of anchovy in half crosswise and crisscross the pieces on top of each egg; garnish with the capers. Serve immediately or chill.

Per egg half. Effective carbohydrates: 0.3 g; Carbohydrates: 0.3 g; Fiber: 0 g; Protein: 7.4 g; Fat: 6.9 g; Calories: 93

OTHER STUFFED-EGG IDEAS

After mashing the egg yolks with mayonnaise, consider adding one of these things to taste.

Chopped fresh tarragon or dill	Minced garlic, olive oil, and parsley
Crisp crumbled bacon and Parmesan	Mushroom Tapenade (page 22)
Curry powder	Pesto
Dijon mustard	Prepared horseradish
Grainy mustard	Tapenade
Mashed avocado and salsa	Wasabi paste

THE EASY WAY TO HARD-COOK EGGS

Place large eggs in a saucepan large enough to hold them in a *single layer*—this is very important! Add cold water to cover them by at least 1 inch (2.5 cm). Start cooking over medium-high heat. As soon as a few bubbles appear on the surface, slap on the lid and remove the pan from the heat. Let the eggs sit undisturbed for 15 minutes.

Pour off the water, then run cold water over the eggs until they are cool enough to handle. Rap the bottom—the big rounded part—of each egg against the sink to crack it and return it to the pot. Keep the cold water running over the eggs until they are completely cold.

Tap each egg gently with a spoon or against the counter or sink until it's cracked all over. Under running water, remove the shell and rinse off any shell fragments.

CAPONATA

Makes about 2 cups (480 ml)

Many years ago, a supplier of excellent wines and olive oils gave me a jar filled with a miracu-lous eggplant dish that his mother made. It was a perfect blend of sweet, sour, and salty, with a creamy texture. I was so impressed that I immediately set to work replicating it. It seemed like that's all I ate for a whole summer—with meat and fish, on salads, with cheese, as an appetizer. This is one of my favorite eggplant dishes of all time, and I am sure you will find a myriad of uses for it, too. It keeps for up to a week in a tightly closed container in the refrigerator.

Note: *If you can find the Sicilian eggplants that appear in the late summer, you should use them—they are the sweetest.*

1 1-lb.	**(454-g)**	**eggplant**
¼ cup	**(60 ml)**	**extra-virgin olive oil**
1		**celery rib, cut into julienne strips, 2 × ¼ inch (5 × 0.6 cm)**
1		**medium onion, cut into ½-inch (1.2-cm) lengthwise wedges**
1½ cups	**(360 ml)**	**drained canned Italian plum tomatoes, pureed and sieved**
8		**green olives, pitted**
8		**black olives, pitted**
1 Tbsp.	**(15 ml)**	**drained small capers**
		Sea salt and freshly ground black pepper
1 tsp.	**(5 ml)**	**balsamic vinegar**
1½ tsp.	**(7.5 ml)**	**coarsely chopped fresh parsley**
½ cup	**(120 ml)**	**fresh basil leaves**

◦§ Preheat the oven to 350°F (175°C).

◦§ Prick the eggplant several times with a fork and place on a baking sheet. Bake for 30 to 45 minutes, until the eggplant is completely soft and collapsing. Remove from the oven and slit the eggplant open on one side. Place in a colander, slit side down, to drain and cool completely.

◦§ While the eggplant is cooling, heat the oil in a large saucepan over medium heat. Add the celery and onion and sauté for 5 minutes, or until translucent. Add the tomato puree,

olives, and capers. Cook, stirring occasionally, for about 10 minutes, or until slightly thickened and the oil starts to separate from the tomato mixture.

◦⟨ When the eggplant has cooled, peel off the skin. Chop the eggplant crosswise into 2-inch (5-cm) pieces and stir gently into the tomato mixture. Simmer for 10 minutes. Season to taste with salt and pepper. Add the vinegar, parsley, and basil and remove from the heat.

Per 2 Tbsp. (30 ml). Effective carbohydrates: 2.6 g; Carbohydrates: 3.8 g; Fiber: 1.1 g; Protein: 0.7 g; Fat: 4 g; Calories: 53

WHAT TO SNACK ON?

A big part of low-carb eating is making sure to keep your blood sugar level. The best way to do that is to eat every 3 hours or so. These snacks will help you stay on track.

- ◦⟨ Low-carb "bridge mixture"—salami, cheese, and celery, cut into small, nibbly pieces and mixed with macadamia nuts or toasted almonds
- ◦⟨ Cold cuts—naked, smeared with cream cheese, or rolled with cheese
- ◦⟨ Chicken wings
- ◦⟨ Pork rinds with salsa or other dips
- ◦⟨ Small cans of flavored or olive oil–packed tuna
- ◦⟨ Hard-cooked eggs
- ◦⟨ Deviled eggs
- ◦⟨ Leftovers—always make extra food at dinner for snacks and breakfast the next day
- ◦⟨ A small plate of pickles, crisp bacon, and peanuts
- ◦⟨ Celery sticks filled with cream cheese, blue cheese, tuna salad, egg salad, salmon salad, nut butter, or peanut butter (Mix peanut butter with unsalted butter or mayonnaise to make your carbs go further.)
- ◦⟨ Pumpkin and sunflower seeds in the shell
- ◦⟨ Macadamia nuts, almonds, walnuts, pecans, hazelnuts, and brazil nuts (Leave nuts in the shell, when possible. It takes longer to eat them, so it's harder to overindulge!)

SOUPS

SOUPS ARE WHAT WE SHOULD TURN TO WHEN WE'RE PRESSED FOR TIME. Hot soups fit the bill when it's cold outside or when we just need something warm and soothing. Chilled soups are great for hot-weather eating. Many of the soups in this chapter are one-bowl meals and can be frozen so you'll always have a quick meal on hand.

For best flavor, don't wait until vegetables are on their "last legs" before using them. As for what to make, let your vegetable drawer be your guide. You can cram a lot more celery, for instance, into a soup than you can eat raw (and it's a sure way to finish that whole bunch sitting in the crisper)!

Garnishes are a way of turning a good soup into a great soup. Fairly plain vegetable soups, like Italian Egg Drop and Parmesan Soup (page 49), can benefit from a spoonful of Basil Pesto (page 240). I think almost any soup is good with a little diced avocado added to your bowl! And fresh herbs like basil, dill, or mint stirred in just before serving will give the zing of freshness.

Here are some soups that can be main meals all by themselves.

Escarole Soup with Turkey Meatballs (pages 54 and 55)

Winter Vegetable Soup (pages 56 and 57)

Thai Prawn Soup (page 61)

Lisa N.'s Double Italian Sausage Soup (page 64)

Quick Korean-Style Beef and Spinach Soup (page 65)

CHICKEN STOCK

Makes 8 cups (1.9 L)

Although I'm including a recipe for chicken stock, there's a ready-made product that I've fallen in love with. It's Imagine Natural Organic Chicken Broth in a tetra pack. The carton is 32 oz. (946 ml) or about 4 cups. It's delicious in soups and sauces, and I've used it exclusively in all the recipes in this book. It is salted, so make sure you taste any dish that you've used it in before adding salt.

I think adding the vegetables in the last hour gives a sprightly, herbal flavor to the stock. When they're cooked for 4 hours, the taste becomes sweet and dull.

Note: *You can make a richer stock and have the bonus of the meat by using a whole chicken instead of the bones. Or when the stock is finished, cook more bones in the stock.*

Store the finished stock, tightly covered, in the fridge for up to 3 days or freeze it for up to 6 months.

2 lb.	**(908 g)**	**chicken backs, necks, and wings**
8 cups	**(1.9 L)**	**water**
1		**small onion, cut in half**
½ cup	**(120 ml)**	**chopped carrot**
2		**celery ribs with leaves, chopped**
1		**sprig fresh parsley**

◄§ In a large pot, combine the chicken and water. Bring to a boil over high heat and skim off any residue that rises to the surface. Reduce the heat, partially cover the pot, and cook at a bare simmer for 3 hours, replenishing the water as the level lowers and skimming the surface occasionally.

◄§ Add the onion, carrot, celery, and parsley. Cook for 1 hour longer.

◄§ Strain out the bones and vegetables. Place the stock in a large bowl and refrigerate until the fat on the surface hardens. Remove it with a spoon. (Save the fat for frying!)

Per 1 cup (240 ml). Effective carbohydrates: 1 g; Carbohydrates: 2 g; Fiber: 1 g; Protein: 1 g; Fat: 0.5 g; Calories: 20

ITALIAN EGG DROP AND PARMESAN SOUP

Makes 4 servings

This classic Italian soup is known as stracciatella. *It's quick and easy to make from things that are staples—at least in my kitchen. You can add cooked chicken cut into bite-size pieces if you want something a bit heartier.*

Note: *For garnish, a thin slice of lemon floating on top is very good.*

4 cups	(960 ml)	chicken stock
		Sea salt and freshly ground black pepper
2		large eggs
¼ cup	(60 ml)	freshly grated Parmesan cheese
2 tsp.	(10 ml)	chopped fresh parsley

Bring the stock to a boil in a large saucepan over high heat. Season to taste with salt and pepper.

In a small bowl, beat the eggs, cheese, and parsley with a fork to mix well. Season with salt and pepper. Reduce the heat to a bare simmer and slowly stir the egg mixture into the soup. Continue to stir for a few minutes until the eggs float to the top and form tiny "flakes." Serve immediately.

Per serving. Effective carbohydrates: 1.4 g; Carbohydrates: 1.5 g; Fiber: 0.1 g; Protein: 10.5 g; Fat: 5.7 g; Calories: 104

LOW-CARB SOUP SUCCESS

Consider daikon radish in place of carrots in your soup recipes.

If you miss noodles in your chicken soup, add finely shredded cabbage, julienned firm tofu, or shirataki noodles (konnyaku) instead.

For thickening soups, I always rely on cauliflower. Cook it well and puree it, then stir in enough to reach the desired thickness. (Try it in a chowder, for example.)

If you're going to freeze a cream soup, don't add the cream until after you thaw and heat the soup.

CHILLED CUCUMBER AND AVOCADO SOUP

Makes 4 servings

Cold soups are great to have in the summer. They're all the better if they require no cooking—like this one.

Note: *For a more complete hot weather meal, add a handful of leftover chopped cooked chicken or cooked shrimp to this soup.*

1		English cucumber, peeled, seeded, and chopped
2		ripe Haas avocados, pitted, peeled, and chopped
2		green onions, chopped
2 Tbsp.	(30 ml)	freshly squeezed lime juice
1 cup	(240 ml)	sour cream
1 cup	(240 ml)	cold water
		Sea salt and freshly ground black pepper
2 Tbsp.	(30 ml)	chopped fresh cilantro leaves

◦§ In a blender or food processor, combine the cucumber, avocados, green onions, lime juice, sour cream, and water. Process until smooth. Season to taste with salt and pepper. If the soup is too thick for your liking, thin it with water. Stir in the cilantro. Serve immediately or cover and let chill.

Per serving. Effective carbohydrates: 6.1 g; Carbohydrates: 11 g; Fiber: 4.9 g; Protein: 4.1 g; Fat: 25.2 g; Calories: 270

CREAM OF BROCCOLI SOUP

Makes 8 servings

Other vegetables can replace the broccoli: asparagus, spinach, red bell peppers, tomatoes, or more cauliflower (for Cream of Cauliflower Soup). I once made this soup with red Swiss chard stalks, and it was delicious!

Options for garnishing: bacon bits, chunks of chicken or ham, dollops of sour cream, crispy prosciutto or pancetta, pieces of smoked salmon, or a sprinkling of cheese. Blue cheese is great with plain cauliflower, and smoked salmon is elegant on asparagus. Dijon mustard adds a special, cheesy zing to the soup without using cheese.

1 lb.	(454 g)	cauliflower
1½ lb.	(680 g)	broccoli
2 Tbsp.	(30 ml)	extra-virgin olive oil
2		garlic cloves, minced
10 cups	(2.4 L)	chicken stock
1 tsp.	(5 ml)	sea salt
1 Tbsp.	(15 ml)	Dijon mustard
1 tsp.	(5 ml)	dried tarragon or other herb
		Freshly ground black pepper
		Whipping cream (optional)

◦§ Trim the cauliflower and broccoli and chop coarsely. (Peel and use the cauliflower core and the broccoli stems. Save a few tiny broccoli florets for garnishing.)

◦§ Heat the oil in a large pot over medium heat. Add the garlic and sizzle until it smells fragrant. Add the cauliflower, broccoli, stock, and salt. Bring to a boil. Reduce the heat and cook at a lively simmer for about 20 minutes, or until the vegetables are tender. Stir in the mustard and tarragon. Let cool slightly.

◦§ Working in batches, transfer to a blender and process until smooth. Return the mixture to the pot. (If you're using a fibrous vegetable like asparagus, you may want to press it through a sieve to make it smoother.) Add the reserved broccoli florets and season to taste

with pepper and additional salt. Thin with stock or water if the soup is too thick. Stir in the cream (if using).

Per serving (without cream). Effective carbohydrates: 3.6 g; Carbohydrates: 7 g; Fiber: 3.4 g; Protein: 8.2 g; Fat: 4.7 g; Calories: 100

DOTTIE'S CREAM OF MUSHROOM SOUP

Makes about 1 cup (240 ml)

This isn't really a soup that you eat from a bowl. Rather, it's an excellent replacement for canned cream of mushroom soup in casseroles like Norma June's Spaghetti Squash Breakfast Casserole (page 13).

It comes from Norma June's friend Dottie, who says, "After adding the cream, make sure you simmer it long enough so that the cream is no longer white and takes on the light brownish color of the mushrooms." This recipe can make a very rich, tasty sauce for everything from chicken and meatballs to fish and vegetables.

2 Tbsp.	**(30 ml)**	**unsalted butter**
¼ lb.	**(112 g)**	**small mushrooms, thinly sliced**
½ cup	**(120 ml)**	**finely chopped celery**
2 Tbsp.	**(30 ml)**	**finely chopped onion**
½ cup	**(120 ml)**	**chicken stock**
¾ cup	**(180 ml)**	**whipping cream**
		Sea salt and freshly ground black pepper

◆ Melt the butter in a medium frying pan over medium heat. Add the mushrooms, celery, and onion and sauté for 5 minutes, or until soft. Add the stock and cook over medium-high heat until reduced by half. Stir in the cream; bring to a boil and cook until reduced slightly, stirring frequently. Season to taste with salt and pepper.

Per 1 cup (240 ml). Effective carbohydrates: 10.3 g; Carbohydrates: 12 g; Fiber: 1.6 g; Protein: 6.6 g; Fat: 94.9 g; Calories: 914

ESCAROLE SOUP WITH TURKEY MEATBALLS

Makes 4 servings

I think escarole, chicory, kale, and Swiss chard make delicious soups. The meatballs turn this soup into a meal.

Note: *You can use spinach, zucchini, or a combination of both in place of the escarole.*

1 Tbsp.	(15 ml)	extra-virgin olive oil
½ cup	(120 ml)	finely chopped onion
2		garlic cloves, minced
1 tsp.	(5 ml)	chopped fresh rosemary leaves or ½ tsp. (2.5 ml) dried rosemary, crumbled
1½ lb.	(680 g)	escarole, washed, dried, and chopped into 1-inch (2.5-cm) pieces
6 cups	(1.4 L)	chicken stock
1 lb.	(454 g)	ground turkey
1		large egg
2 Tbsp.	(30 ml)	minced green onion
1 Tbsp.	(15 ml)	finely chopped fresh parsley
⅓ cup	(80 ml)	freshly grated Parmesan cheese
		Sea salt and freshly ground black pepper
		Lemon slices (optional)

◦§ Preheat the oven to 350°F (175°C).

◦§ Heat the oil in a large pot over medium heat. Add the onion, garlic, and rosemary and cook for 5 minutes, or until the onion is soft but not brown. Add the escarole and stock. Bring to a boil. Reduce the heat, partially cover the pot, and simmer for about 10 minutes, or until the escarole is tender.

◦§ In a medium bowl, mix the turkey, egg, green onion, parsley, and cheese. Form into 1-inch (2.5-cm) balls. Lightly oil a baking dish large enough to hold the meatballs in a single layer. Add the meatballs. Bake for 10 minutes.

Add the meatballs to the soup and simmer, partially covered, for 5 minutes. Season to taste with salt and pepper. Serve garnished with lemon slices (if using).

Per serving. Effective carbohydrates: 4.3 g; Carbohydrates: 10 g; Fiber: 5.7 g; Protein: 34 g; Fat: 18.4 g; Calories: 346

WHAT TO EAT WHEN YOU'RE SICK

Eating when you're under the weather can be a challenge when you first start low-carbing. Here are some tempting foods to help you out.

- Clear chicken soup with an egg or two beaten into it
- Hot chicken stock pureed with an avocado and lemon juice or pureed with silken tofu (You can add cooked chicken to this and puree it, too.)
- Cream of Broccoli Soup (page 52)—or its variation, Cream of Cauliflower Soup
- Basic Cauliflower Mash (page 112), alone or as a bed for poached eggs
- Custard—sweet or savory
- Poached or scrambled eggs
- Chicken stew
- Yogurt, ricotta, or cottage cheese (Ricotta mixed with cream, sweetener, and cinnamon will remind you of rice pudding.)
- Hot protein drinks (Use boiling water and cream with protein powder; add xanthan gum to thicken it up.)

WINTER VEGETABLE SOUP

Makes 8 servings

It's wonderful to have a hearty soup like this, especially in the winter. I like to cut the vegetables into small pieces to get the flavor of them all in each mouthful. This soup is especially delicious with a swirl of Basil Pesto (page 240).

By grating your own Parmesan or Grana Padano cheese, you will have the added bonus of the rinds. Save the rinds when you can grate no more cheese from them and freeze them. Add them to soups, stews, and tomato sauces. They will provide a savory flavor, aroma, and succulence.

3 Tbsp.	(45 ml)	extra-virgin olive oil
½ cup	(120 ml)	finely diced celery
½ cup	(120 ml)	finely diced onion
1 Tbsp.	(15 ml)	finely chopped fresh parsley
2		garlic cloves, finely minced
8 cups	(1.9 L)	chicken stock or water
2 cups	(480 ml)	canned Italian plum tomatoes with juice, finely chopped
1 cup	(240 ml)	diced turnips
1 cup	(240 ml)	diced daikon radish
2 cups	(480 ml)	finely chopped green cabbage
2 cups	(480 ml)	finely chopped green kale leaves
2		large Parmesan or Grana Padano rinds
1		bay leaf
		Sea salt and freshly ground black pepper
		Freshly grated Parmesan cheese

◦§ Heat the oil in a very large pot over medium heat. Add the celery, onion, parsley, and garlic and sauté until lightly browned. Add the stock or water and tomatoes. Bring to a boil.

◦§ Add the turnips, daikon, cabbage, kale, cheese rinds, and bay leaf. Season lightly with salt. Simmer for 1 hour, or until the vegetables are very tender and the soup has thickened. (If it is too thick, add additional water or stock.) Season to taste with pepper and additional salt. Remove the bay leaf and cheese rinds. Serve with cheese sprinkled on top.

Per serving. Effective carbohydrates: 7.5 g; Carbohydrates: 9.7 g; Fiber: 1.2 g; Protein: 1.8 g; Fat: 5.3 g; Calories: 88

DAIKON RADISH, CHINESE CABBAGE, AND TOFU SOUP

Makes 4 servings

This soup has become my winter staple. It is easy to make and can be the recipient of many leftover meats.

If you like Chinese flavor, add a few drops of roasted sesame oil just before serving. For a Southeast Asian flair—my favorite—crack an egg into each person's bowl and pour the boiling soup over it. Season with chopped cilantro, green onions, chile peppers, and a squeeze of lime juice. Then beat the egg into the broth to create a frothy cream.

Taking a trick from Vietnamese beef noodle soup, the boiling soup can be poured over extremely thinly sliced raw beef. The heat of the soup will cook it through.

7 cups	(1.6 L)	chicken stock
¾ lb.	(340 g)	daikon radish, peeled and cut into ½-inch (1.2-cm) cubes
4		fresh ginger slices, ¼ inch (0.6 cm) thick
		Sea salt
½ lb.	(227 g)	Chinese cabbage, cored and coarsely chopped
8 oz.	(227 g)	soft tofu, sliced

◦§ In a large pot, combine the stock, daikon, and ginger. Bring to a boil over high heat. Season lightly with salt. Reduce the heat and simmer for 20 to 30 minutes, or until the daikon is tender.

◦§ Add the cabbage, return to a boil, and cook for 5 minutes. Add the tofu and heat through. Remove the ginger slices, adjust the seasoning, and serve.

Per serving. Effective carbohydrates: 6.4 g; Carbohydrates: 9.5 g; Fiber: 3.1 g; Protein: 13 g; Fat: 4.3 g; Calories: 129

SHIRATAKI, SUKIYAKI-STYLE

Makes 2 servings

I like to use white tofu shirataki noodles for this.

1 8-oz.	(227-g)	package shirataki noodles
¼ cup	(60 ml)	water
¼ cup	(60 ml)	soy sauce
1 tsp.	(5 ml)	*each* Splenda and Canadian Sugar Twin or 4 tsp. (20 ml) Splenda
2 Tbsp.	(30 ml)	sake
4		green onions, cut into 2-inch (5-cm) pieces

ஃ Drain the shirataki noodles in a sieve and pour boiling water over them to refresh them.

ஃ In a small pot, combine the water, soy sauce, sweetener, and sake. Bring to a boil and drop in the noodles. Simmer over very low heat for 10 minutes. Stir in the green onion, simmer a minute longer, and serve.

Per serving. Effective carbohydrates: 1.2 g; Carbohydrates: 6 g; Fiber: 4.8 g; Protein: 4 g; Fat: 0 g; Calories: 66

JAPANESE GEMS

ஃ **Sake lees or kasu.** This is what's left over from sake production when fermented rice is pressed to make sake. It comes in tubs or "sheets." The sheets have to be soaked in a little cold water. When you can mash it to a paste, mix it with a little salt and use it as a marinade. Scrape off the marinade before broiling or grilling.

ஃ **Shirataki noodles.** Also called konnyaku, they're thin, gelatinous noodles. They have no discernible taste but absorb the flavors of the seasonings they are used with. They are almost completely fiber, almost no calories—depending on the brand—and are anywhere from about 1 gram of carbohydrate per 15 grams (.5 oz.) of noodles to 1 gram of carbohydrate per 100 grams (3.5 oz.) of noodles. Use them in soups, stir-fries, and chilled salads. Try them in a salad with cucumber, shredded chicken, and peanut dressing. One of their most traditional uses is in sukiyaki.

CHAWAN MUSHI

Makes 4 servings

This is a pared-down version of Japanese egg custard. It can contain spinach, mushrooms, and bits of chicken, fish, or prawns. You can drizzle a little soy sauce on top before serving. Hot or cold, it is a good thing to eat after dental work or when you're feeling sick.

Note: *This is best made in a steamer, but if you don't have one, you can bake the custards. Cover the bowls with aluminum foil and place in a baking dish. Pour boiling water into the dish to come halfway up the sides of the bowls. Bake at 350°F (175°C) for 5 minutes. Reduce the heat to 325°F (165°C) and bake for another 15 minutes.*

3		**large eggs**
2¾ cups	**(660 ml)**	**chicken stock**
½ tsp.	**(2.5 ml)**	**sea salt**

◃ Place the eggs in a medium bowl and beat gently with a fork or chopsticks; you don't want them to get foamy. Gently stir in the stock and salt. Pour into 4 small heatproof serving bowls or cups and cover each tightly with plastic wrap.

◃ Place the bowls in a steaming basket. Bring 2 inches (5 cm) of water to a boil in the bottom of a steamer. Place the steaming basket on top, cover with the lid, and turn the heat down to medium.

◃ Steam for 12 to 15 minutes, or until set. The mixture won't be as firm as a traditional custard or quiche dish, so be careful not to overcook it.

Per serving. Effective carbohydrates: 1 g; Carbohydrates: 1 g; Fiber: 0 g; Protein: 6.2 g; Fat: 4 g; Calories: 68

THAI PRAWN SOUP

Makes 4 servings

There is a wealth of opportunity for good eating from Southeast Asia when you stop focusing on the rice and noodles. This soup is a good example, and it's fast and easy, too!

Lemongrass is easy for me to find, but I always keep frozen kaffir lime leaves and galingale root. You can also freeze lemongrass. You can find these ingredients in well-stocked supermarkets or Southeast Asian grocery stores.

6 cups	(1.4 L)	water
3		shallots, thinly sliced
2		lemongrass stalks, lightly pounded and cut into 1-inch (2.5-cm) pieces
2 Tbsp.	(30 ml)	fish sauce
4		fresh or dried galingale root slices
¾ lb.	(340 g)	medium prawns, peeled with tails intact
½ lb.	(227 g)	small mushrooms, halved
6		kaffir lime leaves
3 Tbsp.	(45 ml)	freshly squeezed lime juice
2 or 3		whole Thai chile peppers
2 Tbsp.	(30 ml)	coarsely chopped cilantro leaves
3		green onions, thinly sliced

◦§ In a large saucepan, combine the water, shallots, lemongrass, fish sauce, and galingale root. Bring to a boil over medium heat and cook for 3 minutes.

◦§ Add the prawns and mushrooms. Cook, stirring occasionally, until the prawns turn pink and are cooked all the way through, about 3 to 4 minutes. Add the lime leaves, lime juice, and chiles. Cover and remove from the heat. Let sit for 1 minute. Ladle into bowls and sprinkle with the cilantro and green onion.

Per serving. Effective carbohydrates: 4.3 g; Carbohydrates: 5 g; Fiber: 0.7 g; Protein: 18.3 g; Fat: 1.5 g; Calories: 109

MORE ENTERTAINING LOW-CARB STYLE

Here are a few more menus—ranging from exotic and elegant to homey and comforting—to help you plan dinner for family and friends. Find more suggestions on pages 24 and 207.

Sit-Down Fancy French Dinner

Chilled Cucumber and Avocado Soup, page 51

Tomato, Olive, and Goat Cheese Salad with Capers, page 80

Pancetta-Wrapped Salmon with Red Wine Butter page 152

Basic Cauliflower Mash with Hollandaise Sauce, page 112

Braised Fennel with White Wine and Parmesan, page 120

Chilled Lemon Meringue Soufflé, page 301

Spicy Thai

Thai Prawn Soup, page 61

Sesame Snow Pea and Daikon Radish Salad, page 84

Thai BBQ Chicken Bundles, pages 186 to 187

Lime and Coconut Cheesecake, page 278

East Indian

Simple Chicken and Coconut Milk Curry, page 175

Basic Cauli-flied Rice with Curry, page 110

Spicy Roasted and Mashed Eggplant, page 119

Kheema (Spiced Ground Beef), page 200

Chai Panna Cotta, page 287

LISA N.'S DOUBLE ITALIAN SAUSAGE SOUP

Makes 6 servings

Lisa is one of the marvelous moderators at lowcarber.org. She says her whole family (which includes two children under 10) likes this. She also gave me the brilliant tip of using scissors to cut the sausage and bacon into small pieces. Now, why didn't I think of that?

½ lb.	(227 g)	hot Italian sausage, cut into small pieces
½ lb.	(227 g)	sweet Italian sausage, cut into small pieces
6		bacon slices, chopped
½ cup	(120 ml)	chopped onion
2		garlic cloves, minced
4 cups	(960 ml)	chicken stock
1 10-oz.	(285-g)	package frozen chopped spinach
1 cup	(240 ml)	whipping cream
		Freshly grated Parmesan cheese

◆§ In a large heavy saucepan, brown the sausage and bacon pieces over medium heat until no longer pink. Add the onion and garlic and continue to cook for 5 minutes, or until the onion softens.

◆§ Add the stock and spinach (which does not have to be thawed). Bring to a boil, then reduce the heat and simmer, stirring occasionally, for 15 minutes, or until the spinach is thawed. Add the cream and heat through, but do not allow the soup to boil. Serve with a sprinkle of cheese.

Per serving. Effective carbohydrates: 4.9 g; Carbohydrates: 6.4 g; Fiber: 1.5 g; Protein: 25.9 g; Fat: 47 g; Calories: 559

QUICK KOREAN-STYLE BEEF AND SPINACH SOUP

Makes 4 servings

If you are a kim chee lover, it is the perfect accompaniment to this soup.

1 Tbsp.	(15 ml)	toasted sesame oil
½ lb.	(227 g)	lean ground beef
1		green onion, finely chopped
1		garlic clove, minced
1 Tbsp.	(15 ml)	soy sauce
3 cups	(720 ml)	water or chicken stock
½ lb.	(227 g)	fresh spinach, washed and trimmed
2		large eggs, beaten
2 tsp.	(10 ml)	toasted sesame seeds
		Sea salt and freshly ground black pepper

◦ʃ Heat the oil in a large heavy pot over medium heat. Add the beef and brown it, breaking up the pieces with a wooden spoon. Add the green onion, garlic, and soy sauce and stir for 30 seconds. Add the water or stock, bring to a boil, and add the spinach. Cover and simmer for 5 minutes.

◦ʃ In a small bowl, mix the eggs and sesame seeds with a fork. Season with salt and pepper. Slowly pour into the pot while swirling the soup with the wooden spoon. Continue to stir for a few minutes until the eggs float to the top and form tiny "flakes."

Per serving. Effective carbohydrates: 2.1 g; Carbohydrates: 3.9 g; Fiber: 1.8 g; Protein: 19.1 g; Fat: 19.8 g; Calories: 274

SALADS
AND DRESSINGS

THERE'S MORE TO LIFE THAN ICEBERG LETTUCE. Not that there is anything wrong with iceberg, especially a nice crisp wedge with a good blob of blue cheese dressing on it. There are, however, different types of lettuce to discover—some great baby lettuce mixes, red leaf lettuce, romaine, endive, radicchio, chicory, watercress, escarole, Boston, Bibb, arugula, and mizuna.

No excuses—a quick tip is to wash and dry your lettuce all at once and store it in a resealable plastic bag lined with a paper towel, pressing the air out of it. You'll always have it ready when you want it.

There's no need to ever be bored with the salads. These are the real workhorses of low-carb cuisine. Also, I'm a salad dressing snob. I don't buy bottled salad dressing and never have. I know that preparing dressings makes people nervous, but with the right recipe, you will have something more delicious and fresher-tasting than anything you could buy. If you're taking the time to make a wonderful, fresh salad, you should honor it by using a wonderful, fresh dressing.

Here are a few ideas to get you started.

PINE NUT AND PARSLEY SALAD

Makes 6 servings

This is the low-carb version of tabbouli, the wonderful Middle Eastern parsley salad. It's excellent with grilled or roasted chicken. A traditional way of eating this is to wrap it up in leaf lettuce. Try it with Hummus (page 23).

You can mix the vegetables 4 to 6 hours in advance and add the dressing just before serving.

Note: *For variety, serve this salad minus the pine nuts and add a few chopped black olives. Or add a sprinkling of feta cheese and diced avocado.*

SALAD

2 cups	(480 ml)	fresh parsley leaves, finely chopped
1 cup	(240 ml)	fresh mint leaves, coarsely chopped
⅓ cup	(80 ml)	seeded and finely chopped tomatoes
⅓ cup	(80 ml)	seeded and finely diced English cucumber
¼ cup	(60 ml)	thinly sliced green onion
½ cup	(120 ml)	pine nuts, coarsely chopped

DRESSING

2 Tbsp.	(30 ml)	freshly squeezed lemon juice
½ tsp.	(2.5 ml)	finely chopped garlic
¼ tsp.	(1.2 ml)	sea salt
5 Tbsp.	(75 ml)	extra-virgin olive oil
½ tsp.	(2.5 ml)	ground allspice
¼ tsp.	(1.2 ml)	ground cinnamon

➔ *To make the salad:* In a large bowl, mix the parsley, mint, tomatoes, cucumber, and green onion. Sprinkle with the pine nuts. Cover and refrigerate until needed.

➔ *To make the dressing:* Just before serving, combine the lemon juice, garlic, and salt in a small bowl. Stir well. Slowly beat in the oil. Stir in the allspice and cinnamon. Pour over the parsley mixture and toss to coat.

Per serving. Effective carbohydrates: 3.6 g; Carbohydrates: 5.6 g; Fiber: 2 g; Protein: 4.3 g; Fat: 18.3 g; Calories: 192

MOM'S CAULIFLOWER SALAD

Makes 6 servings

My mother never made this salad, but she did make a great potato salad in exactly the same way. I think she would have enjoyed my new version.

		Sea salt
2 lb.	(908 g)	**cauliflower, trimmed**
3		**hard-cooked large eggs, peeled and grated**
⅓ cup	(80 ml)	**mayonnaise**
⅓ cup	(80 ml)	**sour cream**
1 Tbsp.	(15 ml)	**Dijon mustard**
¼ cup	(60 ml)	**finely diced celery**
2 Tbsp.	(30 ml)	**minced green onion**
2 Tbsp.	(30 ml)	**finely chopped fresh dill or 1½ tsp. (7.5 ml) dried dill**
		Freshly ground black pepper

⊷ Bring a large pot of water to a boil and season liberally with salt. (It should taste like sea water.) Cut the cauliflower, including the core, into 4 wedges and add to the pot. Cook for about 10 to 12 minutes, or until it's barely tender and still somewhat crisp. Drain and let cool completely.

⊷ In a large bowl, mix the eggs, mayonnaise, sour cream, mustard, celery, green onion, and dill. Season to taste with salt and pepper.

⊷ Shred the cauliflower, using the large holes on the grater, and add to the bowl. Mix well. Check the seasoning if it sits for a while. The water drains from the cauliflower as it sits, so it will taste less salty.

Per serving. Effective carbohydrates: 5.2 g; Carbohydrates: 8.9 g; Fiber: 3.7 g; Protein: 6.8 g; Fat: 15 g; Calories: 191

WARM CAULIFLOWER, BACON, AND EGG SALAD WITH SPINACH

Makes 6 servings

This is a very succulent salad with great texture. I think it goes very well with white fish like halibut or cod. And leftovers are very good cold.

1½ lb.	(680 g)	cauliflower, trimmed
6		hard-cooked large eggs, peeled
1 10-oz.	(285-g)	bag ready-to-use spinach
8		bacon slices, cut into ½-inch (1.2-cm) pieces
¼ cup	(60 ml)	finely chopped green onion
½ cup	(120 ml)	extra-virgin olive oil
⅓ cup	(80 ml)	white wine vinegar
1 Tbsp.	(15 ml)	Dijon mustard
		Sea salt and freshly ground black pepper

◅ Cut the cauliflower evenly into 1-inch (2.5-cm) pieces and set aside.

◅ Cut the eggs into ¼ -inch (0.6-cm) slices. Place the spinach in a large bowl and add the eggs.

◅ Fry the bacon in a medium frying pan over medium heat until crisp. Remove the bacon with a slotted spoon and add to the spinach. Add the green onion, oil, vinegar, and mustard to the pan and bring to a simmer, stirring constantly. Remove from the heat.

◅ Bring a large pot of water to a boil and season liberally with salt. (It should taste like sea water.) Add the cauliflower and cook for about 6 to 7 minutes, or until it is tender but still has some texture. Drain immediately, tossing well to remove the water. Add to the spinach.

◅ Bring the contents of the frying pan to a boil and pour over the salad. Toss gently. Season to taste with salt and pepper. Serve immediately.

Per serving. Effective carbohydrates: 4.6; Carbohydrates: 8.6 g; Fiber: 4 g; Protein: 12.6 g; Fat: 28 g; Calories: 327

COLE SLAW
WITH BACON BUTTERMILK DRESSING

Makes 4 servings

Salting and rinsing cabbage for cole slaw prevents it from turning watery and thinning out the dressing. It also gives the cabbage a toothsome crunch.

SALAD

1 lb.	(454 g)	green cabbage, cored and finely shredded
½ cup	(120 ml)	thinly sliced red onion
1 tsp.	(5 ml)	sea salt
8		bacon slices, cut into ½-inch (1.2-cm) pieces

DRESSING

¼ cup	(60 ml)	buttermilk
¼ cup	(60 ml)	mayonnaise
2 Tbsp.	(30 ml)	vegetable oil
1 tsp.	(5 ml)	Dijon mustard
		Pinch *each* of Splenda and Canadian Sugar Twin or a larger pinch of Splenda
		Sea salt and freshly ground black pepper

◦§ *To make the salad:* In a large bowl, mix the cabbage, onion, and salt. Transfer to a large sieve or colander to drain. Let sit for at least 1 hour and up to 4 hours.

◦§ Rinse under cold running water. Drain well and pat dry with paper towels. Place in a large bowl.

◦§ Cook the bacon in a medium frying pan over medium heat until crisp. Remove from the pan with a slotted spoon and drain on paper towels; discard the fat in the pan. Add the bacon to the bowl with the cabbage.

◦§ *To make the dressing:* Combine the buttermilk, mayonnaise, oil, mustard, and sweetener. Mix well.

◦§ Pour the dressing over the cabbage and toss gently. Season to taste with salt and pepper. Cover and refrigerate.

Per serving. Effective carbohydrates: 6.1 g; Carbohydrates: 9 g; Fiber: 2.9 g; Protein: 6.4 g; Fat: 24.6 g; Calories: 277

WEIGHING IN ON MEASURING VEGETABLES

I'm a heavy supporter of weighing vegetables. You don't have to be tied to the scale for life—use it until you get a feel for carb counting. With weighing, you get the real picture instead of a subjective take on what ½ cup (120 ml) of broccoli or 2 cups (480 ml) of lettuce is. Sixteen ounces, or 1 pound, of salad weighed on a scale would be an incredible amount, depending on the lettuce used.

Keep in mind that volume and mass are two different things. One cup—8 oz.—of liquid measurement or dry measurement does not equal 8 oz. of weight. The weight of 1 cup of solids will vary according to whether you're measuring tomatoes or cauliflower. Those amounts can be pitifully small by volume, but 3½ oz. (100 g) of romaine lettuce is a generous serving, very low in carbs, high in fiber, and greatly exceeds 2 cups in volume. And it contains only 0.7 g of effective carbohydrate.

SPINACH SALAD WITH BACON, TOMATO, AVOCADO, AND RANCH DRESSING

Makes 4 servings

You can make this salad even more scrumptious by adding chopped hard-cooked eggs and a few shavings of red onion. It goes well with a steak or simply cooked chicken.

1 10-oz.	(285-g)	bag ready-to-use spinach
1		large ripe tomato, cut into thin wedges
1		ripe Haas avocado, pitted, peeled, and cut into thin wedges
½ lb.	(227 g)	bacon, cooked until crisp and crumbled
2 Tbsp.	(30 ml)	unsalted roasted peanuts (optional)
½ cup	(120 ml)	Ranch Dressing (page 95)

◦§ Place the spinach in a large bowl. Top with the tomato, avocado, bacon, and peanuts (if using). Pour the dressing over the salad, toss well, and serve.

Per serving. Effective carbohydrates: 4 g; Carbohydrates: 7.5 g; Fiber: 3.5 g; Protein: 7.3 g; Fat: 32 g; Calories: 334

CUCUMBER SALAD WITH PEANUTS, COCONUT, AND LIME

Makes 4 servings

This is one of my favorite salads. I think it's just delicious with prawns or shrimp. Serve it with simple meat dishes or as part of a Thai or Indian feast. If you don't have the black mustard seeds, don't sweat it! But do try to use freshly roasted peanuts for best flavor.

2 Tbsp.	(30 ml)	dried unsweetened shredded coconut
¼ cup	(60 ml)	boiling water
1½ cups	(360 ml)	English cucumber cut into ¼-inch (0.6-cm) cubes
½ cup	(120 ml)	unsalted roasted peanuts
2		small chile peppers, finely chopped
2 Tbsp.	(30 ml)	freshly squeezed lime juice
½ tsp.	(2.5 ml)	sea salt
1 Tbsp.	(15 ml)	vegetable oil
¼ tsp.	(1.2 ml)	black mustard seeds

In a small bowl, combine the coconut and boiling water. Let sit until cool.

In a large bowl, combine the cucumber, peanuts, and chiles. Add the coconut and mix well.

In a cup, mix the lime juice and salt. Just before serving, heat the oil over high heat in a small frying pan. Add the mustard seeds. When they pop, pour them into the lime mixture. Pour over the cucumber mixture and toss gently. Serve immediately.

Per serving. Effective carbohydrates: 5.2; Carbohydrates: 7.1 g; Fiber: 1.9 g; Protein: 4.7 g; Fat: 13.6 g; Calories: 159

CUCUMBER SALAD WITH UMEBOSHI AND BONITO FLAKES

Makes 4 servings

If you're buying bonito flakes and umeboshi plums, get some Japanese cucumbers, too. Then you can make this simple salad.

2 cups	(480 ml)	**Japanese or English cucumbers cut into ½-inch (1.2-cm) cubes**
½ tsp.	(2.5 ml)	**sea salt**
4		**umeboshi plums**
1 Tbsp.	(15 ml)	**soy sauce**
1½ tsp.	(7.5 ml)	**sake**
3 Tbsp.	(45 ml)	**small bonito flakes**

•§ Mix the cucumbers and salt. Transfer to a sieve and let drain for 1 hour. Rinse and pat dry. Place in a large bowl.

•§ Pit the plums and mash to a paste. Place in a small bowl and mix with the soy sauce, sake, and bonito. Pour over the cucumbers, toss to mix, and serve immediately.

Per serving. Effective carbohydrates: 1.4 g; Carbohydrates: 1.9 g; Fiber: 0.5 g; Protein: 1.4 g; Fat: 0.2 g; Calories: 17

UMEBOSHI PLUMS: SALTY LITTLE TREATS

Umeboshi plums are green immature plums that are cured in salt for about 2 weeks. Then they're packed with shiso (beefsteak plant) leaves to impart a red color and shiso flavor and marinated for 4 more weeks. Their salty tartness really wakes up your taste buds! They are commonly eaten as part of breakfast in Japan. If you ever have a huge craving for sweets, an umeboshi plum will kill it instantly!

One umeboshi plum has 0.8 gram of carbohydrate, 0.1 gram of fiber, and 3 calories. The fat and protein are negligible.

ROASTED RED PEPPER
AND PRESERVED LEMON SALAD

Makes 4 servings

Serve this with grilled chicken, lamb, or game fish—such as tuna, marlin, or swordfish. Roasted peppers and preserved lemons can be found in gourmet food stores (see page xvii).

6		canned, jarred, or freshly roasted and peeled red peppers
1		garlic clove, minced
¼ cup	(60 ml)	extra-virgin olive oil
¾ tsp.	(3.6 ml)	ground cumin
¼ tsp.	(1.2 ml)	smoked or regular paprika
¼ tsp.	(1.2 ml)	freshly ground black pepper
1		Moroccan preserved lemon, pulp removed and rind diced
		Sea salt and freshly ground black pepper
½ cup	(120 ml)	coarsely chopped fresh parsley

◄§ Coarsely chop the peppers and place in a large bowl. Stir in the garlic, oil, cumin, paprika, pepper, and lemon rind. Season to taste with salt and pepper and toss in the parsley. Cover and refrigerate.

Per serving. Effective carbohydrates: 4.5 g; Carbohydrates: 5.7 g; Fiber: 1.2 g; Protein: 1.3 g; Fat: 14.1 g; Calories: 152

TOMATO, OLIVE, AND GOAT CHEESE SALAD WITH CAPERS

Makes 6 servings

While this is great with the goat cheese, you can use your favorite soft cheese. Brie, gorgonzola, feta, and herbed Boursin are all good choices.

3		large ripe tomatoes
2 Tbsp.	(30 ml)	balsamic vinegar
¼ tsp.	(1.2 ml)	sea salt
1 Tbsp.	(15 ml)	finely chopped shallot
5 Tbsp.	(75 ml)	extra-virgin olive oil
½ cup	(120 ml)	pitted black olives, cut in half
⅓ cup	(80 ml)	crumbled fresh goat cheese
2 Tbsp.	(30 ml)	drained capers

◦§ Cut the tomatoes into thick slices and arrange on a platter. In a small bowl, whisk the vinegar, salt, and shallot together. Whisk in the oil. Drizzle over the tomatoes. Scatter the olives, cheese, and capers over the salad. Serve immediately.

Per serving. Effective carbohydrates: 3.3 g; Carbohydrates: 4.5 g; Fiber: 1.2 g; Protein: 2 g; Fat: 14.9 g; Calories: 155

OLIVE, WALNUT, AND PARSLEY SALAD

Makes 6 servings

This is delicious with Cinnamon-Spiced Lemon Chicken (page 171). I prefer to use a combination of black and green olives. And by all means, get good-quality ones.

2		bunches fresh parsley, stemmed
1 cup	(240 ml)	pitted olives, coarsely chopped
1 cup	(240 ml)	walnuts, coarsely chopped
2		green onions, minced
1		large tomato, seeded and diced
⅓ cup	(80 ml)	extra-virgin olive oil
2 Tbsp.	(30 ml)	red wine vinegar
2 Tbsp.	(30 ml)	freshly squeezed lemon juice
1		small garlic clove, minced
½ tsp.	(2.5 ml)	ground cumin
		Sea salt and freshly ground black pepper

◅§ Coarsely chop the parsley so it remains fluffy looking. Place in a large bowl and toss with the olives, walnuts, green onions, and tomato.

◅§ In a small bowl, beat together the oil, vinegar, lemon juice, garlic, and cumin. Season to taste with salt and pepper. Pour over the salad and toss well.

Per serving. Effective carbohydrates: 5.8 g; Carbohydrates: 8.8 g; Fiber: 3 g; Protein: 4.5 g; Fat: 29.2 g; Calories: 301

TO STORE PARSLEY . . .

I think we've all faced limp or even rotten bunches of parsley with the twist tie being the only thing that's still sassy about the bunch. Here's a great method for keeping parsley. Pluck the parsley clusters from the stems—and I mean the little clusters of leaves from the little branched stems—then wash and dry thoroughly. Place in a large plastic container—a yogurt container works well for this—and punch several holes in the lid. The parsley will stay fresh and ready to use for at least 3 weeks.

CLASSIC CELERY ROOT RÉMOULADE

Makes 8 servings

Substituting a few tablespoons of walnut oil for a few tablespoons of the olive oil is absolutely delicious. You can also add a little chopped fresh dill or parsley for color and freshness. This keeps well in the fridge for a few days.

1 lb.	(454 g)	**celery root**
2 tsp.	(10 ml)	**freshly squeezed lemon juice**
1½ tsp.	(7.5 ml)	**sea salt**
¼ cup	(60 ml)	**Dijon mustard**
3 Tbsp.	(45 ml)	**boiling water**
2 Tbsp.	(30 ml)	**red wine vinegar**
½ cup	(120 ml)	**extra-virgin olive oil**
¼ cup	(60 ml)	**sour cream**
		Freshly ground black pepper

◦§ Peel the celery root. Cut in half and remove the spongy core. Slice thinly, stack up the slices, and cut into thin matchstick strips. Place in a large bowl and toss with the lemon juice and 1½ tsp. (7.5 ml) salt. Let sit for 20 minutes.

◦§ Place the mustard in a small bowl and slowly whisk in the water. Dribble in the vinegar and the oil, whisking constantly. Stir in the sour cream.

◦§ Rinse the celery root under cold water and drain well. Pat dry and toss with the dressing. Season to taste with salt and pepper. Refrigerate for at least 30 minutes.

Per serving. Effective carbohydrates: 6 g; Carbohydrates: 7.1 g; Fiber: 1.1 g; Protein: 1.8 g; Fat: 17.3 g; Calories: 184

CELERY ROOT:
WHERE TASTE EXCEEDS GLAMOUR

One of the more unusual vegetables that you may cross paths with is celery root—also known as celeriac. It's bumpy and a little hairy-looking. Although it seems to be available year-round, it's best in the fall, when it's fresh. It tends to get a little soft when stored too long, so squeeze it before buying to check for firmness and inspect it for soft spots. To use, peel it deeply, cut it in half, and remove the spongy core.

The carbohydrate count for an average 1-lb. (454-g) root is 28 g of effective carbs, or around 8 g per raw chopped cup.

Celery root can be diced and used in soups and stews. It's great roasted. It makes an excellent puree when combined with cauliflower or can be used raw in a salad. (It can be a little tough when raw, so grate it or cut it into fine, matchstick strips.) Celery root discolors quickly, so toss it with a little vinegar or lemon juice to preserve its whiteness.

For an excellent vegetable dish, substitute half of the cauliflower in the Basic Cauliflower Mash (page 112) with cooked celery root. Delicious!

SESAME, SNOW PEA, AND DAIKON RADISH SALAD

Makes 6 servings

Colorful and cool on the eyes, this goes well with roast pork and fits into any Asian-style meal.

		Sea salt
1 lb.	(454 g)	snow peas, stringed and trimmed
¾ lb.	(340 g)	daikon radish, peeled and cut into thin matchstick strips, about 1½ cups (360 ml)
1		large red bell pepper, cored and cut into thin strips
2 Tbsp.	(30 ml)	freshly squeezed lemon juice
2 tsp.	(10 ml)	grated fresh ginger
2 Tbsp.	(30 ml)	soy sauce
¼ cup	(60 ml)	toasted sesame oil
		Freshly ground black pepper
1 Tbsp.	(15 ml)	toasted sesame seeds

◆§ Bring a large pot of water to a boil and season liberally with salt. (It should taste like sea water.) Add the snow peas and cook only until they turn bright green. Drain immediately and cool under cold running water. Drain again and pat dry.

◆§ Place the snow peas in a large bowl. Add the daikon and red pepper. Cover and refrigerate for up to 6 hours.

◆§ In a small bowl, whisk together the lemon juice, ginger, and soy sauce. Slowly whisk in the oil and season to taste with salt and pepper. When you are ready to serve the salad, pour over the vegetables and toss well. Sprinkle with the sesame seeds.

Per serving. Effective carbohydrates: 5.5 g; Carbohydrates: 8.6 g; Fiber: 3.1 g; Protein: 3.5 g; Fat: 10.1 g; Calories: 136

WARM TURKEY, BACON, AND MUSHROOM SALAD

Makes 4 servings

This is an excellent way to use up leftover turkey. It's also great with chicken.

½ lb.	(227 g)	bacon slices, cut into ½-inch (1.2-cm) pieces
1 lb.	(454 g)	mushrooms, coarsely chopped
2 cups	(480 ml)	coarsely shredded cooked turkey
⅓ cup	(80 ml)	balsamic vinegar
1 tsp.	(5 ml)	sea salt
½ tsp.	(2.5 ml)	freshly ground black pepper
1		medium head romaine lettuce, coarsely shredded
1		bunch watercress, stemmed

⚬§ Cook the bacon in a large frying pan over medium heat until crisp. Remove from the pan with a slotted spoon and drain on paper towels.

⚬§ Add the mushrooms to the fat in the pan and cook over very low heat until the water evaporates and the mushrooms brown. Add the turkey and bacon. Cook over medium-low heat until warmed through. Add the vinegar, salt, and pepper and toss well.

⚬§ Place the lettuce and watercress in a large salad bowl. Add the turkey mixture and toss quickly. Serve immediately.

Per serving. Effective carbohydrates: 8.6 g; Carbohydrates: 11.5; Fiber: 2.9; Protein: 43.8; Fat: 26.5; Calories: 450

DO AS THE FRENCH DO

In France, a common dressing for salads is the pan juices left from roasting chicken. The salad is then served with the chicken. This works with any roasted meat. Heat the juices gently and season with salt and pepper and a few drops of lemon juice or vinegar for tartness. This dressing is fantastic on spinach or sturdier greens like arugula, escarole, or chicory.

WARM STEAK SALAD
WITH CREAMY SALSA DRESSING

Makes 2 servings

This is also delish served with leftover roast beef or chicken instead of the steak.

¾ lb.	(340 g)	sirloin steak
		Extra-virgin olive oil
		Sea salt and freshly ground black pepper
1 cup	(240 ml)	seeded and finely chopped ripe tomato
6 Tbsp.	(90 ml)	sour cream or crème fraîche
2 Tbsp.	(30 ml)	cilantro leaves, finely chopped
1 Tbsp.	(15 ml)	freshly squeezed lime or lemon juice
1		jalapeño pepper, seeded and finely chopped
4 cups	(960 ml)	shredded romaine lettuce

⌐§ Rub the steak on both sides with the oil and season with salt and pepper. Broil, barbecue, or sear until done to your liking.

⌐§ In a small bowl, mix the tomato, sour cream or crème fraîche, cilantro, lime or lemon juice, jalapeño pepper to taste, and ½ tsp. (2.5 ml) salt.

⌐§ Place the lettuce on a platter. Slice the steak and arrange it on the lettuce. Spoon the tomato mixture over the steak.

Per serving. Effective carbohydrates: 7 g; Carbohydrates: 10.6 g; Fiber: 3.6 g; Protein: 42.8 g; Fat: 17.7 g; Calories: 374

BEEF SALAD
WITH CREAMY HORSERADISH DRESSING

Makes 4 servings

You can add other vegetables to this salad—such as cooked green beans, radishes, or peppers—and use other greens in place of the spinach.

DRESSING

½ cup	(120 ml)	white wine vinegar
2 Tbsp.	(30 ml)	Dijon mustard
½ tsp.	(2.5 ml)	sea salt
¼ tsp.	(1.2 ml)	*each* Splenda and Canadian Sugar Twin or 1 tsp. (5 ml) Splenda
6 Tbsp.	(90 ml)	finely grated fresh horseradish or ¼ cup (60 ml) prepared horseradish
2 cups	(480 ml)	sour cream or crème fraîche
½ cup	(120 ml)	extra-virgin olive oil

SALAD

2 lb.	(908 g)	flank steak or top sirloin
2		garlic cloves
½ tsp.	(2.5 ml)	sea salt
½ tsp.	(2.5 ml)	freshly ground black pepper
1 Tbsp.	(15 ml)	Worcestershire sauce
2 Tbsp.	(30 ml)	vegetable oil
1 10-oz.	(285-g)	bag ready-to-use spinach
2		ripe tomatoes
1		medium red onion

To make the dressing: In a medium bowl, combine the vinegar, mustard, salt, sweetener, horseradish, sour cream or crème fraîche, and oil. Whisk until smooth. Cover and refrigerate until needed. The dressing may be prepared up to 3 days in advance.

To make the salad: If you are using flank steak, score it lightly with a sharp knife on both sides in a diamond pattern at 2-inch (5-cm) intervals. Place the meat on a plate.

Finely chop the garlic. Sprinkle with the salt and crush to a paste using the flat side of a knife blade. Place in a small bowl and mix in the pepper, Worcestershire sauce, and oil. Rub on both sides of the steak. Cover and refrigerate until ready to cook. The steak may be prepared up to 2 days in advance.

To serve, place the spinach on a large platter. Cut the tomatoes into 8 wedges each. Slice the onion into thick slices and separate into rings. Arrange the tomatoes and onion over the spinach.

Heat a large heavy frying pan (preferably cast iron) over medium heat. When it is hot, add the steak. Cook until browned on one side, about 4 to 5 minutes. If the steak is browning too quickly, adjust the heat accordingly. Turn the steak over and brown the other side. Cook until the steak is done to your liking. These instructions will produce a medium-rare steak. Remove from the pan and let rest for 5 minutes.

Slice the steak thinly across the grain and arrange on the salad. Serve immediately with the dressing on the side.

Per serving. Effective carbohydrates: 15.4; Carbohydrates: 18.9 g; Fiber: 3.5 g; Protein: 56.6 g; Fat: 71.8 g; Calories: 941; Made with Splenda only: Add 0.12 g carbohydrates

MICHELLE'S BROCCOLI AND CHICKEN SALAD

Makes 2 main-course servings

A real winner from Michelle—one of lowcarber.org's alumni. It's very portable for lunch.

SALAD

4		bacon slices, chopped
2 cups	(480 ml)	cooked bite-size broccoli florets
1½ cups	(360 ml)	bite-size pieces cooked chicken
½ cup	(120 ml)	coarsely shredded cheddar cheese
1 cup	(240 ml)	thinly sliced celery

DRESSING

⅓ cup	(80 ml)	mayonnaise
⅓ cup	(80 ml)	sour cream
½ tsp.	(2.5 ml)	celery seeds
2 Tbsp.	(30 ml)	apple cider vinegar
1 tsp.	(5 ml)	Dijon mustard
		Sea salt and freshly ground black pepper

To make the salad: Cook the bacon in a medium frying pan over medium heat until crisp. Remove from the pan with a slotted spoon and drain on paper towels.

In a large bowl, combine the broccoli, chicken, cheese, and celery. Toss lightly.

To make the dressing: In a small bowl, mix the mayonnaise, sour cream, celery seeds, vinegar, and mustard. Season to taste with salt and pepper.

Pour over the salad and toss to combine. Add the bacon and toss lightly again.

Per serving. Effective carbohydrates: 7.4 g; Carbohydrates: 13 g; Fiber: 5.6 g; Protein: 58 g; Fat: 59 g; Calories: 807

BASIC VINAIGRETTE

Makes ¾ cup (180 ml)

You can go wild with variations of a basic vinaigrette dressing recipe. Fresh or dried herbs, garlic, shallots, or pesto will make your salads come alive. A few spoonfuls of sour cream turn it into a creamy dressing. You can make Greek dressing by adding garlic and oregano. You can even add mashed raspberries or strawberries and a touch of sweetener to the basic vinaigrette.

You can also add dimensions of flavor with different vinegars and oils, singly or blending several into the vinaigrette. Use balsamic vinegar in place of the red wine vinegar. Or substitute walnut oil for half of the olive oil and you'll have vinaigrette that's great on asparagus or broccoli.

The most important element in the vinaigrette—or any salad dressing, for that matter—is salt. The dressing should taste slightly salty in the bowl. Remember, it has to cover a lot of water-filled vegetables. And in my humble opinion, a lot of vinaigrettes go a little too heavy on the vinegar.

2 tsp.	(10 ml)	Dijon mustard
2 Tbsp.	(30 ml)	red wine vinegar
¼ tsp.	(1.2 ml)	sea salt
½ cup	(120 ml)	extra-virgin olive oil
1 tsp.	(5 ml)	freshly squeezed lemon juice
		Freshly ground black pepper

◄ In a small bowl, mix the mustard, vinegar, and salt. Let sit until the salt dissolves.

◄ While whisking or mixing with a hand-held blender, slowly pour the oil into the vinegar mixture. The dressing should thicken a bit and be evenly mixed. Add the lemon juice. Season with pepper and additional salt, if needed.

Per 1 Tbsp. (15 ml). Effective carbohydrates: 0.3 g; Carbohydrates: 0.3 g; Fiber: 0 g; Protein: 0 g; Fat: 9 g; Calories: 81

CAESAR DRESSING

Makes about ¾ cup (180 ml)

This recipe is for my favorite classic Caesar dressing. My true dressing snobbery comes through here—I frown upon creamy Caesar dressing.

Note: *The egg is not cooked in this dressing. If that is a concern, look for pasteurized eggs in the grocery store.*

1½ tsp.	(7.5 ml)	finely chopped garlic
¼ tsp.	(1.2 ml)	sea salt
1		large anchovy fillet, finely chopped, or ½ tsp. (2.5 ml) anchovy paste
1 Tbsp.	(15 ml)	Dijon mustard
2 Tbsp.	(30 ml)	freshly squeezed lemon juice
6		drops hot-pepper sauce
8		drops Worcestershire sauce
5 Tbsp.	(75 ml)	extra-virgin olive oil
1		large egg
		Freshly ground black pepper

⋙ Place the garlic and salt in a small bowl. Mash to a paste with the back of a spoon. Add the anchovy and crush again. With a fork, stir in the mustard. Stir in the lemon juice, hot-pepper sauce, and Worcestershire sauce.

⋙ Slowly beat in the oil. Then add the egg and beat like a madman to emulsify it into the dressing. Season to taste with pepper.

Per 1 Tbsp. (15 ml). Effective carbohydrates: 0.5 g; Carbohydrates: 0.5 g; Fiber: 0 g; Protein: 0.7 g; Fat: 6.2 g; Calories: 59

GREEN GODDESS DRESSING

Makes about 1½ cups (360 ml)

When I was a kid, green goddess was my favorite dressing. Sadly, it fell out of fashion, but it's here again and better than ever. It makes a great dip or a sauce for meat or vegetables, especially steak and asparagus.

½ cup	(120 ml)	mayonnaise
½ cup	(120 ml)	sour cream
¼ cup	(60 ml)	chopped green onion tops
2 Tbsp.	(30 ml)	chopped fresh chives
2 Tbsp.	(30 ml)	chopped fresh parsley
2 tsp.	(10 ml)	chopped fresh tarragon or 1 Tbsp. (15 ml) dried tarragon
3		anchovy fillets or 1 Tbsp. (15 ml) anchovy paste
1 Tbsp.	(15 ml)	freshly squeezed lemon juice
		Sea salt and freshly ground black pepper

◦§ In a blender or food processor, combine the mayonnaise, sour cream, green onion, chives, parsley, tarragon, anchovy, and lemon juice. Process until smooth and light green. Season to taste with salt and pepper. Transfer to a bowl and refrigerate.

Per 1 Tbsp. (15 ml). Effective carbohydrates: 0.4 g; Carbohydrates: 0.4 g; Fiber: 0 g; Protein: 0.3 g; Fat: 4.7 g; Calories: 45

BLUE CHEESE DRESSING

Makes 1½ cups (360 ml)

This dressing tastes best when allowed to sit overnight so the flavors can blend. A must with Buffalo-Style Wings (page 176).

4 oz.	(112 g)	blue cheese, crumbled
1 cup	(240 ml)	sour cream
¼ cup	(60 ml)	mayonnaise
1 Tbsp.	(15 ml)	red wine vinegar
1 tsp.	(5 ml)	minced garlic
		Sea salt and freshly ground black pepper

◦§ Place the cheese in a small bowl and mash to a paste using a fork. Stir in the sour cream, mayonnaise, vinegar, and garlic. Season to taste with salt and pepper. Cover and refrigerate.

Per 1 Tbsp. (15 ml). Effective carbohydrates: 0.5 g; Carbohydrates: 0.5 g; Fiber: 0 g; Protein: 2.6 g; Fat: 9.9 g; Calories: 103

THOUSAND ISLAND DRESSING

Makes about 2 cups (480 ml)

Once you've had the "real thing," you'll never want to go back to the stuff in bottles.

1¼ cups	(300 ml)	mayonnaise
⅓ cup	(80 ml)	Ketchup (page 233) or store-bought
¼ cup	(60 ml)	finely chopped drained pimiento or roasted red pepper
3 Tbsp.	(45 ml)	finely chopped dill pickle
2 Tbsp.	(30 ml)	Dijon mustard
2 Tbsp.	(30 ml)	finely chopped green onion
1		hard-cooked large egg, peeled and grated
		Dash of hot-pepper sauce
		Sea salt and freshly ground black pepper

✑ In a medium bowl, combine all ingredients together and mix well. Season to taste with salt and pepper. Cover and refrigerate.

Per 1 Tbsp. (15 ml). Effective carbohydrates: 0.3 g; Carbohydrates: 0.4 g; Fiber: 0.1 g; Protein: 0.4 g; Fat: 7.2 g; Calories: 67

RANCH DRESSING

Makes about 2 cups (480 ml)

Why buy when you can make a versatile dressing that tastes this good?

You can add a couple of cloves of crushed garlic to turn this into a creamy garlic dressing. Or a few spoonfuls of Basil Pesto (page 240) for a creamy basil dressing that is excellent on tomatoes and cucumbers. Or some crumbled feta cheese and oregano for a creamy Greek dressing.

¾ cup	(180 ml)	sour cream
½ cup	(120 ml)	mayonnaise
½ cup	(120 ml)	water
½ cup	(120 ml)	vegetable oil
2 Tbsp.	(30 ml)	white vinegar
2 Tbsp.	(30 ml)	finely chopped green onion tops
2 tsp.	(10 ml)	garlic powder
1 tsp.	(5 ml)	Worcestershire sauce
¾ tsp.	(3.6 ml)	sea salt
½ tsp.	(2.5 ml)	dried basil
		Hot-pepper sauce

✑ In a small bowl, combine the sour cream, mayonnaise, water, oil, vinegar, green onion, garlic powder, Worcestershire sauce, salt, basil, and hot-pepper sauce to taste. Whisk until smooth. Cover and refrigerate.

Per 1 Tbsp. (15 ml). Effective carbohydrates: 0.1 g; Carbohydrates: 0.5 g; Fiber: 0.4 g; Protein: 0.3 g; Fat: 3.9 g; Calories: 38

JAPANESE-STYLE
SESAME GINGER DRESSING

Makes 1½ cups (360 ml)

Great as a dip or dressing for meat, fish (especially salmon), and vegetables. It can be addictive!
Note: This dressing will thicken as it sits. You can use water to thin it out.

⅓ cup	(80 ml)	soy sauce
¼ cup	(60 ml)	tahini
1½ tsp.	(7.5 ml)	toasted sesame oil
1 Tbsp.	(15 ml)	brown rice or white wine vinegar
1 Tbsp.	(15 ml)	finely grated fresh ginger
¾ tsp.	(3.6 ml)	*each* Splenda and Canadian Sugar Twin or 1 Tbsp. (15 ml) Splenda
¼ cup	(60 ml)	water
⅓ cup	(80 ml)	vegetable oil
2 Tbsp.	(30 ml)	toasted sesame seeds

◦§ In a food processor or blender, combine the soy sauce, tahini, sesame oil, vinegar, ginger, sweetener, and water. Blend until smooth. With the motor running, pour in the vegetable oil in a thin stream. Add the sesame seeds and pulse only to combine.

Per 1 Tbsp. (15 ml). Effective carbohydrates: 0.5 g; Carbohydrates: 0.8 g; Fiber: 0.3 g; Protein: 0.8 g; Fat: 4.9 g; Calories: 48

CREAMY SESAME MISO DRESSING

Makes ¾ cup (180 ml)

Good with asparagus and green beans or as a dressing for cabbage.

5 oz.	(140 g)	soft tofu
2 Tbsp.	(30 ml)	dark miso
2 Tbsp.	(30 ml)	water
1 Tbsp.	(15 ml)	rice vinegar
1 tsp.	(5 ml)	toasted sesame oil
1 Tbsp.	(15 ml)	toasted sesame seeds

In a blender or food processor, blend the tofu, miso, water, vinegar, oil, and sesame seeds until smooth. Store in the refrigerator.

Per 1 Tbsp. (15 ml). Effective carbohydrates: 0.9 g; Carbohydrates: 1.1 g; Fiber: 0.2 g; Protein: 1.2 g; Fat: 1.2 g; Calories: 21

VEGETABLES

It was a wise person who said, "I didn't get fat from eating vegetables!"

One of the most fascinating and delicious aspects of low-carbing is taking the deep dive into the world of vegetables. A plainly cooked piece of chicken can be quite sexy when it's sitting beside a luscious vegetable dish such as Parmesan-Crusted Cauliflower (page 109) or Spaghetti Squash, Carbonara-Style (page 131).

Vegetables don't always have to be crunchy. Many are delicious when cooked until soft, like Twice-Baked Cauliflower (page 113) and Butter-Wrinkled Beans (page 101). And roasting is a way to bring different character to familiar vegetables. And it's easy to add flair to vegetables with little effort: Try fresh herbs, sour cream, toasted nuts, and a matching nut oil.

Though not a vegetable, soy beans do grow on a plant and are another source of protein. So I've included a handful of tofu recipes, including Tofu-roni and Cheese (page 136) and Tofu "Egg" Salad (page 141), to give you reason to experiment with it.

Here are a few of my favorites to get you started.

Green Beans with Eggs and Nutmeg (pages 102 and 103)
Daikon Cakes (pages 116 and 117)
Braised Fennel with White Wine and Parmesan (page 120)
Roasted Mushrooms with Garlic and Thyme (page 126)
Broiled Spinach with Four Cheeses (page 129)

STIR-FRIED CELERY WITH SESAME

Makes 2 servings

Besides going well with other Asian dishes, this is also good cold. Try it as a topping for tofu.
    Note: *If you don't have any sake around, just use water.*

4		**large celery ribs**
1 Tbsp.	**(15 ml)**	**vegetable oil**
2 tsp.	**(10 ml)**	**sake**
		Pinch of Splenda
4 tsp.	**(20 ml)**	**soy sauce**
		Ground dried chile peppers
2 Tbsp.	**(30 ml)**	**sesame seeds, lightly toasted and crushed**

🍃 Remove the strings from the celery using a vegetable peeler (no, you don't have to—but it makes a better dish!) and cut each piece into 2-inch (5-cm) segments. Cut each segment lengthwise into ¼-inch (0.6-cm) strips.

🍃 Heat the oil in a large frying pan over high heat and add the celery. Stir-fry until just tender, about 1 minute. Add the sake and Splenda and stir until the liquid has evaporated. Add the soy sauce and stir until the liquid is almost gone. Stir in the chile peppers to taste. Transfer to a dish and sprinkle with the sesame seeds.

Per serving. Effective carbohydrates: 1.5 g; Carbohydrates: 2.8 g; Fiber: 1.3 g; Protein: 1.8 g; Fat: 5.9 g; Calories: 74

BUTTER-WRINKLED BEANS

Makes 4 servings

The beans develop a richly browned exterior and soft, silky texture with this cooking method. One of the nice things about this recipe is that you can pretty much leave the beans unattended while you are doing other things. I find this is a good use for my old cast-iron frying pan.

		Sea salt
1½ lb.	(680 g)	green beans, trimmed
4 Tbsp.	(60 ml)	unsalted butter
		Freshly ground black pepper
		Freshly squeezed lemon juice

❧ Bring a large pot of water to a rapid boil and season liberally with salt. (It should taste like sea water.) Add the beans and cook for only a minute or so after they come to a boil. They should be bright green and still raw in the center. Cool under cold water. Drain well and pat dry.

❧ Melt the butter in a large frying pan over medium heat. Add the beans and spread them out evenly. As soon as they start to sizzle, turn the heat to low. After 5 minutes, check to see if the beans that are in contact with the pan have browned. If so, give them a stir to redistribute them. If not, leave for a few more minutes. Let the beans cook for 5 minutes longer. Some will be browned and wrinkled and others not. Season to taste with salt and pepper and add a squeeze of lemon juice.

Per serving. Effective carbohydrates: 4 g; Carbohydrates: 10 g; Fiber: 6 g; Protein: 2 g; Fat: 7 g; Calories: 115

GREEN BEANS WITH EGGS AND NUTMEG

Makes 6 servings

I really like the combination of nutmeg and vinegar that the Dutch use to season beans. This recipe takes it one step further. You can serve this at room temperature as well as warm, and it's great with salmon or other distinctively flavored fish.

3		hard-cooked large eggs, peeled
1 Tbsp.	(15 ml)	coarsely chopped fresh parsley
1 Tbsp.	(15 ml)	finely chopped green onion tops
⅛ tsp.	(0.6 ml)	freshly grated nutmeg, or more to taste
		Sea salt and freshly ground black pepper
1 lb.	(454 g)	green beans, trimmed
3 Tbsp.	(45 ml)	extra-virgin olive oil
1 Tbsp.	(15 ml)	red wine vinegar

⋙ Grate the eggs into a bowl and toss with the parsley, green onion, and nutmeg. Season to taste with salt and pepper.

⋙ Bring a large pot of water to a boil and season liberally with salt. (It should taste like sea water.) Add the beans and cook until tender but still crisp, about 4 to 5 minutes. Drain well and toss with the oil and vinegar. Add the egg mixture and toss well to coat the beans.

Per serving. Effective carbohydrates: 5.9 g; Carbohydrates: 9.7 g; Fiber: 5.8 g; Protein: 4.1 g; Fat: 14.5 g; Calories: 189

BROCCOLI DIJON

Makes 4 servings

This dish is excellent with roast chicken. You can use whole-grain mustard in place of the Dijon. A sprinkle of toasted sliced almonds or pine nuts is good, too.

1 lb.	(454 g)	broccoli
		Sea salt
4 Tbsp.	(60 ml)	unsalted butter
2 Tbsp.	(30 ml)	Dijon mustard
2 Tbsp.	(30 ml)	freshly squeezed lemon juice
		Freshly ground black pepper

∾ Cut the florets from the broccoli stalks and peel the stalks. Cut the florets and stalks into bite-size pieces.

∾ Bring a large pot of water to a boil and season liberally with salt. (It should taste like sea water.) Add the broccoli and cook until it's barely tender. Drain and cool under cold water; drain.

∾ Melt the butter in a large frying pan over medium-high heat. Add the broccoli; toss and stir until heated through. Move the broccoli to the sides of the pan and stir in the mustard and lemon juice. Stir the broccoli around to coat it with the sauce and season to taste with salt and pepper.

Per serving. Effective carbohydrates: 3.8 g; Carbohydrates: 7.2 g; Fiber: 3.4 g; Protein: 4 g; Fat: 13.1 g; Calories: 151

BROCCOLI ITALIANISSIMO

Makes 4 servings

Delicious with anything remotely Italian. If you don't like anchovies, just leave them out.

1 lb.	(454 g)	broccoli
3 Tbsp.	(45 ml)	extra-virgin olive oil
2		garlic cloves, minced
2		anchovy fillets, finely chopped
		Sea salt and freshly ground black pepper
¼ cup	(60 ml)	freshly grated Parmesan cheese

⋙ Cut the florets from the broccoli stalks and peel the stalks. Cut the florets and stalks into bite-size pieces.

⋙ Bring a large pot of water to a boil and season liberally with salt. (It should taste like seawater.) Add the broccoli and cook until it's barely tender. Drain and cool under cold water; drain.

⋙ Heat the oil in a large frying pan over medium-high heat. Add the garlic and anchovies and sauté until the garlic starts to turn pale gold. Add the broccoli and season to taste. Stir and toss the broccoli until heated through. Sprinkle with the cheese.

Per serving. Effective carbohydrates: 3.1 g; Carbohydrates: 6.4 g; Fiber: 3.3 g; Protein: 6.1 g; Fat: 12.2 g; Calories: 150

WINNING WAYS WITH BROCCOLI

⋙ Sauté with garlic, ginger, and chiles

⋙ Toss with lemon and oregano

⋙ Add to tomatoes, anchovies, and basil

⋙ Mash with cheese and cream cheese

⋙ Puree with eggs, cream, and cheese; bake

⋙ Toss with cooked bacon, bacon fat, and green onion

⋙ Cover with Dottie's Cream of Mushroom Soup (page 53) and top with shredded cheese

⋙ Dribble with tomato sauce, add bits of cooked sausage, and broil with cheese

BRUSSELS SPROUTS SAUTÉED WITH GARLIC, PINE NUTS, AND BALSAMIC VINEGAR

Makes 4 servings

Delicious with Italian-style meat preparations.

1 lb.	(454 g)	**Brussels sprouts**
½ cup	(120 ml)	**water**
		Sea salt
2 Tbsp.	(30 ml)	**extra-virgin olive oil**
2		**garlic cloves, minced**
2 Tbsp.	(30 ml)	**toasted pine nuts**
2 tsp.	(10 ml)	**balsamic vinegar**
		Freshly ground black pepper

Trim the stem ends of the sprouts and remove any discolored leaves. If the sprouts are very large, cut them in half.

Place the sprouts, water, and ½ tsp. (2.5 ml) salt in a pot that will hold (or will almost hold) the sprouts in a single layer. Bring to a gentle boil, then turn down to a simmer. Cover and cook the sprouts for 8 to 10 minutes, or until the sprouts are tender when pierced with a knife. Shake and stir the pot to prevent the sprouts from sticking and keep the heat low. Drain well and cut the sprouts into quarters.

Heat the oil in a large frying pan over medium heat. Add the garlic and let it sizzle for a minute. Stir in the sprouts until heated through and glistening. Add the pine nuts and vinegar and season to taste with salt and pepper.

Per serving. Effective carbohydrates: 6.8 g; Carbohydrates: 11.8 g; Fiber: 5 g; Protein: 5.1 g; Fat: 9.6 g; Calories: 140

MARY'S BRUSSELS SPROUTS WITH CREAM CHEESE, TOASTED ALMONDS, AND NUTMEG

Makes 4 servings

This is a very good way of serving Brussels sprouts to first-time eaters. Even people who are suspect of them find this dish delicious. Mary is a friend of mine who owns a wonderful bakery—but I don't hold that against her!

1 lb.	(454 g)	Brussels sprouts
		Sea salt
½ cup	(120 ml)	cream cheese, cut into small pieces
2 Tbsp.	(30 ml)	unsalted butter
		Freshly ground black pepper
		Freshly grated nutmeg
¼ cup	(60 ml)	slivered almonds, toasted

◦§ Trim the stem ends of the sprouts and remove any discolored leaves. Cut the sprouts in half.

◦§ Bring a pot of water to a boil and season liberally with salt. (It should taste like sea water.) Add the sprouts and cook until tender when pierced with a knife. Drain and return to the pot.

◦§ Stir in the cream cheese and butter. Season to taste with salt, pepper, and nutmeg. Transfer to a warmed serving dish and sprinkle with the almonds.

Per serving. Effective carbohydrates: 7 g; Carbohydrates: 12.6 g; Fiber: 5.6 g; Protein: 7.7 g; Fat: 20.9 g; Calories: 253

SCALLOPED SAVOY CABBAGE

Makes 6 servings

Savoy cabbage is the crinkly-leafed cabbage, but regular green cabbage works just fine, too.

Scalloped vegetables are great when the weather turns cold. This cabbage goes well with all meats, but especially with pork, ham, and sausages. Add a sprinkling of cheese, if you like, for the last 30 minutes of baking. To turn this into a meal, place sausages that you have browned on top of the cabbage for the last 30 minutes of cooking.

1 lb.	(454 g)	Savoy cabbage
½ cup	(120 ml)	thinly sliced onion
½ cup	(120 ml)	freshly grated Parmesan cheese
2½ cups	(600 ml)	whipping cream
¾ tsp.	(3.7 ml)	sea salt
		Freshly ground black pepper

◦ᶘ Preheat the oven to 350°F (175°C). Cover a rimmed baking sheet with foil.

◦ᶘ Remove the outer leaves of the cabbage and cut the head into quarters. Core and slice thinly. Place in a large bowl and toss with the onion and cheese. Transfer to a 13 × 9-inch (32.5 × 22.5-cm) baking dish.

◦ᶘ In a medium saucepan, bring the cream, salt, and pepper to taste to a boil. Pour over the cabbage and cover tightly with foil. Place on the prepared baking sheet.

◦ᶘ Bake for 45 minutes. Remove the foil and bake for 30 minutes longer. Let the cabbage sit for 10 minutes before serving.

Per serving. Effective carbohydrates: 6.2 g; Carbohydrates: 8.7 g; Fiber: 2.5 g; Protein: 6.4 g; Fat: 38.8 g; Calories: 398

PARMESAN-CRUSTED CAULIFLOWER

Makes 6 servings

This is a very attractive-looking cauliflower dish: large lacy wedges of cauliflower crusted with cheese. You can add spices to the cheese—garlic powder, oregano, basil—if you like or serve it with Simple Tomato Sauce (page 242).

2 lb.	(908 g)	cauliflower, trimmed
2 Tbsp.	(30 ml)	extra-virgin olive oil
1		large egg
1 Tbsp.	(15 ml)	whipping cream
2 cups	(480 ml)	freshly grated Parmesan cheese

◆§ Slice the cauliflower into very thin wedges, keeping the pieces no thicker than ½ inch (1.2 cm). A few florets will crumble, and that's fine. Just set them aside.

◆§ Preheat the oven to 400°F (200°C). Spread the oil on a rimmed baking sheet (preferably nonstick), or on a parchment-lined, rimmed baking sheet.

◆§ Beat the egg with the cream in a shallow bowl and spread the cheese out on a plate. Dip each side of the cauliflower wedges into the egg mixture, then press each side into the cheese. Lay the pieces on the baking sheet. When you are finished, mix the crumbled florets with the remaining eggs and cheese and drop small spoonfuls onto the baking sheet, flattening them slightly.

◆§ Bake for 15 to 20 minutes, or until browned on the bottom and easy to turn without the cheese sticking to the pan. Turn over and bake for 10 minutes longer.

VARIATION
Add ½ tsp. (2.5 ml) turmeric, 2 tsp. (10 ml) Garam Masala (page 249), and 1 Tbsp. (15 ml) cumin seeds to give this dish an Indian flair.

Per serving. Effective carbohydrates: 5.1 g; Carbohydrates: 8.5 g; Fiber: 3.4 g; Protein: 15.2 g; Fat: 14.5 g; Calories: 219

BASIC CAULI-FLIED "RICE"

Makes 6 servings

This goes with almost anything saucy. My sous chef and good buddy Wayne just loves it with crumbled feta, olive oil, and chopped tomato on top. The variations are endless: a bit of curry powder, some grated lemon rind to go with fish, or some chili powder.

2 lb.	(908 g)	cauliflower, trimmed
4 Tbsp.	(60 ml)	unsalted butter
2		garlic cloves, minced
1 tsp.	(5 ml)	sea salt
2		green onions, thinly sliced
		Freshly ground black pepper

🍃 Grate the cauliflower, including the core, using the medium holes of a grater or the grater attachment of a food processor. With your hands, squeeze out as much water as you can. (This may not be necessary for some cauliflower as they vary in degree of wetness.)

🍃 Melt the butter in a large heavy frying pan over medium heat. Add the garlic and sauté until the garlic sizzles. Add the cauliflower, sprinkle with the salt, and stir-fry until tender-crisp, about 5 to 8 minutes. The length of time will depend on the cauliflower.

🍃 Stir in the green onions and season to taste with pepper. Check the seasoning and serve.

VARIATION

For a Pan-Asian taste, use oil instead of butter. Scramble 2 eggs in the oil after sautéeing the garlic. Add chopped, cooked meat or shrimp, give a few stirs, then add the cauliflower. Serve with soy sauce at table.

Per serving. Effective carbohydrates: 4.3 g; Carbohydrates: 7.8 g; Fiber: 3.5 g; Protein: 3.1 g; Fat: 8.4 g; Calories: 109

BASIC CAULIFLOWER MASH

Makes 6 servings

The marvelous thing about mashed-cauliflower dishes is that they can be reheated beautifully.

To make a puree that's very thick, puree the cauliflower alone. Spoon it into a cheesecloth-lined sieve, place over a bowl to catch the drips, cover, and refrigerate overnight. Then reheat gently and add the remaining ingredients.

You can season Cauliflower Mash with roasted garlic, Basil Pesto (page 240), fresh garlic, chopped sun-dried tomatoes, wasabi paste, and Dijon mustard.

2 lb.	**(908 g)**	**cauliflower, trimmed**
		Sea salt
¼ cup	**(60 ml)**	**whipping cream**
4 Tbsp.	**(60 ml)**	**unsalted butter**
¼ cup	**(60 ml)**	**freshly grated Parmesan cheese**
¼ cup	**(60 ml)**	**cream cheese**

◦§ Cut the cauliflower, including the core, into 1-inch (2.5-cm) pieces. Bring a large pot of water to a boil and salt lightly. Add the cauliflower and cook over medium heat until completely tender, 20 to 30 minutes.

◦§ Drain the cauliflower in a colander. With a bowl or small plate, press on the cauliflower to remove all the water. Toss the cauliflower and continue pressing out the water. This step is very important to the texture of the dish.

◦§ Transfer the cauliflower to a food processor. Add the cream and puree until completely smooth. If you like a chunkier texture, mash by hand, adding the cream after the cauliflower is mashed. Return to the pot.

◦§ When you are ready to serve the puree, heat over low heat, stirring constantly. Add the butter, Parmesan, and cream cheese. Stir until incorporated. Season to taste with salt, if necessary. Serve immediately.

Per serving. Effective carbohydrates: 4.6 g; Carbohydrates: 8 g; Fiber: 3.4 g; Protein: 5.4 g; Fat: 16.6 g; Calories: 193

TWICE-BAKED CAULIFLOWER

Makes 6 servings

Okay, I admit it's not exactly twice-baked, because the cauliflower is boiled and then baked, but it sounds good as a title. And it's much tastier than a twice-baked potato!

2 lb.	(908 g)	cauliflower, trimmed and cut into florets
4 oz.	(112 g)	cream cheese
2 Tbsp.	(30 ml)	unsalted butter
½ cup	(120 ml)	sour cream
¼ cup	(60 ml)	minced green onion
¼ cup	(60 ml)	freshly grated Parmesan cheese
8		bacon slices, cooked until crisp and crumbled
1 cup	(240 ml)	shredded aged cheddar cheese

⏷ Preheat the oven to 350°F (175°C).

⏷ Cook the cauliflower in a large pot of rapidly boiling water until tender. Drain well and mash. (Or puree in a food processor if you want a smoother texture.) Mix in the cream cheese, then the butter, sour cream, green onion, Parmesan, and all but 1 Tbsp. (15 ml) of the bacon.

⏷ Spread evenly in an 8 × 8-inch (20 × 20-cm) baking dish. Sprinkle with the cheddar and reserved bacon. Bake for 30 to 35 minutes, or until hot and bubbly around the sides.

Per serving. Effective carbohydrates: 5.9 g; Carbohydrates: 9.5 g; Fiber: 3.6 g; Protein: 13.8 g; Fat: 26.3 g; Calories: 320

CAULIFLOWER CHAMELEON

There is no other vegetable in the low-carb repertoire that is as versatile as cauliflower. It can be stir-fried, mashed, roasted, and more. It's obvious salad material and a less-obvious thickener for gravies, soups, or sauces.

One cup (240 ml) of cooked cauliflower pieces has only 1.8 g of effective carbohydrates. And it's not too shabby in potassium, with 176 mg in that same cupful—more than many supplements.

CHAYOTE WITH TOMATOES AND MINT

Makes 4 servings

This dish goes really well with sausages. For variety, try young, firm zucchini in place of the chayote. You can use fresh basil or parsley instead of the mint.

1 8-oz.	(227-g)	chayote
2 Tbsp.	(30 ml)	extra-virgin olive oil
1		garlic clove, minced
½ cup	(120 ml)	cherry tomato halves
		Sea salt and freshly ground black pepper
2 Tbsp.	(30 ml)	coarsely chopped fresh mint
1 Tbsp.	(15 ml)	freshly squeezed lemon juice

◦§ Peel the chayote. Cut lengthwise in half and remove the seed. Cut crosswise into thin slices.

◦§ Heat the oil in a large heavy frying pan over high heat. Add the garlic. When it sizzles, add the chayote and stir for a minute or so. Reduce the heat to medium and cook, stirring occasionally, until the chayote is crisp-tender.

◦§ Add the tomatoes and cook until softened. Season to taste with salt and pepper and stir in the mint and lemon juice.

Per serving. Effective carbohydrates: 2.7 g; Carbohydrates: 4 g; Fiber: 1.3 g; Protein: 0.7 g; Fat: 6.9 g; Calories: 77

CHAYOTE: THE AZTEC ZUCCHINI

Chayote squash is used extensively in Mexico, the Caribbean, Louisiana, and other southern states. It's known by many names: custard marrow, christophene, brione, cho-cho, and mirliton, to name a few.

The best way to describe its qualities is to say it's like a very firm zucchini that holds its shape well during cooking. It's a slightly flattened pear-shape that's mildly lobed and a beautiful light green. The seed can be eaten as well as the flesh, and it does not have to be peeled if you're grilling or frying. It can be cooked in soups and stews or eaten raw in salads.

CHAYOTE STUFFED WITH SPICY SAUSAGE

Makes 6 servings

While this can be a meal in itself, try it with Basic Cauliflower Mash (page 112) and a simple salad. Leftovers are fantastic cold.

3 8-oz.	(227-g)	chayotes
1 lb.	(454 g)	spicy Italian, chorizo, or other sausage, casings removed
½ cup	(120 ml)	finely diced onion
½ cup	(120 ml)	diced tomato
		Sea salt and freshly ground black pepper
1		large egg
1 cup	(240 ml)	shredded Monterey Jack or mozzarella cheese

◦§ Cut the chayotes lengthwise in half and remove the seeds. Steam or cook in rapidly boiling water until tender, about 20 minutes. Drain and set aside until cool enough to handle. Use a spoon to remove the inside flesh, leaving about a ¼ -inch (0.6-cm) shell. Dice the flesh from the chayotes; set the shells aside.

◦§ In a large frying pan, cook the sausage and onion over medium-high heat, crumbling the meat with a spoon as you cook it. Add the tomato and continue to cook until the tomato pieces are soft. Add the flesh from the chayotes. Season to taste with salt and pepper. Let cool. Beat in the egg.

◦§ Preheat the oven to 350°F (175°C).

◦§ Stuff the cooled mixture into the chayote shells. Place in a baking dish that will hold the shells snugly. Pour in just enough water to be about ½-inch (1.2-cm) deep. Cover with a tight-fitting lid and bake for 40 minutes.

◦§ Remove the lid, sprinkle with the cheese, and bake for another 5 to 10 minutes, or until the tops are golden brown.

Per serving. Effective carbohydrates: 6.2 g; Carbohydrates: 8.5 g; Fiber: 2.3 g; Protein: 21 g; Fat: 24.5 g; Calories: 339

DAIKON CAKES

Makes 6 cakes

These are pretty tasty on their own or with a dab of sour cream or mayonnaise. They are also good cold.

Daikon contains a lot of water, and 1½ lb. (680 g) makes only 6 cakes. Because of the water content, it is important to get the grated daikon as dry as you can or the cakes will fall apart when you fry them.

Note: *An excellent dipping sauce for fish, especially salmon, is finely grated daikon mixed with soy sauce, a little grated ginger, and a touch of sweetener. It's also very tasty with green vegetables such as asparagus, broccoli, and snow peas.*

1½ lb.	(680 g)	daikon radish
1 tsp.	(5 ml)	sea salt
1		large egg
5 Tbsp.	(75 ml)	finely ground pork rinds
2 Tbsp.	(30 ml)	finely minced green onion
		Freshly ground black pepper
2 Tbsp.	(30 ml)	olive or vegetable oil

Peel and grate the daikon into a bowl. Combine with 1 tsp. (5 ml) salt and let sit for 30 minutes.

Squeeze the water out of the daikon with your hands. The more water you squeeze, the better the cakes will be. Mix the daikon with the egg, pork rinds, green onion, and salt and pepper to taste. Let sit for 10 minutes.

Preheat the oven to 350°F (175°C).

Heat a large ovenproof heavy frying pan—a cast-iron pan is ideal—over medium-low heat. Swirl the oil around the pan. Fill a ¼ -cup (60-ml) dry measuring cup with some of the mixture, packing it slightly. Turn out into the frying pan. You should have a nicely

shaped cake that stands a bit more than 1 inch (2.5 cm) high. Continue with the remaining mixture.

◦§ Fry the cakes on one side without disturbing them too much until browned on the bottom, 5 to 6 minutes. Very carefully turn the cakes over and fry for 2 to 3 minutes longer. Place the whole pan in the oven and bake the cakes for 15 minutes.

Per cake. Effective carbohydrates: 3.2 g; Carbohydrates: 5 g; Fiber: 1.8 g; Protein: 2.8 g; Fat: 3.6 g; Calories: 63

DAIKON: THE WONDER RADISH!

Daikon radish is used frequently in all sorts of ways in Japanese and Chinese cooking. It's simmered in soups and stews, made into steamed cakes, grated and used as an ingredient in dipping sauces, and employed as a fluffy garnish beside sushi and sashimi.

Daikon is mild and sweet. Like celery root, it's best from late summer to fall. The roots are fairly long and pure white. They shouldn't be soft or overly blemished. Small daikons are best, as the larger ones can be tough with a spongy core. If you have a Chinese or Japanese grocery store near you, buy daikon there since the turnover is very high.

Use this root in the same way the Japanese do—in soups and stews—as well as roasting large chunks of it or dicing it and frying it to make something similar to hash-brown potatoes. It's very tasty fried in bacon fat or the drippings from a roast. When cut into matchstick pieces, it can be used in stir-fries or salads. Sliced, it's a good dipping vegetable.

I did use daikon once in a "carrot cake" recipe I was developing. I don't advise repeating this.

A 1-lb. (454-g) daikon radish contains only 11 g of effective carbohydrates, so it's definitely a bargain.

EGGPLANT WITH SOUR CREAM DRESSING

Makes 8 servings

A fantastic summer dish that makes great leftovers. It is especially good with lamb.

4		**small eggplants, about 3 lb. (1.3 kg) total**
		Extra-virgin olive oil
1 cup	(240 ml)	**sour cream**
½ tsp.	(2.5 ml)	**sea salt**
¼ tsp.	(1.2 ml)	**freshly ground black pepper**
¼ cup	(60 ml)	**fresh basil leaves, chopped**
¼ cup	(60 ml)	**fresh mint leaves, chopped**
2		**garlic cloves, minced**
1		**large tomato, finely diced**

➺ Cut the ends off the eggplants and cut into ¾-inch (1.9-cm) slices.

➺ Preheat the broiler. Lightly brush both sides of the eggplant slices with oil and broil about 6 inches (15 cm) from the heat, turning only once, until golden brown on both sides and completely tender. Remove from the heat and arrange attractively on a platter.

➺ In a small bowl, mix the sour cream, salt, pepper, basil, mint, and garlic. Drizzle the dressing over the eggplant and scatter the chopped tomatoes over the top.

Per serving. Effective carbohydrates: 8.9 g; Carbohydrates: 13.5 g; Fiber: 4.6 g; Protein: 3 g; Fat: 6.4 g; Calories: 116

SPICY ROASTED AND MASHED EGGPLANT

Makes 6 servings

Lovers of Indian food will recognize this as bharta. This dish is great served warm or cold as a dip.

2		medium eggplants, about 2 lb. (908 g) total, cut in half lengthwise
⅓ cup	(80 ml)	vegetable oil
½ cup	(120 ml)	finely chopped onion
2 Tbsp.	(30 ml)	finely chopped fresh ginger
1 Tbsp.	(15 ml)	minced garlic
2 tsp.	(10 ml)	ground cumin
1 tsp.	(5 ml)	sweet paprika
1 tsp.	(5 ml)	ground coriander
½ tsp.	(2.5 ml)	cayenne pepper
½ lb.	(227 g)	tomatoes, coarsely chopped
⅓ cup	(80 ml)	chopped fresh cilantro
		Sea salt and freshly ground black pepper

◆§ Preheat the oven to 350°F (175°C).

◆§ Oil a pan large enough to hold the eggplant halves in a single layer. Place the halves, cut side down, in the pan. Roast until the flesh is soft, about 1 hour. Cool slightly. Scoop the pulp from the eggplant skin into a sieve and let drain while you prepare the rest of the ingredients.

◆§ Heat the oil in a large heavy skillet over medium-high heat. Add the onion and sauté until golden brown. Add the ginger, garlic, cumin, paprika, coriander, and cayenne. Stir for a minute longer. Add the tomatoes and cook over high heat, stirring frequently, until the tomatoes thicken and become pulpy.

◆§ Mash in the eggplant, reduce the heat, and stir until slightly thickened. Remove from the heat and stir in the cilantro. Season to taste with salt and pepper.

Per serving. Effective carbohydrates: 8.5 g; Carbohydrates: 13.5 g; Fiber: 5 g; Protein: 2.4 g; Fat: 12.7 g; Calories: 168

BRAISED FENNEL
WITH WHITE WINE AND PARMESAN

Makes 6 servings

Fennel is a great vegetable served raw and crunchy in salads or softly braised as in this recipe. It goes well with chicken, pork, or fish.

Fennel is usually sold with most of the long fronds removed, but occasionally you get to see the bulbs in their full glory.

2 1-lb.	(454-g)	fennel bulbs
4 Tbsp.	(60 ml)	unsalted butter
		Sea salt and freshly ground black pepper
½ cup	(120 ml)	dry white wine or chicken stock
½ cup	(120 ml)	freshly grated Parmesan cheese

⋅§ Preheat the oven to 325°F (165°C).

⋅§ Trim the base and stems from the fennel and cut each bulb into 6 wedges.

⋅§ In a frying pan large enough to hold the fennel comfortably, melt the butter over medium heat. Add the fennel and season to taste with salt and pepper. Add the wine or stock and bring to a simmer.

⋅§ Cover, lower the heat, and let the fennel cook for about 15 minutes. Turn the wedges over, cover, and cook until the liquid has evaporated and the fennel starts to turn golden. Turn over and color the other side. Sprinkle with the cheese and serve. (You can also pop the pan under the broiler to brown the cheese if you like.)

Per serving. Effective carbohydrates: 6.7 g; Carbohydrates: 11.3 g; Fiber: 4.6 g; Protein: 4.6 g; Fat: 11.8 g; Calories: 175

BUTTERED SESAME KALE

Makes 4 servings

Kale is eaten more commonly in the southern United States and Europe, with Scotland being the largest consumer. It makes frequent appearances in Portuguese and Italian soups. Kale is quite chewy unless cooked for a long time into tenderness. If you happen to find very young and tender kale, you don't have to remove the ribs. (Its cousin the collard green can be prepared the same way.)

1 lb.	(454 g)	flat-leaf kale
2 Tbsp.	(30 ml)	vegetable oil
2		garlic cloves, minced
½ cup	(120 ml)	chicken stock or water
1 Tbsp.	(15 ml)	soy sauce
1 Tbsp.	(15 ml)	unsalted butter
1 tsp.	(5 ml)	toasted sesame oil
1 Tbsp.	(15 ml)	toasted sesame seeds
		Freshly ground black pepper

◈ Remove the thick ribs from the kale and cut the leaves crosswise into 1-inch (2.5-cm) strips.

◈ Heat the vegetable oil in a wok or large heavy frying pan over high heat. Add the garlic; when it sizzles, add the kale and stir until it's glistening with oil. Add the stock or water. Turn the heat to low, cover, and steam until the kale is tender but still chewy, about 15 to 20 minutes.

◈ Add the soy sauce and stir for a minute or so to evaporate some of the liquid. Stir in the butter and sesame oil, then sprinkle with the sesame seeds, and season to taste with the pepper.

Per serving. Effective carbohydrates: 1.6; Carbohydrates: 5.9 g; Fiber: 4.3 g; Protein: 3.7 g; Fat: 4.3 g; Calories: 76

GREEN GREENS PUREE

Makes 6 servings

I like to have this with roasted salmon basted with butter.

1 cup	(240 ml)	chicken stock or water
½ lb.	(227 g)	kale (any type), ribs removed and leaves chopped
2 cups	(480 ml)	shredded green cabbage
2 10-oz.	(285-g)	bags ready-to-use spinach
2 oz.	(56 g)	cream cheese
2 Tbsp.	(30 ml)	whipping cream
		Sea salt and freshly ground black pepper

◆§ Bring the stock or water to a boil in a large pot. Add the kale, cabbage, and spinach. Cook, stirring occasionally, until the kale wilts.

◆§ Turn the heat to low, cover, and cook until the vegetables are very tender, about 45 minutes to 1 hour. Check the water level occasionally. There should be enough to keep the vegetables just juicy and prevent them from sticking to the pan. If there is too much water near the end of the cooking time, remove the lid and allow it to evaporate.

◆§ Transfer the mixture to a food processor and puree until smooth. Add the cream cheese and cream. Season to taste with salt and pepper. Blend again to mix smoothly. Return to the pot and stir over low heat until piping hot.

Per serving. Effective carbohydrates: 3.1 g; Carbohydrates: 7.8 g; Fiber: 4.7 g; Protein: 5 g; Fat: 6.4 g; Calories: 98

KOHLRABI AND CELERY GRATIN

Makes 6 servings

The flavors of the celery and kohlrabi play off each other in this dish. Don't be intimidated— gratin is just a fancy name for "scalloped."

Note: *If you are so inclined, peel the strings from the celery ribs using a vegetable peeler. It makes them a little less chewy but is not essential.*

6		large celery ribs, trimmed
4		medium kohlrabi, about 1½ lb. (680 g) total, peeled
1 cup	(240 ml)	whipping cream
⅓ cup	(80 ml)	water
2		garlic cloves, minced
½ tsp.	(2.5 ml)	sea salt
		Freshly ground black pepper
½ cup	(120 ml)	freshly grated Parmesan cheese

•ᔑ Preheat the oven to 350°F (175°C). Butter a 13 × 9-inch (32.5 × 22.5-cm) baking dish and place on a rimmed baking sheet to catch any spills.

•ᔑ Cut the celery into ¼-inch (0.6-cm) slices. Cut the kohlrabi into ¼-inch (0.6-cm) slices. Layer the celery and kohlrabi in the baking dish.

•ᔑ In a medium saucepan, combine the cream, water, garlic, salt, and pepper to taste. Bring to a boil over medium heat. Pour over the vegetables and sprinkle with the cheese.

•ᔑ Bake for 50 to 60 minutes, or until the top is golden and the vegetables are tender. Remove from the oven and let settle for 10 minutes before serving.

Per serving. Effective carbohydrates: 5.4 g; Carbohydrates: 10.1 g; Fiber: 4.7 g; Protein: 5.8 g; Fat: 16.8 g; Calories: 205

KOHLRABI: THE SPACE-AGE TURNIP

Many people look at kohlrabi and wonder what in the world to do with it. It's that light green or purple, turnipy, Sputnik-shaped vegetable. It's actually an ancient vegetable that's very much admired in Germany, Hungary, China, and India. Although it has been in North America since the early nineteenth century, we can only guess at why its popularity waned.

It's sweeter than both turnip and rutabaga and can be cooked and mashed like cauliflower. You can use it raw in a salad or slaw or as a crisp snack with a piece of cheese. You can either cook kohlrabi until it's tender or prepare it so its crispness is retained. It can be shredded and quickly sautéed, seasoning it as you please, or it can be cut into wedges and roasted along with beef, pork, or chicken to soak up their flavorful juices.

Choose baseball-size kohlrabi over giants or babies. Cracks indicate a woody heart. Peel kohlrabi deeply to remove the tough outer skin. The leaves can be eaten, too.

One cup (240 g) of chopped raw kohlrabi has only 2.6 g of effective carbohydrates.

KOHLRABI, THREE WAYS

Makes 4 servings

1½ lb.	(680 g)	kohlrabi, peeled and cut into 1-inch (2.5-cm) cubes

❧ Bring a large pot of water to a boil and drop in the kohlrabi. Cook for 8 to 10 minutes, or until tender but still with a bite. Drain well and proceed with one of the recipes below.

KOHLRABI WITH CREAM AND THYME

½ cup	(120 ml)	whipping cream
1 tsp.	(5 ml)	fresh thyme leaves or ½ tsp. (2.5 ml) dried thyme
1½ lb.	(680 g)	kohlrabi, cooked as above
		Sea salt and freshly ground black pepper

◈ In a large saucepan, bring the cream and thyme to a boil and simmer until thickened. Add the kohlrabi and simmer until heated through. Season to taste with salt and pepper.

Per serving. Effective carbohydrates: 4 g; Carbohydrates: 8.5 g; Fiber: 4.5 g; Protein: 2.7 g; Fat: 11 g; Calories: 136

KOHLRABI WITH BUTTER AND PARMESAN

2 Tbsp.	(30 ml)	unsalted butter
1½ lb.	(680 g)	kohlrabi, cooked as above
		Sea salt and freshly ground black pepper
3 Tbsp.	(45 ml)	freshly grated Parmesan cheese

◈ Melt the butter in a large frying pan over medium heat and add the kohlrabi. Sauté until the butter lightly browns. Season to taste with salt and pepper and sprinkle with the cheese.
◈ Remove from the heat and stir to coat with the cheese.

Per serving. Effective carbohydrates: 3.5 g; Carbohydrates: 7.9 g; Fiber: 4.4 g; Protein: 4.2 g; Fat: 7.3 g; Calories: 106

KOHLRABI WITH TARRAGON AND DIJON

2 Tbsp.	(30 ml)	unsalted butter
1½ lb.	(680 g)	kohlrabi, cooked as above
2 tsp.	(10 ml)	Dijon mustard
2 tsp.	(10 ml)	chopped fresh tarragon or ½ tsp. (2.5 ml) dried tarragon

◈ Melt the butter in a large frying pan over medium heat. Add the kohlrabi and stir until it's glistening with the butter. Add the mustard and tarragon.

Per serving. Effective carbohydrates: 3.5 g; Carbohydrates: 8 g; Fiber: 4.5 g; Protein: 2.3 g; Fat: 6 g; Calories: 87

ROASTED MUSHROOMS
WITH GARLIC AND THYME

Makes 4 servings

While these mushrooms won't win any prizes for beauty, they will for taste. Of course, they're fabulous with beef or added to a salad. Lining the baking sheet with foil makes cleanup easy.

1 lb.	(454 g)	small mushrooms
2 Tbsp.	(30 ml)	extra-virgin olive oil
		Sea salt and freshly ground black pepper
1		garlic clove, minced
1 Tbsp.	(15 ml)	balsamic vinegar
1 Tbsp.	(15 ml)	fresh thyme leaves or 1 tsp. (5 ml) dried thyme

∙⸕ Preheat the oven to 450°F (225°C). Line a rimmed baking sheet with foil.

∙⸕ In a large bowl, combine the mushrooms, oil, and salt and pepper to taste. Toss to mix well. Spread evenly in the prepared baking sheet.

∙⸕ Place on the lowest rack in the oven. Roast for 10 to 15 minutes, or until the juice from the mushrooms has almost evaporated. Turn the mushrooms over and continue roasting for an additional 10 minutes, or until they are browned all over. Toss with the garlic, vinegar, and thyme. Check and adjust the seasoning.

Per serving. Effective carbohydrates: 5.4 g; Carbohydrates: 6.8 g; Fiber: 1.4 g; Protein: 2.4 g; Fat: 7.2 g; Calories: 98

SOY, SAKE, AND BUTTER-GLAZED MUSHROOMS

Makes 4 small servings

A wonderful accompaniment to Asian meals, these mushrooms are also good as an appetizer or thinly sliced and tossed in with a salad.

1 lb.	(454 g)	extra-large white mushrooms
1 cup	(240 ml)	water
¼ cup	(60 ml)	soy sauce
½ cup	(120 ml)	sake
½ tsp.	(2.5 ml)	*each* Splenda and Canadian Sugar Twin or 2 tsp. (10 ml) Splenda
4		fresh ginger slices, ½-inch (1.2-cm) thick
2 Tbsp.	(30 ml)	unsalted butter
1 tsp.	(5 ml)	toasted sesame seeds

◆ Trim the mushroom stems flush with the caps and save the stems for another use.

◆ In a large pot, combine the water, soy sauce, sake, sweetener, and ginger. Bring to a boil and add the mushrooms. Cook at a medium boil, turning the mushrooms over every 5 minutes, for about 20 minutes, or until the liquid turns into a light glaze. Remove the ginger. Stir in the butter and sesame seeds.

Per serving. Effective carbohydrates: 8 g; Carbohydrates: 9.4 g; Fiber: 1.4 g; Protein: 4.2 g; Fat: 7 g; Calories: 144

RUTABAGA WITH BALSAMIC VINEGAR AND BROWNED BUTTER

Makes 8 servings

Rutabagas are those large waxed golden and purple roots that are frequently called turnips. Regular turnips are the smaller white-bottomed and purple-topped roots. You can substitute them for the rutabagas here, if you like.

The balsamic vinegar balances the sweetness of the vegetable. Cut the rutabagas into quarters with a cleaver or a large heavy knife before you peel them. This makes them much easier to handle.

You can make the rutabaga puree up to 2 days ahead, cover, and refrigerate. Bring to room temperature and reheat, covered, in a 400°F (200°C) oven for 20 to 30 minutes.

I serve this for Thanksgiving and Christmas dinners, which is why the recipe makes a large amount.

4 lb.	(1.8 kg)	rutabagas, peeled and cut into 1-inch (2.5-cm) cubes
8 Tbsp.	(120 ml)	unsalted butter
2 Tbsp.	(30 ml)	sour cream
		Sea salt and freshly ground black pepper
2 Tbsp.	(30 ml)	balsamic vinegar

⋙ Place the rutabagas in a large pot and cover with cold water. Bring to a boil and cook at a moderate boil until the pieces are tender, 45 minutes to 1 hour. Drain well.

⋙ Mash by hand or puree in a food processor. Return to the pot and stir in 4 Tbsp. (60 ml) of the butter, the sour cream, and salt and pepper to taste. Stir over low heat until hot. Transfer the puree to a large gratin or baking dish.

⋙ Melt the remaining 4 Tbsp. (60 ml) butter in a small saucepan over low heat until it turns a nut brown. Add the vinegar. Drizzle over the puree and serve immediately.

Per serving. Effective carbohydrates: 7.8 g; Carbohydrates: 12.3 g; Fiber: 4.5 g; Protein: 1.8 g; Fat: 13.1 g; Calories: 161

BROILED SPINACH WITH FOUR CHEESES

Makes 6 servings

This is quick, easy, and delicious. You can change the cheeses depending on your mood.
Monterey Jack with chiles and cheddar is a good combination.

½ cup	(120 ml)	grated Gruyère cheese
½ cup	(120 ml)	ricotta cheese
¼ cup	(60 ml)	crumbled gorgonzola or blue cheese
2 Tbsp.	(30 ml)	freshly grated Parmesan cheese
2 Tbsp.	(30 ml)	chopped fresh dill
1		large egg yolk
2 Tbsp.	(30 ml)	unsalted butter
1		garlic clove, minced
2 10-oz.	(285-g)	bags ready-to-use spinach
		Sea salt and freshly ground black pepper

◖ Preheat the broiler. Lightly butter an 11 × 7-inch (27.5 × 17.5-cm) baking dish.

◖ In a large bowl, mix the Gruyère, ricotta, gorgonzola or blue cheese, Parmesan, dill, and egg yolk.

◖ Melt the butter in a large pot over medium-high heat. Add the garlic and stir for a minute until fragrant. Pour into the baking dish. Add the spinach to the pot and sauté until wilted. Transfer to a strainer; drain well. Add to the baking dish and toss to coat with the butter. Season to taste with salt and pepper.

◖ Evenly spread the spinach in the dish and dab with the cheese mixture. Broil about 6 inches (15 cm) from the heat until cheese is golden on top and the spinach is heated thoroughly.

Per serving. Effective carbohydrates: 2 g; Carbohydrates: 4.5 g; Fiber: 2.5 g; Protein: 10.5 g; Fat: 8.2 g; Calories: 177

BASIC SPAGHETTI SQUASH

Makes 10 servings

My grandmother would stuff spaghetti squash with cooked ground beef and bake it until the squash was tender. She only did this occasionally, so it was a treat.

With the way it turns into tender but crisp shreds, spaghetti squash makes an interesting medium for different flavors. While I don't miss pasta—and I used to eat it almost every day—I do miss some of the flavor combinations. Spaghetti squash, as well as cauliflower, fits the bill as the vehicle.

After you cook the squash, you can package the pasta-like shreds into small portions and freeze them.

Note: To microwave the squash, place the cut and seeded halves in a microwaveable dish and add ½ inch (1.2 cm) of water. Cover tightly with plastic wrap and microwave on high power for 10 minutes. The squash is done when the skin yields to firm pressure. Uncover and let cool before scraping out the shreds with a spoon.

1 3-lb.	(1.3-kg)	spaghetti squash

✺ Preheat the oven to 350°F (175°C).

✺ With a sharp, sturdy knife, trim the stem end from the squash and split the squash in half lengthwise. Scoop out the seeds with a spoon. Lay each half, cut side down, in a large baking dish and add ½ inch (1.2 cm) water to the pan. Cover tightly with foil and bake for 40 minutes. Remove from the oven, uncover, and let cool.

✺ With a spoon, scrape out the spaghetti-like shreds.

Per serving. Effective carbohydrates: 5.2 g; Carbohydrates: 6.6 g; Fiber: 1.4 g; Protein: 0.6 g; Fat: 0.6 g; Calories: 29

SPAGHETTI SQUASH, CARBONARA-STYLE

Makes 8 servings

Carbonara was one of my favorite pastas—spaghetti enrobed in a sauce of eggs, prosciutto or pancetta, Parmesan cheese, and black pepper. This casserole has all the flavor and none of the side effects from pasta eating.

I prefer to dice the prosciutto from a thick slice for this rather than use thin slices. You can also use bacon in place of prosciutto. If you do, cook 6 slices until almost crisp and drain off the fat before adding to the egg mixture.

2 oz.	(56 g)	**prosciutto, finely diced**
2 Tbsp.	(30 ml)	**extra-virgin olive oil**
1		**large egg**
1		**large egg yolk**
½ cup	(120 ml)	**whipping cream**
¼ cup	(60 ml)	**water**
¼ tsp.	(1.2 ml)	**sea salt**
½ tsp.	(2.5 ml)	**freshly ground black pepper**
1 cup	(240 ml)	**freshly grated Parmesan cheese**
½ recipe		**Basic Spaghetti Squash (opposite page)**

◦§ Preheat the oven to 350°F (175°C).

◦§ Combine the prosciutto and oil in a small frying pan. Cook over medium-low heat until the prosciutto starts to brown. Remove from the heat.

◦§ In a large bowl, beat together the egg, egg yolk, cream, water, salt, pepper, and Parmesan. Stir in the prosciutto and oil. Stir in the squash.

◦§ Transfer to an 8 × 8-inch (20 × 20-cm) baking dish. Bake for 35 to 40 minutes, or until the center barely jiggles. Let sit for 10 minutes before serving.

Per serving. Effective carbohydrates: 5.5 g; Carbohydrates: 6.7 g; Fiber: 1.2 g; Protein: 6.1 g; Fat: 13.7 g; Calories: 170

SPAGHETTI SQUASH ARRABBIATA

Makes 8 servings

Arrabbiata means "angry" in Italian. While the sauce may anger the squash, it will make your taste buds very happy! Spaghetti squash is a good-natured and mild-mannered vegetable that gets along with seasonings from all over the world. I don't think of it as a substitute for pasta but as a wonderful vegetable in its own right. Try flavoring it with butter and nutmeg, Parmesan or Jack cheese, chili powder, coconut milk and curry powder. This recipe does make a lot of servings, but the leftovers freeze just fine.

2 Tbsp.	(30 ml)	extra-virgin olive oil
2		garlic cloves, minced
2 oz.	(56 g)	prosciutto, finely diced
1 to 2		hot chile peppers, finely chopped
1 cup	(240 ml)	canned Italian plum tomatoes with juice, pureed
		Sea salt and freshly ground black pepper
½ recipe		Basic Spaghetti Squash (page 130)
½ cup	(120 ml)	freshly grated Parmesan cheese

•§ Heat the oil in a large pot over medium heat. Add the garlic, prosciutto, and chiles to taste. Cook until the garlic turns golden.

•§ Add the tomatoes. Turn the heat to low and cook until the mixture thickens slightly, about 20 minutes. Season to taste with salt and pepper.

•§ Add the spaghetti squash and simmer until heated through, about 5 minutes. Stir in the cheese and serve.

Per serving. Effective carbohydrates: 6.2 g; Carbohydrates: 7.8 g; Fiber: 1.6 g; Protein: 4.8 g; Fat: 6.3 g; Calories: 102

BROILED TOMATOES WITH GOAT CHEESE, PANCETTA, AND FENNEL

Makes 4 servings

These can be served with lamb or chicken and are outstanding as an appetizer with a handful of lightly dressed mixed greens.

4		small ripe tomatoes, about ½ lb. (227 g) total
4 Tbsp.	(60 ml)	extra-virgin olive oil
		Sea salt and freshly ground black pepper
4 oz.	(112 g)	soft unripened goat cheese, cut into 8 slices
¼ cup	(60 ml)	finely julienned pancetta
1 tsp.	(5 ml)	fennel seeds

◦§ Preheat the broiler.

◦§ Cut the tomatoes in half crosswise and scoop out the seeds using a small spoon. Place, cut side up, on a baking sheet or heatproof pan. Drizzle with 2 Tbsp. (30 ml) of the oil and season to taste with salt and pepper. Broil close to the heat until sizzling and browned, about 3 to 4 minutes.

◦§ Remove from the oven and top with the cheese. Scatter the pancetta over the cheese and then the fennel seeds. Drizzle with the remaining 2 Tbsp. (30 ml) oil. Broil until the cheese turns golden.

Per serving. Effective carbohydrates: 2.3 g; Carbohydrates: 3.1 g; Fiber: 0.8 g; Protein: 3.1 g; Fat: 21.5 g; Calories: 239

ZUCCHINI, SOUR CREAM, AND JACK CHEESE BAKE

Makes 4 servings

Jack cheese is fairly mild, but you can use a cheese that packs more punch, like an aged cheddar or Asiago. Or try hot pepper Jack.

4 Tbsp.	(60 ml)	unsalted butter
½ cup	(120 ml)	finely chopped green onion
1		garlic clove, minced
1 lb.	(454 g)	zucchini, trimmed and sliced ⅛ inch (0.3 ml) thick
1 cup	(240 ml)	grated Jack cheese
1		large egg
½ cup	(120 ml)	sour cream
½ tsp.	(2.5 ml)	sea salt
2 Tbsp.	(30 ml)	chopped fresh basil or 1 tsp. (5 ml) dried

⊷ Preheat the oven to 350°F (175°C). Butter an 8 × 8-inch (20 × 20-cm) baking dish.

⊷ Melt 1 Tbsp. (15 ml) of the butter in a large frying pan over medium heat. Add the onion and garlic and sauté until the onion is translucent. Scrape into a large bowl.

⊷ In the same frying pan, melt the remaining 3 Tbsp. (45 ml) butter over medium-high heat. Add the zucchini and cook, stirring frequently, until the moisture has evaporated and the zucchini is tender. Transfer to a food processor and pulse until smooth.

⊷ Add the cheese, egg, sour cream, salt, and basil. Pulse to combine. Add the onions and pulse once. Pour into the prepared baking dish.

⊷ Bake for 30 minutes, or until lightly golden.

Per serving. Effective carbohydrates: 4.7 g; Carbohydrates: 6.3 g; Fiber: 1.6 g; Protein: 11.3 g; Fat: 28.7 g; Calories: 320

TOFU-RONI AND CHEESE

Makes 4 servings

Suspend judgment and you'll find this to be a cheesy dream of a dish. Leftovers are great fried until the cheese gets all nice and crispy, just like you would have done with Kraft Macaroni & Cheese Dinner if there were any leftovers! You can add florets of cooked cauliflower or broccoli to this, too, or bake it over a bed of cooked spinach.

2 12-oz.	(340-g)	containers firm tofu, drained
4 oz.	(112 g)	cream cheese, diced
1¼ cups	(300 ml)	whipping cream
4 oz.	(112 g)	shredded aged cheddar cheese
1 Tbsp.	(15 ml)	Dijon mustard
½ tsp.	(2.5 ml)	sea salt
2		large egg yolks
1½ oz.	(42 g)	freshly grated Parmesan cheese

◆ Preheat the oven to 325°F (165°C). Butter a 9 × 9-inch (22.5 × 22.5-cm) baking dish.

◆ Bring a large pot of water to a boil. Cut the tofu into skinny, macaroni-shaped pieces. Add to the pot. When the water returns to a full boil, drain the tofu.

◆ Combine the cream cheese and cream in a medium saucepan. Cook over medium heat, whisking occasionally, until the cream cheese melts and the mixture simmers.

◆ Remove from the heat and whisk in the cheddar until melted. Whisk in the mustard, salt, and egg yolks. Fold in the tofu and transfer to the prepared baking dish. Sprinkle with the Parmesan.

◆ Bake for 25 minutes. Turn on the broiler and brown the top. Let settle for a few minutes before serving.

Per serving. Effective carbohydrates: 7.5 g; Carbohydrates: 11.4 g; Fiber: 3.9 g; Protein: 43.6 g; Fat: 67.7 g; Calories: 799

THE MANY FACES OF TOFU

I am a tofu lover. Before you say "blech!", try some of these recipes. I have a friend who was a tofu hater. It became my personal challenge to feed her tofu in many forms to show her its potential and also to see the look on her face when I said there was tofu in the dish after she finished eating it!

There are many different flavored types of tofu available now. Herb and garlic, sun-dried tomato, smoked tofu, Indonesian-style, and the list goes on. There are pros and cons to using soy products, but the jury is still out. What I would say is to not overdo soy, but please enjoy it when you do have it. Here are the basic types.

Extra-firm tofu is well-pressed and maintains its shape, making it ideal for slicing, dicing, frying, and broiling. Extra-firm tofu generally has the most protein and fat. It can be frozen; when thawed, it has a porous, spongy texture. It then can be finely chopped and added to dishes in place of ground meat.

Firm tofu is not as dense, but it also holds its shape for slicing, dicing, and frying. Firm tofu works well as a substitute for fresh cheese, such as cottage cheese, ricotta, or cream cheese.

Regular or "cotton" tofu is probably the first tofu the Western world became familiar with. I still remember buying it by the piece out of plastic-lined cans over 25 years ago. It's good for stir-fries and for deep-frying.

Soft tofu is much less dense—good for blending into dressings and sauces. It can be used to replace a portion of the egg in a recipe and to replace sour cream or yogurt. Soft tofu is lower in both protein and fat.

Silken tofu has a much finer consistency than other forms of tofu. Silken tofu also is available in extra-firm, firm, and soft. It's good for desserts, sauces, and dressings.

Fried, puffy tofu is available in most Asian markets and some larger supermarkets. It comes in two styles: either flat rectangles or squares. You can carefully split the tofu and fill it with cheese, mayonnaise, and a swipe of Dijon mustard. Then pop the tofu under the broiler until it's crispy and browned. Delicious!

Other tofu recipes:

Curried Tofu, Mashroom, and Pepper Scramble (page 18)

Hummus (page 23)

Daikon Radish, Chinese Cabbage, and Tofu Soup (page 58)

Creamy Sesame Miso Dressing (page 97)

Silken Chocolate Pudding (page 292)

TOFU-LAFELS

Makes 14 tofu-lafels

There are few things that I miss, but I do sigh a little when I go past a falafel joint. These fit the bill completely, even down to the crunchy exterior. Serve with Hummus (page 23).

1 12-oz.	(340-g)	container firm tofu, drained
½ tsp.	(2.5 ml)	sea salt
2 tsp.	(10 ml)	ground coriander
1 tsp.	(5 ml)	ground cumin
¼ tsp.	(1.2 ml)	freshly ground black pepper
½ tsp.	(2.5 ml)	sweet paprika
		Large pinch of ground cinnamon
1		garlic clove, finely grated
1 Tbsp.	(15 ml)	finely chopped fresh parsley
2 Tbsp.	(30 ml)	flaxseed meal
		Vegetable oil

•ᔆ In a large bowl, mash the tofu with a potato masher or your hands until finely crumbled. Add the salt, coriander, cumin, pepper, paprika, cinnamon, garlic, and parsley. Mix well. Stir in the flaxseed meal until well-combined.

•ᔆ Shape into 14 flattened oval disks, using a heaping tablespoon of the mixture for each.

•ᔆ In a heavy frying pan, heat ½ inch (1.2 cm) oil over medium-high heat. Add the disks and fry until crispy and browned on one side. Turn over and fry on the other side. Remove from the pan and place on paper towels to drain.

Per tofu-lafel. Effective carbohydrates: 1 g; Carbohydrates: 2.1 g; Fiber: 1.1 g; Protein: 4.3 g; Fat: 2.9 g; Calories: 48

KOREAN-STYLE TOFU

Makes 2 servings

This delicious dish makes a good introduction for people who think they don't like tofu. Try it for breakfast!

1 12-oz.	(340-g)	container medium-firm tofu, drained
2 Tbsp.	(30 ml)	soy sauce
1½ tsp.	(7.5 ml)	toasted sesame oil
2 Tbsp.	(30 ml)	thinly sliced green onion
1½ tsp.	(7.5 ml)	toasted sesame seeds
1½ tsp.	(7.5 ml)	dried chile flakes, or to taste
2		large eggs
¼ tsp.	(1.2 ml)	sea salt
1 Tbsp.	(15 ml)	vegetable oil

Slice the tofu into 6 pieces and lay out on several layers of paper towels to drain.

In a small bowl, mix the soy sauce, sesame oil, green onion, sesame seeds, and chile flakes.

In a shallow bowl, beat the eggs and salt with a fork.

Heat the vegetable oil in a large frying pan (preferably nonstick) over medium heat. Dip the tofu slices into the egg and place in the pan. Pour the remaining egg mixture over the tofu. Fry until golden brown on one side. Flip over and cook until golden brown on the other side. Transfer to a plate and drizzle with the soy sauce mixture.

Per serving. Effective carbohydrates: 4 g; Carbohydrates: 7.1 g; Fiber: 3.1 g; Protein: 26.1 g; Fat: 27.3 g; Calories: 363

TO-FRITES

Makes 3 servings

Serve with Ketchup (page 233)—or Aioli (page 248), if you're in a European kind of mood.

1 12-oz.	(340-g)	container firm tofu, drained
1		large egg
1 Tbsp.	(15 ml)	mayonnaise
1 Tbsp.	(15 ml)	Dijon mustard
¼ tsp.	(1.2 ml)	sea salt
½ tsp.	(2.5 ml)	paprika
½ tsp.	(2.5 ml)	garlic powder
		Freshly ground black pepper
1 cup	(240 ml)	freshly grated Parmesan cheese
		Sea salt

◅ Preheat the oven to 400°F (200°C). Line a baking sheet with parchment paper.

◅ Cut the tofu into long, thin french fry–like sticks.

◅ In a large shallow dish, beat the egg, mayonnaise, mustard, salt, paprika, garlic powder, and pepper to taste until well-combined. Spread the cheese out on a plate.

◅ Add a few tofu sticks at a time to the egg mixture and roll them gently to coat on all sides. Transfer to the cheese plate and roll to coat on all sides. Transfer to the baking sheet.

◅ Bake for 20 minutes. Pop under the broiler for a minute or so to brown the tops. Sprinkle with the salt and serve. These are best served hot.

Per serving. Effective carbohydrates: 4.5 g; Carbohydrates: 7.2 g; Fiber: 2.7 g; Protein: 36 g; Fat: 26.9 g; Calories: 400

TOFU "EGG" SALAD

Makes about 2 cups (480 ml)

Incredibly similar to the real thing! This keeps for 3 to 4 days in the fridge.

2 12-oz.	(340-g)	containers firm tofu, drained
¼ tsp.	(1.2 ml)	turmeric
2 Tbsp.	(30 ml)	finely minced green onion
2 Tbsp.	(30 ml)	finely minced celery
½ cup	(120 ml)	mayonnaise
2 tsp.	(10 ml)	Dijon mustard
1 Tbsp.	(15 ml)	chopped fresh dill
¼ tsp.	(1.2 ml)	sea salt
		Freshly ground black pepper

In a large bowl, mash the tofu with a potato masher or your hands until finely crumbled. Sprinkle with the turmeric and mix well. Add the green onion and celery.

In a small bowl, mix the mayonnaise, mustard, dill, salt, and pepper to taste. Add to the tofu and mix well. Cover and refrigerate.

Per ½ cup (120 ml). Effective carbohydrates: 4.2 g; Carbohydrates: 8.3 g; Fiber: 4.1 g; Protein: 27.4 g; Fat: 37.1 g; Calories: 452

USING YOUR NOODLE

Lasagna needn't be a distant memory. Using Donald's Deep-Dish Pizza Quiche (page 213) as the basis for "noodles" was the brainchild of Lisa (aka Digwig), a long-term lowcarber.org member. Absolutely brilliant!

DIGWIG'S COLLABORATION LASAGNA NOODLES
Makes 8 servings

The recipe makes 2 large egg sheets. You may think that isn't enough for a lasagna, but believe me, it is.

The egg sheets can be made a day in advance. You can use your favorite lasagna fillings with them. Or try them in Spinach, Ricotta, and Pesto Lasagna (page 143) or Bolognese Lasagna (page 205).

8 oz.	(227 g)	cream cheese, at room temperature
12		large eggs
1 cup	(240 ml)	whipping cream
½ tsp.	(2.5 ml)	sea salt
		Freshly ground black pepper
1 cup	(240 ml)	shredded full-fat mozzarella cheese
1 cup	(240 ml)	shredded Asiago or aged cheddar cheese

Preheat the oven to 350°F (175°C). Generously butter two 13 × 9-inch (32.5 × 22.5-cm) nonstick baking pans. (If you don't have nonstick pans, line yours with parchment paper and then butter the paper.)

Place the cream cheese in a food processor and pulse until smooth. Beat in the eggs, one at a time. Add the cream and salt and pepper to taste. Divide the mixture evenly between the prepared pans. Sprinkle evenly with the mozzarella and Asiago or cheddar.

Bake for 20 minutes, or until set. Remove from the oven. Invert each egg sheet onto a separate baking sheet. Let cool on wire racks. Cover and refrigerate.

Per serving. Effective carbohydrates: 3.3 g; Carbohydrates: 3.5 g; Fiber: 0.2 g; Protein: 17.7 g; Fat: 36 g; Calories: 408

SPINACH, RICOTTA, AND PESTO LASAGNA

Makes 8 servings

If you can get really good ricotta, usually sold sealed in a plastic basket, I think it makes a huge difference. It's creamier than ricotta sold in a carton.

Homemade pesto and tomato sauce are best, but if you don't have them, use store-bought.

2 10-oz.	(285-g)	bags ready-to-use spinach
1½ lb.	(680 g)	ricotta cheese
2		large eggs
⅛ tsp.	(0.6 ml)	freshly grated nutmeg
½ tsp.	(2.5 ml)	sea salt
½ cup	(120 ml)	freshly grated Parmesan cheese
½ cup	(120 ml)	Basil Pesto (page 240)
1½ cups	(360 ml)	Simple Tomato Sauce (page 242)
		Digwig's Collaboration Lasagna Noodles (page 142)
1½ cups	(360 ml)	shredded full-fat mozzarella cheese

◦§ Preheat the oven to 350°F (175°C).

◦§ Place the spinach and a scant amount of water in a large pot. Cover and cook over medium-high heat until wilted. Cool, squeeze out the water, and chop finely.

◦§ Place the spinach in a large bowl. Stir in the ricotta, eggs, nutmeg, salt, Parmesan, and pesto. Cover and refrigerate for up to 1 day.

◦§ Spread one-quarter of the tomato sauce in a 13 × 9-inch (32.5 × 22.5-cm) baking dish. Carefully transfer 1 lasagna noodle to the dish. Spread with another quarter of the tomato sauce. Evenly spread the spinach filling on top.

◦§ Add more tomato sauce, the remaining lasagna noodle, and the rest of the tomato sauce.

◦§ Bake for 35 minutes. Sprinkle with the mozzarella and bake for 10 minutes longer. Remove from the oven and let rest for 10 minutes before serving.

Per serving. Effective carbohydrates: 14.5 g; Carbohydrates: 18 g; Fiber: 3.5 g; Protein: 43.3 g; Fat: 66.6 g; Calories: 836

FISH

ONE OF MY FAVORITE FOODS TO WORK WITH IS FISH. Fish cooking makes a lot of people nervous, and rightly so. Fish is usually one of the more expensive proteins, and no one wants to mess it up. My one huge piece of advice when cooking fish is this: It's better to undercook it than overcook it. And remember that any food will continue cooking once you take it off the heat. It's better to return it to the heat to cook more than have a dry and chewy piece of fish on your plate.

Fatty fish like salmon and mackerel are rich in omega-3 fatty acids, and all fish are an excellent choice for low-carbers. If you've never tried them, swordfish and tuna are wonderfully "meaty" fish. Fresh tuna will be a revelation as it in no way resembles canned tuna.

I always look forward to halibut season. While many fish are just fine frozen, I think that halibut loses its wonderful delicate texture after freezing. Cod, when it's treated gently and not overcooked to a state where it resembles cotton, can be as wonderful as halibut.

Clams and mussels are quick to prepare, and their broth is always delicious. In these recipes, clams and mussels can be used interchangeably.

These recipes will impress you fish lovers on any occasion.

BASIC STEAMED FISH

Makes 4 servings

One of the pieces of equipment I find indispensable is a large two-tiered aluminum steamer, found in Chinese food stores. It's lightweight and easy to use. With it, a whole dinner can be cooked in under half an hour. It's great for cooking a large quantity and assortment of vegetables at the same time.

2		green onions, cut into 2-inch (5-cm) pieces
2		button or shiitake mushrooms, sliced
6		large Chinese cabbage leaves, cut into 3-inch (7.5-cm) pieces
4 6-oz.	(170-g)	fish fillets, such as halibut, salmon, or cod
2		fresh ginger slices, minced
¼ cup	(60 ml)	soy sauce
		Fresh cilantro sprigs

◦§ Place half of the green onions in the bottom of a heatproof vessel large enough to hold the fish snugly in a single layer. Add half of the mushrooms and cabbage. Place the fish on top and sprinkle with the ginger. Cover with the remaining green onions, mushrooms, and cabbage. Pour on the soy sauce.

◦§ Bring 2 inches (5 cm) of water to a boil in the bottom of the steamer. Place the fish in the top of the steamer and place over the water. Cover and steam for 15 to 20 minutes, or until the fish flakes easily. Garnish with the cilantro sprigs.

Per serving. Effective carbohydrates: 0.5 g; Carbohydrates: 1 g; Fiber: 0.5 g; Protein: 25.3 g; Fat: 2.6 g; Calories: 137

KAREN'S TOP 10 REASONS FOR LIVING A LOW-CARB LIFE

1. Achieving permanent fat loss and looking radiantly fabulous

2. Feeling a great sense of accomplishment about what you have achieved

3. Gaining the ability to move freely and having consistent energy all day

4. Preventing heart disease and high-blood pressure

5. Eliminating mood swings

6. Living long enough to see your children and grandchildren into adulthood

7. Watching aches and pains, headaches, and sometimes even migraines mysteriously disappear and skin clear up

8. Being able to shop in regular stores for clothing and to do all the things that "normal" size people do

9. Controlling or preventing diabetes and eliminating the symptoms of Polycystic Ovary Syndrome (PCOS)

10. Living each day to the fullest with newfound health and spreading the word!

BAKED HALIBUT
WITH LEMON BASIL VINAIGRETTE

Makes 4 servings

The vinaigrette is also good with salmon or swordfish.

FISH

4 6-oz.	(170-g)	halibut fillets
		Sea salt and freshly ground black pepper

VINAIGRETTE

1 tsp.	(5 ml)	grated lemon zest
2 Tbsp.	(30 ml)	freshly squeezed lemon juice
¼ tsp.	(1.2 ml)	sea salt
		Freshly ground black pepper
2		garlic cloves, cut in half
2 Tbsp.	(30 ml)	extra-virgin olive oil
3 Tbsp.	(45 ml)	thinly sliced fresh basil leaves
1 Tbsp.	(15 ml)	drained capers
½ cup	(120 ml)	finely diced tomatoes

◦§ *To make the fish:* Preheat the oven to 350°F (175°C). Lightly oil a baking dish large enough to hold the fillets in a single layer.

◦§ Season the fillets with salt and pepper. Place in the prepared baking dish. Bake for 15 to 18 minutes, or until the fish is opaque all the way through.

◦§ *To make the vinaigrette:* While the fish is baking, combine the lemon zest, lemon juice, salt, and pepper to taste in a small bowl. Spear the garlic on the tines of a fork and use it to beat the lemon juice mixture. Beat in the oil and then stir in the basil, capers, and tomatoes.

◦§ Place the fillets on heated plates, spoon on the vinaigrette, and serve.

Per serving. Effective carbohydrates: 2.1 g; Carbohydrates: 2.5 g; Fiber: 0.4 g; Protein: 35.7 g; Fat: 10.7 g; Calories: 256

HALIBUT WITH PINE NUT
AND PARMESAN CRUST

Makes 4 servings

*There are few people who would turn down fresh halibut, especially prepared like this.
When halibut is unavailable, you can use cod.*

½ cup	(120 ml)	pine nuts, coarsely chopped
¼ cup	(60 ml)	freshly grated Parmesan cheese
1 Tbsp.	(15 ml)	finely chopped fresh basil, mint, or dill
1		garlic clove, minced
4 6-oz.	(170-g)	halibut fillets
		Sea salt and freshly ground black pepper
2 Tbsp.	(30 ml)	mayonnaise

•§ Preheat the oven to 425°F (220°C). Lightly oil a baking dish large enough to hold the fillets in a single layer.

•§ In a small bowl, mix the pine nuts, cheese, herb, and garlic.

•§ Season the fillets with salt and pepper. Place in the prepared baking dish. Smear the top of each fillet with mayonnaise. Pat the pine nut mixture onto the mayonnaise, pressing lightly to make it adhere.

•§ Bake for 10 to 15 minutes, or until the fish is opaque all the way through.

Per serving. Effective carbohydrates: 2.4 g; Carbohydrates: 3.3 g; Fiber: 0.9 g; Protein: 42.3 g; Fat: 21 g; Calories: 364

SOLE WITH HORSERADISH CREAM SAUCE

Makes 4 servings

You can also use cod, salmon, or halibut for this dish. Just increase the cooking time.

Note: If you don't have a frying pan large enough to hold the fillets in a single layer, use two smaller ones.

1½ lb.	(680 g)	sole fillets, rinsed and patted dry
		Sea salt and freshly ground black pepper
2 Tbsp.	(30 ml)	unsalted butter
2 Tbsp.	(30 ml)	thinly sliced green onion
1 Tbsp.	(15 ml)	white wine vinegar
⅔ cup	(160 ml)	whipping cream
2 Tbsp.	(30 ml)	prepared horseradish
1 Tbsp.	(15 ml)	minced fresh parsley

◦§ Season the fillets with salt and pepper.

◦§ Heat a large frying pan over medium heat. Add the butter and watch carefully for the foaming to subside. As soon as it does, add the fillets. Cook until lightly golden. Using a wide turner, flip the fillets over. If the fillets are very thin, remove the pan from the heat and let the residual heat finish the cooking. If not, cook for 1 to 2 minutes longer and remove from the pan to a plate.

◦§ Add the green onion to the pan and stir until softened. Add the vinegar and let it bubble, then add the cream, horseradish, and any juice that has accumulated around the fillets on the plate. Let the sauce simmer until thickened, about 1 to 2 minutes. Stir in the parsley, pour over the fillets, and serve.

Per serving. Effective carbohydrates: 1.6 g; Carbohydrates: 1.7 g; Fiber: 0.1 g; Protein: 31.5 g; Fat: 23.2 g; Calories: 345

PANCETTA-WRAPPED SALMON WITH RED WINE BUTTER

Makes 4 servings

Pancetta is unsmoked Italian bacon that is rolled and tied. Its taste is very similar to prosciutto. You can use prosciutto or bacon, if you prefer. This treatment can be used on other fish, such as cod or halibut.

Serve with sautéed spinach and mushrooms.

1 Tbsp.	(15 ml)	minced shallot
1 cup	(240 ml)	dry red wine
4 Tbsp.	(60 ml)	unsalted butter, at room temperature
		Sea salt and freshly ground black pepper
4 6-oz.	(170-g)	skinless salmon fillets
1 tsp.	(5 ml)	fresh thyme leaves or ½ tsp. (2.5 ml) dried thyme
8		very thin pancetta slices
1 Tbsp.	(15 ml)	extra-virgin olive oil

⋆ Combine the shallot and wine in a small saucepan. Bring to a boil over medium-high heat. Cook until the wine is greatly reduced and turns into a syrupy glaze. Remove from the heat and pour into a small bowl. Stir in the butter until the butter is melted and emulsified. Season to taste with salt and pepper.

⋆ Season the salmon with salt and pepper and sprinkle with the thyme. Wrap 2 pancetta slices around each fillet.

⋆ In a frying pan large enough to hold the fillets in a single layer, heat the oil over medium heat. Add the fillets and cook until the pancetta is browned on all sides and the fillets are cooked through, about 8 to 10 minutes. Place the fillets on heated plates and spoon on the sauce.

Per serving. Effective carbohydrates: 1.2 g; Carbohydrates: 1.3 g; Fiber: 0.1 g; Protein: 38.2 g; Fat: 39.4 g; Calories: 315

DOREEN'S INCREDIBLY EASY SALMON OR TUNA PATTIES

Makes 4 patties

Doreen, a fellow founder of lowcarber.org, has many delicious and easy recipes.

Some people swear by these patties for breakfast. But they're good for lunch and dinner, too. They can be eaten hot or cold with any of the sauce suggestions for Fresh Salmon Cakes (page 154).

1 6-oz.	(170-g)	can salmon or tuna
1		large egg, lightly beaten
2 Tbsp.	(30 ml)	minced green onion
		Sea salt and freshly ground black pepper
1 Tbsp.	(15 ml)	extra-virgin olive oil
1 Tbsp.	(15 ml)	unsalted butter

⋙ Drain the fish well, place in a medium bowl, and mash it up with a fork. Stir in the egg and green onion. Season to taste with salt and pepper.

⋙ Heat the oil and butter in a large frying pan (preferably nonstick) over medium to medium-high heat until bubbly. Drop the fish mixture from a large spoon to make 4 equal mounds. Press them flat with the back of the spoon. Cook until golden brown underneath. Use a large pancake turner to gently turn the patties over; turn them only once or they'll break. Brown the other side.

Per patty. Effective carbohydrates (made with salmon): 0.5 g; Carbohydrates: 0.6 g; Fiber: 0.1 g; Protein: 10.4 g; Fat: 10.8 g; Calories: 142; Effective carbohydrates (made with tuna): 0.5 g; Carbohydrates: 0.6 g; Fiber: 0.1 g; Protein: 11.6 g; Fat: 7.7 g; Calories: 120

DOREEN'S INCREDIBLY EASY SALMON OR TUNA PATTIES

Makes 4 patties

Doreen, a fellow founder of lowcarber.org, has many delicious and easy recipes.

Some people swear by these patties for breakfast. But they're good for lunch and dinner, too. They can be eaten hot or cold with any of the sauce suggestions for Fresh Salmon Cakes (page 154).

1 6-oz.	(170-g)	can salmon or tuna
1		large egg, lightly beaten
2 Tbsp.	(30 ml)	minced green onion
		Sea salt and freshly ground black pepper
1 Tbsp.	(15 ml)	extra-virgin olive oil
1 Tbsp.	(15 ml)	unsalted butter

∘§ Drain the fish well, place in a medium bowl, and mash it up with a fork. Stir in the egg and green onion. Season to taste with salt and pepper.

∘§ Heat the oil and butter in a large frying pan (preferably nonstick) over medium to medium-high heat until bubbly. Drop the fish mixture from a large spoon to make 4 equal mounds. Press them flat with the back of the spoon. Cook until golden brown underneath. Use a large pancake turner to gently turn the patties over; turn them only once or they'll break. Brown the other side.

Per patty. Effective carbohydrates (made with salmon): 0.5 g; Carbohydrates: 0.6 g; Fiber: 0.1 g; Protein: 10.4 g; Fat: 10.8 g; Calories: 142; Effective carbohydrates (made with tuna): 0.5 g; Carbohydrates: 0.6 g; Fiber: 0.1 g; Protein: 11.6 g; Fat: 7.7 g; Calories: 120

FRESH SALMON CAKES

Makes 8 cakes

These salmon cakes are mild and packed with fresh salmon flavor. The natural collagen in the salmon is what helps them stick together.

Make sure you chop the salmon with a knife. Don't be tempted to use the food processor. The texture will be heavy!

Serve the cakes with Traditional Cocktail Sauce (page 235) or tartar sauce. If you like garlic, Aioli (page 248) is good, too. And, of course, they're fine eaten cold.

1½ lb.	(680 g)	boneless, skinless salmon fillet
2 Tbsp.	(30 ml)	mayonnaise
1 Tbsp.	(15 ml)	finely chopped green onion tops
1 Tbsp.	(15 ml)	finely chopped fresh dill
1 Tbsp.	(15 ml)	freshly squeezed lemon juice
¾ tsp.	(3.7 ml)	sea salt
		Freshly ground black pepper
2 Tbsp.	(30 ml)	vegetable oil

⊸ With a knife, chop the fillet into ¼-inch (0.6-cm) pieces and place in a bowl. Add the mayonnaise, green onion, dill, lemon juice, salt, and pepper to taste. Stir rapidly in the same direction for 1 minute. This helps the cakes stick together. Form into 8 patties. You can refrigerate them, uncovered, for up to 6 hours or until ready to cook.

⊸ Heat the oil in a large heavy or nonstick frying pan over medium-high heat. Add the cakes and cook until lightly browned, 2 to 3 minutes. Turn over and cook for an additional 2 to 3 minutes, or until browned.

Per cake. Effective carbohydrates: 0.3 g; Carbohydrates: 0.3 g; Fiber: 0.1 g; Protein: 17.1 g; Fat: 15 g; Calories: 209

VARIATIONS

Wasabi Salmon Cakes: Omit the dill and add 2 tsp. (10 ml) prepared wasabi. Serve with soy sauce to which you can add some grated ginger.

French Salmon Cakes: Omit the dill and add 1 Tbsp. (15 ml) Dijon mustard and 2 tsp. (10 ml) chopped fresh tarragon or 1 tsp. (5 ml) dried tarragon.

Smokey and Spicy Salmon Cakes: Omit the dill and add 1 finely chopped chipotle chile en adobo and 1 Tbsp. (15 ml) finely chopped fresh cilantro.

SALMON STEAKS WITH GINGER BUTTER

Makes 4 servings

Simple and impressive enough for company. This is equally good with salmon, halibut, or cod fillets in place of the salmon steaks.

8 Tbsp.	(120 ml)	unsalted butter, at room temperature
2 Tbsp.	(30 ml)	grated fresh ginger
3 Tbsp.	(45 ml)	finely chopped green onion
		Sea salt and freshly ground black pepper
4 8-oz.	(227-g)	salmon steaks, 1 inch (2.5 cm) thick
1 Tbsp.	(15 ml)	soy sauce
4		lime wedges

◦§ In a small bowl, mix the butter, ginger, and green onion. Season with salt and pepper. Remove 3 Tbsp. (45 ml) and set aside. Wrap the remainder in plastic wrap, forming a short log. Refrigerate until ready to serve.

◦§ Place the reserved 3 Tbsp. (45 ml) butter in a frying pan large enough to hold the steaks in a single layer. Melt over medium heat. Add the steaks and cook for about 4 minutes on each side, turning once. Add the soy sauce and give the pan a few shakes to glaze the bottom of the steaks.

◦§ Transfer the steaks, glazed side up, to heated plates or a platter. Unwrap the chilled butter and slice into 4 pieces. Top each piece of salmon with the butter and garnish with a lime wedge.

Per serving. Effective carbohydrates: 1.3 g; Carbohydrates: 1.5 g; Fiber: 0.2 g; Protein: 46.2 g; Fat: 48 g; Calories: 630

JAPANESE CONDIMENTS

When you go into a Japanese food store—or even peruse the international aisle in a well-stocked supermarket—you'll find many seasonings and condiments on the shelves. Naturally, you'll find different types of soy sauce—traditional, tamari, and reduced-sodium. (My favorite brand is Kikkoman.) But there's lots more, like these items.

- Agar-agar or kanten is a vegetable gelatin derived from seaweed. It has a "crunchy" texture and sets at room temperature. It's available in powdered flakes or in a square log shape. Once a jelly is made from it, it can be cut into pieces. One teaspoon of agar-agar has 0.3 gram of carbohydrate and not much of anything else.

  For a firm jell, you will need 2 tsp. (10 ml) of powder or 2 Tbsp. (30 ml) of flakes and 2 cups (480 ml) of liquid. Agar-agar should be soaked in the liquid first for 10 to 15 minutes, then gently brought to a boil and simmered (while stirring) until it dissolves completely. This will take about 5 minutes for powder and 10 to 15 minutes for flakes.

- Condiments come in a wide variety. Wasabi, hot mustard—and this is hot!—garlic, ginger, and umeboshi pastes are all conveniently packed in tubes.

- Dried black soybeans are much cheaper than those in cans, and they have a better texture. Cover generously with cold water, soak overnight in the refrigerator, drain, and add fresh water. Cook at a simmer until tender, 1½ to 2 hours.

- Ponzu is a citrus sauce, usually combined with vinegar and soy. Excellent on sashimi and cooked fish.

- Rice vinegar and brown rice vinegar are very complex and full-flavored. Watch out for "seasoned" rice vinegar—it contains sugar.

- Roasted soy flour is darkly roasted and nutty. The flavor is so intense that if you bake using soy flour, use half roasted soy flour and half regular soy flour. Roasted soy flour is traditionally used as a dusting on Japanese sweets.

- Sesame oil (both light and the dark toasted kind) and chili oil (when you want heat but don't have the peppers around) add immeasurable flavor.

- Sesame seeds—black and white—are available raw, roasted, as a paste, or ground. There's also gomashio, a combination of ground sesame seeds and salt that is very tasty.

SALMON WITH MISO GLAZE

Makes 4 servings

I love this glaze with other fatty fish, such as mackerel. It also goes very well with white fish, like halibut and cod. This is the quick version of the recipe, but its charms are really revealed by marinating the fish up to 2 days in the miso mixture, then discarding it all before broiling.

4 6-oz.	(170-g)	salmon fillets or steaks
¼ cup	(60 ml)	white miso paste
2 Tbsp.	(30 ml)	sake
2 Tbsp.	(30 ml)	water
1½ tsp.	(7.5 ml)	*each* Splenda and Canadian Sugar Twin or 1 Tbsp. (15 ml) Splenda
1 Tbsp.	(15 ml)	toasted sesame seeds
		Lemon wedges

•§ Preheat the broiler.

•§ Line a rimmed baking sheet with foil. Lightly oil the foil or coat with nonstick cooking spray. Place the fish on the foil.

•§ In a small bowl, whisk the miso, sake, water, and sweetener into a smooth paste. Brush the fish with half of the miso mixture. Broil 3 to 4 inches (7.5 to 10 cm) from the heat until golden brown, 4 to 5 minutes.

•§ Turn the fish over and brush with the remaining miso mixture. Sprinkle the sesame seeds on top and broil until the fish is opaque in the center, 3 to 4 minutes. Serve with lemon wedges.

Per serving. Effective carbohydrates: 4.7 g; Carbohydrates: 5.3 g; Fiber: 0.6 g; Protein: 35.5 g; Fat: 19.3 g; Calories: 356

SALMON WITH BACON, TOMATO, AND CAPER VINAIGRETTE

Makes 4 servings

This warm vinaigrette will complement many kinds of seafood. Think trout, halibut, cod, snapper, scallops, and prawns.

¼ lb.	(112 g)	bacon
4 6-oz.	(170-g)	salmon fillets
		Extra-virgin olive oil
		Sea salt and freshly ground black pepper
1		ripe tomato, peeled, seeded, and diced
1½ tsp.	(7.5 ml)	small capers
1 Tbsp.	(15 ml)	coarsely chopped fresh parsley
½ tsp.	(2.5 ml)	prepared horseradish
2 tsp.	(10 ml)	balsamic vinegar

◆ Preheat the oven to 350°F (175°C).

◆ Dice the bacon into ¼-inch (0.6-cm) pieces. Cook in a small frying pan over low heat until crisp. Remove from the heat.

◆ Drizzle the fillets with oil and season with salt and pepper. Heat a large ovenproof nonstick frying pan over medium heat. Place the salmon, skin side up, in the pan. Cook until the salmon is lightly browned. Flip the pieces over and cook until the skin is crisp.

◆ Transfer to the oven and bake for 5 to 6 minutes, or until cooked through but still juicy. Remove from the oven.

≈ Add the tomato, capers, parsley, horseradish, and vinegar to the bacon. Heat to a simmer and season with salt and pepper. Transfer the fillets to warm plates and spoon the vinaigrette over each piece.

Per serving. Effective carbohydrates: 1.3 g; Carbohydrates: 1.6 g; Fiber: 0.3 g; Protein: 37.2 g; Fat: 22.4 g; Calories: 367

A-PEELING TOMATOES

There's more than one way to skin a tomato.

≈ The most traditional method of peeling tomatoes starts with bringing a large pot of water to a boil. Score a small × on the bottom of each tomato and drop them into the boiling water, a few at a time. After about 10 seconds, remove them with a slotted spoon, let cool, and slip off the skins.

≈ A second method—the one I prefer—is to use a swivel-headed vegetable peeler. This method is better for tomatoes that are going to be used raw. Starting at the top of the tomato, use the peeler in a back and forth motion to pare the skin away.

After peeling, cut the tomatoes in half crosswise. If using them raw, remove the seeds with a small spoon. If you are going to be cooking them, squeeze the tomato half, cut side downward.

ROSEBUD'S TUNA AND SPINACH BAKE

Makes 4 servings

I found Rosebud's dish especially appealing because my mother used to make something similar, which I in turn was taught to make when just a wee girl.

Rosebud—a lowcarber.org alumna—says you can use any cheese for this, as long as it's tasty! As you can imagine, it makes great leftovers for breakfast. It's also quite good with canned salmon.

2 Tbsp.	(30 ml)	unsalted butter
½ cup	(120 ml)	finely chopped onion
2 10-oz.	(285-g)	bags ready-to-use spinach
2 6-oz.	(170-g)	cans chunk light tuna, drained and flaked
3		large eggs
¾ cup	(180 ml)	whipping cream
½ tsp.	(2.5 ml)	sea salt
4 oz.	(112 g)	aged cheddar cheese, shredded

◦§ Preheat the oven to 350°F (175°C).

◦§ Melt the butter in a large frying pan over medium heat. Add the onion and stir for about 2 minutes, or until the onion is soft. Add the spinach and cook until wilted.

◦§ Spread the spinach mixture in an 8 × 8-inch (20 × 20-cm) baking dish. Top with the tuna.

◦§ In a small bowl, lightly beat the eggs with a fork. Beat in the cream and salt. Pour over the tuna. Sprinkle evenly with the cheese.

◦§ Bake for 40 minutes, or until set and the top is lightly browned.

Per serving. Effective carbohydrates: 4.6 g; Carbohydrates: 8.7 g; Fiber: 4.1 g; Protein: 38.7 g; Fat: 36.9 g; Calories: 515

ALBACORE TUNA MELT

Makes 4 servings

This is a playful take on the tuna melt, using fresh tuna. You can use either albacore or ahi, just make sure it is thickly cut and you don't overcook it or your beautiful piece of tuna will end up tasting like it came from a can.

The lion's share of the carb count comes from the roasted garlic, at 7 grams of effective carbs for the whole recipe. You can omit it or use less.

Note: *To roast garlic, use this easy stove-top method: Choose fresh, firm bulbs with no green sprouts. Separate the cloves and peel them. Put in a small heavy saucepan, cover with vegetable oil or extra-virgin olive oil by ½ inch (1.2 cm), and place over medium-low heat. As soon as bubbles form around the garlic, turn the heat to low and cook until the cloves are golden brown and completely soft—from 20 to 40 minutes. Let cool, cover, and refrigerate.*

¼ cup	(60 ml)	mayonnaise
2 Tbsp.	(30 ml)	coarsely chopped basil leaves
8		roasted garlic cloves, coarsely chopped
¾ cup	(180 ml)	shredded Asiago or other full-flavored cheese
4 6-oz.	(170-g)	albacore tuna steaks, about ¾ inch (1.9 cm) thick
1 Tbsp.	(15 ml)	extra-virgin olive oil
		Sea salt and freshly ground black pepper
1		ripe tomato, seeded and finely diced

◄ Preheat the broiler.

◄ In a small bowl, mix the mayonnaise, basil, garlic, and cheese.

◄ Season the tuna on both sides with the oil, salt, and pepper. Heat a large ovenproof heavy frying pan until almost smoking. Add the tuna in a single layer and sear until lightly brown on one side. Turn over and sear the other side. The tuna should remain rare.

◄ Spread the cheese mixture evenly over each piece of tuna. Broil 4 inches (10 cm) from the heat until the cheese bubbles. Sprinkle with the tomato and serve immediately.

Per serving. Effective carbohydrates: 4.3 g; Carbohydrates: 5 g; Fiber: 0.7 g; Protein: 45.9 g; Fat: 26.6 g; Calories: 451

SEARED TUNA WITH SOY WASABI GLAZE

Makes 4 servings

The sauce is extremely good with other fish, such as salmon and halibut. For vegetables, spinach, asparagus, and snow peas are a good match with the sauce and tuna.

Note: *Make sure your butter is cold or the sauce won't emulsify properly.*

4 6-oz.	(170-g)	fresh ahi or albacore tuna steaks, about ¾ inch (1.9 cm) thick
		Vegetable oil
		Sea salt and freshly ground black pepper
8 Tbsp.	(120 ml)	cold unsalted butter
1 Tbsp.	(15 ml)	freshly squeezed lemon juice
3 Tbsp.	(45 ml)	soy sauce
1 to 2 Tbsp.	(15 to 30 ml)	prepared wasabi
3		green onions, thinly sliced

⊸ Brush the steaks on both sides with the oil and season with salt and pepper.

⊸ Heat a heavy nonstick frying pan over high heat. Place the steaks in the pan and sear until browned. Turn over and sear the other side. Be careful not to overcook the tuna. It's best rare to medium-rare.

⊸ While the tuna is cooking, combine the butter, lemon juice, soy sauce, and wasabi in a small saucepan. Heat over low heat, stirring constantly, until smooth and emulsified. Remove immediately from the heat.

⊸ Serve the tuna immediately, drenched with the sauce. Sprinkle with the green onions.

Per serving. Effective carbohydrates: 2.9 g; Carbohydrates: 3 g; Fiber: 0.1 g; Protein: 40.8 g; Fat: 32.7 g; Calories: 475

CLAMS STEAMED WITH BACON, GREEN OLIVES, AND TOMATOES

Makes 4 servings

Before cooking clams and mussels, check them thoroughly and set aside any that are open. Check through the ones you have set aside again and discard any that did not close. I love this heady, punchy combination of flavors with the smoothness of the cream.

½ lb.	(227 g)	bacon slices, cut into ½-inch (1.2-cm) pieces
4		garlic cloves, minced
¼ cup	(60 ml)	finely chopped onion
½ cup	(120 ml)	dry white wine
½ cup	(120 ml)	drained canned Italian plum tomatoes, finely chopped
12		large green olives, pitted and roughly chopped
½ cup	(120 ml)	whipping cream
3 lb.	(1.3 kg)	Manila clams, scrubbed
2 Tbsp.	(30 ml)	finely chopped fresh parsley

◦§ Cook the bacon in a large pot over low heat until crisp. Remove the bacon and discard all the fat except 1 Tbsp. (15 ml). Turn the heat to high and add the garlic and onion. When they sizzle, add the wine, tomatoes, olives, cream, clams, and parsley.

◦§ Cover tightly and steam until the clams open, shaking the pot occasionally to redistribute the clams. When the clams have opened, add the bacon. Cover and shake a few times. Serve in heated bowls.

Per serving. Effective carbohydrates: 4.7 g; Carbohydrates: 5.2 g; Fiber: 0.5 g; Protein: 13.4 g; Fat: 20.7 g; Calories: 268

STIR-FRIED PRAWNS
WITH TOMATO COCONUT CREAM

Makes 4 servings

Quick and delicious! Try it with Basic Cauli-flied "Rice" (page 110).

1 Tbsp.	(15 ml)	tomato paste
½ tsp.	(2.5 ml)	sea salt
1 tsp.	(5 ml)	Garam Masala (page 249)
½ tsp.	(2.5 ml)	ground toasted cumin seeds
3 Tbsp.	(45 ml)	finely chopped fresh cilantro
1		hot green chile pepper, finely chopped
1 Tbsp.	(15 ml)	freshly squeezed lime juice
1 cup	(240 ml)	canned coconut milk
3 Tbsp.	(45 ml)	vegetable oil
1 tsp.	(5 ml)	black mustard seeds
3		garlic cloves, minced
1¼ lb.	(565 g)	large prawns, 26 to 30 per lb. peeled and deveined

❧ Put the tomato paste in a small bowl. Mix in the salt, garam masala, cumin, cilantro, chile, and lime juice. Gradually stir in the coconut milk.

❧ Heat the oil in a large frying pan over medium-high heat. Add the mustard seeds. When they pop, add the garlic. When the garlic starts to turn golden, add the prawns.

❧ Stir-fry until the prawns turn pink. Add the sauce mixture and bring to a boil. The prawns should be cooked all the way through by this point. Serve immediately.

Per serving. Effective carbohydrates: 5.6 g. Carbohydrates: 6.1 g; Fiber: 0.5 g; Protein: 31.5 g; Fat: 29.3 g; Calories: 421

QUICK PRAWNS, SCAMPI-STYLE

Makes 6 servings

Delicious served over a bed of Basic Cauliflower Mash (page 112) seasoned with goat cheese to soak up the buttery, garlicky juices. The scampi also makes a perfect appetizer.

2 Tbsp.	(30 ml)	extra-virgin olive oil
4		garlic cloves, minced
1¼ lb.	(565 g)	large prawns, 26 to 30 per lb., peeled and deveined
2 Tbsp.	(30 ml)	dry white wine
4 Tbsp.	(60 ml)	unsalted butter, at room temperature
¼ cup	(60 ml)	finely chopped fresh parsley Sea salt and freshly ground black pepper

◆ Heat the oil and garlic in a large frying pan over medium heat until the garlic starts to sizzle. Turn the heat to medium-low and cook until the garlic turns gold. Add the prawns and turn the heat back to medium.

◆ When the prawns start to sizzle, add the wine and continue cooking—stirring occasionally—until they turn pink and plump. Check for doneness by taking a slice from the thick end. It should be opaque. Swirl in the butter and parsley and season to taste with salt and pepper. Serve immediately.

Per serving. Effective carbohydrates: 1.9 g; Carbohydrates: 2 g; Fiber: 0.1 g; Protein: 19.3 g; Fat: 20.5 g; Calories: 273

MUSSELS, PIZZERIA-STYLE

Makes 4 servings

These mussels are "all-dressed." If you want, a little pepperoni added to the sauce would not be out of place. This recipe works with clams, too.

¼ cup	(60 ml)	extra-virgin olive oil
2 Tbsp.	(30 ml)	finely chopped onion
4		garlic cloves, minced
½ cup	(120 ml)	thinly sliced mushrooms
¼ cup	(60 ml)	finely diced red or green pepper
½ cup	(120 ml)	canned plum tomatoes with juice, coarsely chopped
½ cup	(120 ml)	dry white wine
½ tsp.	(2.5 ml)	dried oregano
2 lb.	(908 g)	fresh mussels, debearded if necessary and scrubbed
		Dried chile flakes
2 Tbsp.	(30 ml)	finely chopped fresh parsley
¼ cup	(60 ml)	freshly grated Parmesan cheese

∽ Heat the oil in a large pot over medium-high heat. Add the onion and garlic and sauté until the onion becomes translucent. Add the mushrooms and peppers and cook until both become soft. Add the tomatoes, wine, and oregano. Bring to a boil.

∽ Add the mussels and chile flakes. Cover, turn up the heat, and cook until the mussels open, shaking the pan occasionally. Discard any that stay closed. Stir in the parsley and cheese. Serve immediately.

Per serving. Effective carbohydrates: 3.6 g; Carbohydrates: 3.5 g; Fiber: 0.6 g; Protein: 4.2 g; Fat: 15.2 g; Calories: 195

CHICKEN
AND TURKEY

CHICKEN
AND TURKEY

I'M STATING THE OBVIOUS HERE, BECAUSE WE ALL KNOW THAT CHICKEN IS ONE OF THE MOST VERSATILE MEATS. It's easy to prepare, cooks quickly, suits almost any seasoning, and is universally beloved. Along with hard-cooked eggs, it's good to have a few cooked drumsticks, wings, or breasts in your fridge as a quick meal.

For easy casseroles, add cooked boneless chicken pieces to such dishes as Spaghetti Squash, Carbonara-Style (page 131), Spaghetti Squash Arrabbiata (page 132), and Tofu-roni and Cheese (page 136). Really, most any casserole, vegetable side dish, soup, or salad can be enhanced by chicken.

Equally obvious: Everything that applies to chicken goes double for turkey. Thanksgiving leftovers are never a problem! And speaking of the holidays, the 90-Minute Miracle Turkey (page 188) will take all the stress and work out of yours.

Try these other favorites to warm the hearts of family and friends.

ONE-POT CHICKEN
WITH MUSHROOMS AND SOUR CREAM

Makes 4 servings

Although you don't need the sour cream for this delicious one-pot dish, it is extremely tasty.
Use whatever combination of chicken legs, thighs, and breasts that you prefer.
  Note: *If you lack a large enough pan, work with two smaller ones.*

4 lb.	(1.8 kg)	**bone-in chicken pieces with skin**
½ tsp.	(2.5 ml)	**sea salt**
		Freshly ground black pepper
1 Tbsp.	(15 ml)	**unsalted butter**
1 Tbsp.	(15 ml)	**extra-virgin olive oil**
½ cup	(120 ml)	**thinly sliced onion**
½ lb.	(227 g)	**mushrooms, cut in half**
1½ tsp.	(7.5 ml)	**fresh thyme leaves or ½ tsp. (2.5 ml) dried thyme**
½ cup	(120 ml)	**dry white wine or water**
½ cup	(120 ml)	**sour cream**

•§ Season the chicken with the salt and pepper.

•§ Place the butter and oil in a frying pan or pot large enough to hold the chicken pieces in a single layer. Heat over medium-high heat until the butter melts. Add the chicken pieces and cook until they are brown on both sides, turning once. Remove the chicken to a plate.

•§ Remove all but 2 Tbsp. (30 ml) of fat from the pan. Add the onion and mushrooms. Cook, stirring frequently, until the juice from the mushrooms evaporates.

•§ Return the chicken with any juice to the pan. Add the thyme and wine or water and bring to a boil. Give the pan a shake to redistribute the chicken and vegetables. Turn the heat down to a bare simmer, cover, and cook until the chicken is cooked through, about 25 minutes. Stir in the sour cream and heat through. Taste and adjust the seasoning with salt and pepper.

Per serving. Effective carbohydrates: 4.7 g; Carbohydrates: 5.7 g; Fiber: 1 g; Protein: 95.4 g; Fat: 51.3 g; Calories: 906

CINNAMON-SPICED LEMON CHICKEN

Makes 4 servings

These chicken thighs are a perfect accompaniment to Pine Nut and Parsley Salad (page 68).

8		large bone-in chicken thighs with skin
		Sea salt and freshly ground black pepper
1 tsp.	(5 ml)	ground cinnamon
1 tsp.	(5 ml)	ground cumin
1 tsp.	(5 ml)	sweet or hot paprika
¼ cup	(60 ml)	freshly squeezed lemon juice
2 Tbsp.	(30 ml)	extra-virgin olive oil
2 Tbsp.	(30 ml)	unsalted butter, cut into small pieces

◀ Preheat the oven to 400°F (200°C).

◀ With a sharp knife, slash the thighs once or twice on each side. Place in a large bowl and season liberally with salt and pepper.

◀ In a small bowl, mix the cinnamon, cumin, paprika, lemon juice, and oil. Add to the chicken and toss to coat.

◀ Place the thighs in a single layer in a baking dish. Dot with the butter. Bake for 30 minutes, basting occasionally with the butter.

◀ Turn on the broiler. Broil 4 to 6 inches (10 to 15 cm) from the heat until golden brown. Serve with the pan juices.

Per serving. Effective carbohydrates: 1.7 g; Carbohydrates: 2.3 g; Fiber: 0.6 g; Protein: 31.3 g; Fat: 32.3 g; Calories: 429

FLAT-ROASTED CHICKEN
WITH PROSCIUTTO AND GREEN OLIVES

Makes 4 servings

This chicken dish will have wonderful smells coming from your oven—especially welcoming on a chilly night.

Buy the prosciutto in a single piece, rather than sliced, and cut it into small cubes.

1		chicken, 3½ to 4 lb. (1.6 kg to 1.8 kg)
		Sea salt and freshly ground black pepper
¼ lb.	(112 g)	prosciutto, cut into ½-inch (1.2-cm) cubes
⅓ cup	(80 ml)	minced shallot
2		garlic cloves, minced
½ cup	(120 ml)	unpitted green olives
½ cup	(120 ml)	dry white wine

◦§ Preheat the oven to 350°F (175°C). Lightly oil a large roasting pan.

◦§ With a sharp heavy knife, split the chicken down the backbone and open it up. Turn it breast side up and flatten with the palm of your hand. Cut a slit in the skin in the center, at the bottom of the breast area, and slip both drumstick tips through it. Sprinkle liberally with salt and pepper. Transfer the chicken, breast side down, to the prepared roasting pan.

◦§ Bake for 45 minutes.

◦§ In a small bowl, mix the prosciutto, shallot, garlic, and olives.

◦§ Remove the chicken from the oven and transfer to a plate. Remove any accumulated fat from the pan and discard. Scatter the prosciutto mixture evenly in the pan and add the wine. Place the chicken, skin side up, in the pan. Bake for 45 minutes longer.

◦§ Remove the chicken from the pan. Either carve the meat from the bones or cut the chicken into serving pieces. Pour the prosciutto mixture over the chicken and serve.

Per serving. Effective carbohydrates: 0.4 g; Carbohydrates: 1.2 g; Fiber: 0.8 g; Protein: 52.4 g; Fat: 31.2 g; Calories: 523

DOREEN'S THIGHS WITH LIME, GARLIC, SESAME, AND GINGER

Makes 4 servings

Doreen, fellow founder of lowcarber.org, intentionally makes sure that there are leftovers. You can fight her for them!

She also likes to finish these thighs off with kizami shoga ginger (page 35). It really looks and tastes good with the cilantro and flavors of the chicken.

It's best to bake these thighs in a glass dish and start them in a cold oven.

8		large bone-in, skinless chicken thighs
		Juice and grated rind of 1 large lime
3		large garlic cloves, minced
1-inch	(2.5-cm)	piece fresh ginger, grated
½ tsp.	(2.5 ml)	Garam Masala (page 249)
½ tsp.	(2.5 ml)	dried chile flakes
2 Tbsp.	(30 ml)	vegetable oil
1 Tbsp.	(15 ml)	toasted sesame oil
3 Tbsp.	(45 ml)	chopped fresh cilantro

◦ Place the chicken in a 9 × 9-inch (22.5 × 22.5-cm) glass baking dish.

◦ In a small bowl, mix the lime juice and rind, garlic, ginger, garam masala, chile flakes, vegetable oil, and sesame oil. Pour over the chicken and turn the pieces to coat. Cover and refrigerate for at least 1 hour or up to overnight.

◦ Uncover and place in a cold oven. Turn the heat to 350°F (175°C). Bake, basting occasionally with the pan juices, for 45 to 50 minutes, or until the juices run clear when the thickest part of a thigh is pierced with a fork. Sprinkle with the cilantro.

Per serving. Effective carbohydrates: 1.3 g; Carbohydrates: 1.7 g; Fiber: 0.4 g; Protein: 27.4 g; Fat: 21.7 g; Calories: 317

SIMPLE CHICKEN
AND COCONUT MILK CURRY

Makes 4 servings

This recipe is really easy and really good. It's a gentle dish that doesn't blast your taste buds with heavy spice. If you want to make a "meal in a pot," add some fresh green beans when the chicken is done and cook for 5 minutes or so until the beans are just tender. Adding a squeeze of lime is great.

Note: *Because the whole spices are not eaten, they're not included in the carb count.*

2 Tbsp.	(30 ml)	vegetable oil
1½ tsp.	(7.5 ml)	black peppercorns
3 1½-inch	(3.7-cm)	cinnamon sticks
10		cloves
8		cardamom pods
3		dried red chile peppers
1 Tbsp.	(15 ml)	grated fresh ginger
8		large bone-in, skinless chicken thighs
1 14-oz.	(400-ml)	can coconut milk
		Sea salt

◆§ Heat the oil in a large heavy pot over high heat. Add the peppercorns, cinnamon, cloves, cardamom, and chiles. Stir for a few minutes, until the cardamom darkens slightly. Add the ginger and give a few stirs.

◆§ Add the chicken and coconut milk. Salt very lightly. Add enough water to just cover the chicken pieces. Bring to a boil, turn down to a simmer, and cook for 40 minutes, or until the chicken is cooked through and the sauce thickens slightly. Season to taste with salt.

Per serving. Effective carbohydrates: 1.7 g; Carbohydrates: 2.8 g; Fiber: 1.1 g; Protein: 2.8 g; Fat: 38.7 g; Calories: 425

BUFFALO-STYLE WINGS

Makes 4 servings

The challenge was how to make a wing that was spicy, saucy, and crispy without deep-frying.

Broiling or baking the wings and then tossing them into sauce had no oomph to it. The wings were pale and flabby. I remembered a technique I used to make teriyaki wings years ago: simmering the wings in sauce and then broiling. It worked beautifully.

You can increase the finishing toss of hot sauce to taste. (In my book, Frank's is the only sauce for real Buffalo wings, but you can use the hot sauce that you prefer.) Serve with Blue Cheese Dressing (page 94) or Ranch Dressing (page 95).

Note: If you don't have a large enough pan to hold the wings in a single layer, use two smaller pans and divide the ingredients.

½ cup	(120 ml)	water
1 cup	(240 ml)	Frank's Red Hot Sauce or other hot-pepper sauce
2½ lb.	(1.1 kg)	split chicken wings, wing tips removed

◦⟋ Preheat the broiler. Line a rimmed baking sheet with foil.

◦⟋ Combine the water and ¾ cup (180 ml) of the hot sauce in a nonstick frying pan or pot large enough to hold the wings in a single layer. Bring to a boil over high heat. Add the wings and cook at a rapid boil for 5 minutes. Turn the wings over and cook for 5 minutes longer. The important thing is to regulate the heat so there is enough liquid to cook the wings without evaporating.

◦⟋ If there is still liquid in the pan after 10 minutes, lower the heat and continue to cook, shaking the pan frequently, until the wings are covered with a glaze.

◦⟋ Spread the wings in a single layer on the prepared baking sheet. Broil 4 to 6 inches (10 to 15 cm) from the heat, for 4 to 5 minutes, until the wings are crispy and brown. Turn over and crisp the other side. Transfer to a bowl and toss with the remaining ¼ cup (60 ml) hot sauce.

Per serving. Effective carbohydrates: 1.3 g; Carbohydrates: 1.3 g; Fiber: 0 g; Protein: 58.3 g; Fat: 42.3 g; Calories: 635

CHICKEN WINGS IN PEANUT SAUCE

Makes 6 servings

A great grab-and-go item to have in your fridge.

Note: If you want a dip for the wings, make four times the amount of the peanut butter mixture. Reserve one-quarter of it for cooking the wings and mix the remainder with a bit of mayonnaise or sour cream.

4 lb.	(1.8 kg)	split chicken wings, wing tips removed
2 Tbsp.	(30 ml)	vegetable oil
1 Tbsp.	(15 ml)	finely grated fresh ginger
1		garlic clove, minced
¼ cup	(60 ml)	smooth natural peanut butter
1 Tbsp.	(15 ml)	freshly squeezed lime juice
2 tsp.	(10 ml)	fish sauce
2 tsp.	(10 ml)	soy sauce
1 tsp.	(5 ml)	*each* Splenda and Canadian Sugar Twin or 4 tsp. (20 ml) Splenda
¼ tsp.	(1.2 ml)	sea salt
		Dried chile flakes

◦ Preheat the oven to 500°F (260°C).

◦ In a large bowl, toss together the wings, oil, ginger, and garlic. Spread out on 1 or 2 nonstick, rimmed baking sheets in a single layer. Bake for 25 minutes. Remove from the oven and turn on the broiler.

◦ In a clean bowl large enough to hold the wings, combine the peanut butter, lime juice, fish sauce, soy sauce, sweetener, salt, and chile flakes to taste. Mix until smooth. Add the wings, discarding the pan juices, and toss well to coat with the sauce.

◦ Spread the wings on the baking sheet in a single layer. Broil 4 to 6 inches (10 to 15 cm) from the heat for 4 to 5 minutes on each side or until nicely browned and crispy.

Per serving. Effective carbohydrates: 2.2 g; Carbohydrates: 3.1 g; Fiber: 0.9 g; Protein: 63.9 g; Fat: 53.4 g; Calories: 760

OVEN-FRIED CHICKEN

Makes 6 servings

Move over, Colonel Sanders! The secret to success here is baking the chicken on a wire rack set in a shallow pan.

5½ oz.	(154 g)	pork rinds
6		bone-in chicken thighs with skin, about 2 lb. (908 g)
6		bone-in chicken legs with skin, about 1½ lb. (680 g)
1		large egg
½ cup	(120 ml)	mayonnaise
2 Tbsp.	(30 ml)	Dijon mustard
1½ tsp.	(7.5 ml)	dried thyme
1 tsp.	(5 ml)	sea salt
1 tsp.	(5 ml)	freshly ground black pepper
1 tsp.	(5 ml)	dried oregano
½ tsp.	(2.5 ml)	garlic powder

◦§ Preheat the oven to 400°F (200°C). Place a wire cooling rack in a large rimmed baking sheet.

◦§ In a food processor, grind the pork rinds. (A few larger pieces are desirable. I like to squish them up in the bag first to get the process started.) Spread on a large plate.

◦§ Remove the skin from the chicken pieces. (Using a paper towel to grip the skin helps.)

◦§ In a shallow bowl, mix the egg, mayonnaise, mustard, thyme, salt, pepper, oregano, and garlic powder.

◦§ Dip each piece of chicken in the mayonnaise mixture to coat thoroughly and then roll in the pork rinds to cover completely. Place the chicken on the wire rack, making sure there is enough room around each piece for the chicken to roast evenly and crisply.

Bake for 40 minutes, or until the juice runs clear when the thickest part of the thigh is pricked with a knife.

Per serving. Effective carbohydrates: 0.9 g; Carbohydrates: 1.3 g; Fiber: 0.4 g; Protein: 52.8 g; Fat: 46.9 g; Calories: 650

ROSEBUD'S BUTTER CHICKEN

Makes 4 servings

As Rosebud, another wonderful member of lowcarber.org says, this could not be much simpler to make! Serve it with Cucumber Salad with Peanuts, Coconut, and Lime (page 76) and Basic Cauli-flied "Rice" (page 110) seasoned with curry powder.

Butter chicken usually requires making tandoori chicken first, but you don't have to do that with Rosebud's recipe. Just start with commercially prepared tandoori paste, which you can buy in Indian groceries or well-stocked supermarkets.

2 Tbsp.	**(30 ml)**	**vegetable oil**
1½ lb.	**(680 g)**	**boneless, skinless chicken breast halves, cut into bite-size pieces**
2 Tbsp.	**(30 ml)**	**tandoori paste**
¾ cup	**(180 ml)**	**whipping cream**
1 Tbsp.	**(15 ml)**	**unsalted butter**
2 Tbsp.	**(30 ml)**	**toasted sliced almonds (optional)**

Heat the oil in a large frying pan over medium-high heat. Add the chicken and cook, stirring occasionally, until lightly browned and almost cooked through, for 4 to 5 minutes. Stir in the tandoori paste and then add the cream. Simmer for about 5 minutes, or until the cream is lightly thickened. Stir in the butter and garnish with the almonds (if using).

Per serving. Effective carbohydrates: 2.7 g; Carbohydrates: 3.8 g; Fiber: 1.1 g; Protein: 37.7 g; Fat: 43.1 g; Calories: 558

LEMONGRASS CHICKEN

Makes 4 servings

If you have not yet become acquainted with the flavors of Southeast Asia, this is a good introduction. Serve with Cucumber Salad with Peanuts, Coconut, and Lime (page 76).

2		**fresh lemongrass stalks**
2		**small shallots, coarsely chopped**
2		**garlic cloves, coarsely chopped**
1		**small hot chile pepper, coarsely chopped**
1 Tbsp.	(15 ml)	**fish sauce**
4 8-oz.	(227-g)	**boneless chicken breast halves with skin**
1 Tbsp.	(15 ml)	**vegetable oil**
		Sea salt and freshly ground black pepper

◦§ Remove the fibrous outer covering and top of the lemongrass and chop the tender part as finely as you can. Place in a food processor and add the shallots, garlic, chile, and fish sauce. Pulse to a fine paste.

◦§ Place the chicken in a large bowl and add the paste. Toss to coat well. Cover and refrigerate for at least 2 hours or up to overnight.

◦§ Preheat the oven to 450°F (225°C).

◦§ Pat the chicken dry with paper towels. Heat the oil in a large ovenproof nonstick frying pan over medium-high heat. Add the chicken, skin side down, season with salt and pepper, and cook until lightly browned, about 5 minutes.

◦§ Place the pan in the oven and bake for 5 minutes. Turn the chicken over and bake for an additional 5 minutes, or until cooked through.

Per serving. Effective carbohydrates: 2 g; Carbohydrates: 2.5 g; Fiber: 0.5 g; Protein: 51.2 g; Fat: 16.8 g; Calories: 379

CHICKEN WITH BACON, CREAM, AND THYME

Makes 4 servings

Delicious served with steamed spinach and Basic Cauliflower Mash (page 112) on the side. If you don't have fresh thyme, a light sprinkling of dried thyme will do.

4 8-oz.	(227-g)	boneless chicken breast halves with skin
		Sea salt and freshly ground black pepper
8		bacon slices
8		small fresh thyme sprigs
1 Tbsp.	(15 ml)	vegetable oil
½ cup	(120 ml)	chicken stock or water
1 cup	(240 ml)	whipping cream
1		garlic clove, minced

◦§ Preheat the oven to 350°F (175°C).

◦§ Lightly season the chicken with salt and pepper. Wrap 2 bacon slices around each breast, forming an × in the middle of the skin side. Tuck 2 thyme sprigs per breast behind the bacon.

◦§ Heat the oil in an ovenproof frying pan over medium-high heat. Place the chicken breasts, bacon side down, in the pan and cook until the bacon and chicken skin are browned. Turn over and cook until the other side is browned.

◦§ Drain off the fat and add the stock or water, cream, and garlic. Bring to a boil.

◦§ Transfer the pan to the oven. Bake for 15 to 20 minutes, or until the cream has thickened. Season to taste with salt and pepper. Let sit a few minutes before serving.

Per serving. Effective carbohydrates: 2.1 g; Carbohydrates: 2.1 g; Fiber: 0 g; Protein: 43.7 g; Fat: 41.7 g; Calories: 565

36 WAYS TO DRESS UP CHICKEN

There are times when we want something fast but tasty, and most low-carbers fall back on an old standby: boneless, skinless chicken breasts. Here are 36 quick ways to give them extra oomph. Just top the cooked meat as directed and, if needed, broil until heated through.

- **A la grecque.** Top with feta cheese, black olives, tomatoes, and onions.

- **Aioli.** Top with Cambozola cheese, broil to melt, and serve with Aioli (page 248).

- **All-dressed.** Add pepperoni, sautéed mushrooms and peppers, mozzarella cheese, and tomato sauce; broil until the cheese melts.

- **Benedict.** Assemble as usual, using ham, Blender Hollandaise Sauce (page 245), and a poached egg (if you're daring).

- **Bistro.** Apply caramelized onions and Brie cheese; broil until the cheese melts.

- **BLT.** Top with bacon, tomatoes, and Swiss cheese; broil until the cheese melts and serve on a shredded lettuce salad.

- **Blue moon.** Cover with blue cheese and sautéed mushrooms. Broil until melted, then serve with lettuce, and tomato.

- **Boursin.** Smear on herbed or peppered Boursin cheese and sliced tomatoes.

- **Buzzy.** Apply cream cheese blended with horseradish and top with smoked oysters.

- **Cajun.** Dust Cajun spices over the meat before cooking. Then add jalapeño cheese, broil until melted, and serve with Aioli (page 248).

- **Caprese.** Arrange sliced tomatoes and bocconcini on top. Serve with mayonnaise enhanced with Basil Pesto (page 240).

- **Cubano.** Layer with ham, roast pork, pickles, and mayonnaise; top with Swiss cheese and broil to melt.

- **De-lox.** Spread with cream cheese and top with smoked salmon, avocado, and thin slices of red onion.

- **Divan.** Top with cooked broccoli; add cheddar cheese and melt. Serve with Blender Hollandaise Sauce (page 245), if you're feeling ambitious.

- **Eh?** Add Canadian back bacon, garnish with cheese curds, and broil.

- **Florentine.** Pile on sautéed spinach with garlic and blanket with Blender Hollandaise Sauce (page 245) or cream cheese.

- **Gingersnap.** Use a dipping sauce of soy sauce, ginger, toasted sesame oil, sweetener, and green onion.

◆ **Italiano.** Cover with thinly sliced prosciutto, roasted red bell peppers, and mayonnaise mixed with Basil Pesto (page 240); add mozzarella cheese and broil.

◆ **Japonaise.** Serve with Japanese-Style Sesame Ginger Dressing (page 96) and Cucumber Salad with Umeboshi and Bonito Flakes (page 77).

◆ **Madame.** Top with sliced smoked turkey and Dijon mustard; add Gruyère cheese and broil until melted.

◆ **Milanese.** Coat with Parmesan cheese and oregano before cooking.

◆ **Steakhouse.** Mix mayonnaise mixed with prepared horseradish as a dip and serve with sliced tomatoes.

◆ **Monsieur.** Layer with sliced ham, Swiss cheese, and Dijon mustard.

◆ **Olivada.** Top with Mushroom Tapenade (page 22) and serve with Broccoli Italianissimo (page 105).

◆ **Portobello.** Serve on a grilled or broiled portobello mushroom with Blue Cheese Dressing (page 94).

◆ **Provence.** Spread with goat cheese and sprinkle with walnuts and crisp bacon.

◆ **Reuben.** Top with sauerkraut and Thousand Island Dressing (pages 94 to 95); add Swiss cheese and melt.

◆ **Holsteiner.** Top with a fried egg—add bacon and you have breakfast!

◆ **Smokehouse.** Add bacon and Smoky Barbecue Sauce (page 234); top with cheddar cheese and broil until melted.

◆ **Souvlaki.** Serve with chopped onions, tomatoes, cucumber, and sour cream or yogurt mixed with chopped garlic.

◆ **Stroganoff.** Mix sautéed mushrooms and onions with sour cream and spoon over top.

◆ **Sushi.** Dab with mayo mixed with wasabi; top with cucumber, avocado, and crab.

◆ **Tex-Mex.** Melt cheddar over the top and serve on shredded lettuce with sour cream, avocado, and salsa.

◆ **Thai.** Add peanut sauce (see Chicken Wings in Peanut Sauce, page 177) and sliced cucumber; wrap in a lettuce leaf.

◆ **Turkish.** Toss together garlic, parsley, olive oil, paprika, and artichoke hearts; spoon on top and serve with yogurt or sour cream.

◆ **Verde.** Season with garlic before cooking and top with a piquant sauce made of parsley, onions, and capers.

DONALD'S AWESOME CHICKEN AND BROCCOLI CASSEROLE

Makes 6 servings

From the mouth of Donald—creator of Donald's Deep-Dish Pizza Quiche (page 213): "One of our most craveable meals!"

Donald recommends a combination of Monterey Jack and cheddar as the cheese. You can use cauliflower or green beans instead of the broccoli as a variation.

2 Tbsp.	(30 ml)	extra-virgin olive oil
4 Tbsp.	(60 ml)	unsalted butter
8 6-oz.	(170-g)	boneless, skinless chicken breast halves
3 cups	(720 ml)	broccoli cut into bite-size pieces
1 cup	(240 ml)	thinly sliced onion
4		celery ribs, diced
½ lb.	(227 g)	mushrooms, sliced
½ cup	(120 ml)	whipping cream
½ cup	(120 ml)	mayonnaise
2 cups	(480 ml)	shredded cheese
¼ tsp.	(1.2 ml)	garlic powder
		Sea salt and freshly ground black pepper

◦§ Preheat the oven to 350°F (175°C). Butter a 13 × 9-inch (32.5 × 22.5-cm) baking dish.

◦§ Heat the oil and 2 Tbsp. (30 ml) of the butter in a large frying pan over medium-high heat until the butter melts. Add the chicken and brown on each side, turning once. Transfer to the prepared baking dish. Arrange the broccoli around the chicken.

◦§ Melt the remaining 2 Tbsp. (30 ml) butter in the frying pan. Add the onion, celery, and mushrooms. Cook, stirring occasionally, until the onion is translucent, about 5 minutes. Spread over the chicken and broccoli.

◦§ In a small bowl, mix the cream, mayonnaise, cheese, and garlic powder. Season to taste with salt and pepper. Pour over the chicken and vegetables.

•§ Cover tightly with foil and bake for 40 minutes. Let sit for 5 minutes before serving.

Per serving. Effective carbohydrates: 5.9 g; Carbohydrates: 8.2 g; Fiber: 2.3 g; Protein: 63.7 g; Fat: 45.9 g; Calories: 703

RUTH'S EASY HERBED LEMON CHICKEN

Makes 4 servings

Ruth—a lowcarber.org old-timer—says of her chicken: "This is a very fast and easy dish using ingredients found in almost every kitchen. I've served this dish literally dozens of times to guests and have always received rave reviews. I love it because it tastes delicious and is one of the easiest things for me to serve as a hostess. I'd rather spend my time with guests than in the kitchen."

Ruth says you can substitute basil or rosemary for the thyme.

4 6-oz.	(170-g)	boneless, skinless chicken breast halves
1 tsp.	(5 ml)	dried thyme
½ tsp.	(2.5 ml)	sea salt
½ tsp.	(2.5 ml)	freshly ground black pepper
⅛ tsp.	(0.6 ml)	garlic powder
⅓ cup	(80 ml)	freshly squeezed lemon juice

•§ Preheat the oven to 450°F (225°C).

•§ Arrange the chicken in an 8 × 8-inch (20 × 20-cm) baking dish. In a cup, mix the thyme, salt, pepper, garlic powder, and lemon juice. Pour over the chicken.

•§ Bake for 20 to 25 minutes, until the chicken is no longer pink in the center when cut with a sharp knife.

Per serving. Effective carbohydrates: 1.8 g; Carbohydrates: 2.1 g; Fiber: 0.3 g; Protein: 39.4 g; Fat: 2.2 g; Calories: 194

THAI BBQ CHICKEN BUNDLES

Makes 4 servings

Here's one of my favorite recipes, reworked for fine low-carb dining—the original had noodles, rice papers, and sugar. If you like pork rinds, they are great to eat with the dipping sauce or to put in the lettuce bundles.

Warning! Don't make your bundles too big or they will fall all over the place when you bite into them.

I just love the way the dinner table comes alive when a group is sharing from a communal dish. If you have eaten mu shu pork or chicken or dined in Vietnamese restaurants, you will be familiar with the eating technique.

You can make this dish with boneless chicken thighs in place of the breasts. This is wonderful cooked on the grill, too.

1		small bunch fresh cilantro
2		garlic cloves, smashed
3 Tbsp.	(45 ml)	fish sauce
1 tsp.	(5 ml)	coarsely ground black pepper
6 8-oz.	(227-g)	boneless chicken breast halves with skin
1		large head leaf lettuce or butter lettuce, washed and dried
½		English cucumber, halved lengthwise and cut into thin half moons
1		small bunch fresh mint
		Thai Sweet-and-Sour Chile Dipping Sauce (page 241)
¼ cup	(60 ml)	unsalted roasted peanuts, chopped

◦§ Coarsely chop half of the cilantro and place in a blender or food processor. Add the garlic, fish sauce, and pepper. Process to a paste.

◦§ Place the chicken in a large bowl. Add the paste and toss well to coat. Cover and refrigerate for at least 2 hours or up to overnight.

◦§ Preheat the broiler. Line a rimmed baking sheet with foil.

◦§ Place the chicken on the sheet, skin side down. Broil about 4 to 6 inches (10 to 15 cm) from the heat for 4 to 5 minutes. Turn the pieces over and broil until the skin is crisp

and the chicken is cooked all the way through (the juices should run clear when the thickest area is pricked with a fork).

◦§ Arrange the lettuce, cucumber, and mint on a large platter. Remove the stems from the remaining cilantro and add to the platter. Cut the chicken into ¾-inch (1.9-cm) slices and place on the platter.

◦§ Divide the dipping sauce among individual dipping bowls and sprinkle with the peanuts.

◦§ To eat, take a lettuce leaf and tear it in half. Place a few cucumber slices, a few mint and cilantro leaves, and a slice or two of chicken on the leaf. Roll up into a snug bundle, dip into the sauce, and eat.

Per serving (without sauce). Effective carbohydrates: 4.6 g; Carbohydrates: 7.2 g; Fiber: 2.6 g; Protein: 40.4 g; Fat: 20.2 g; Calories: 372

Per 2 Tbsp. (30 ml) sauce with peanuts. Effective carbohydrates: 1.6 g; Carbohydrates: 1.8 g; Fiber: 0.2 g; Protein: 0.5 g; Fat: 0 g; Calories: 8

CRISPY CHICKEN SKIN

If you like pork rinds, you'll love this!

Save chicken skin in the freezer until you have about a pound or so. Before freezing, cut it into smaller pieces. When it's thawed, toss it with salt and refrigerate it overnight. Drain off the water the next day. Put it into a large nonstick pot—saves on scrubbing later—with a tiny bit of water and place in a 300°F (150°C) oven. The fat renders out of the chicken skin, and the skin starts frying in its own fat. This can take up to 2 hours, so I usually do it when I am using the oven for other things. If you have a Crock-Pot, you can use it instead. Drain well through a sieve, then transfer to paper towels and sprinkle with salt. Store in the refrigerator. This is great with salsa or Guacamole (page 27)!

90-MINUTE MIRACLE TURKEY

Makes 10 servings

A miracle because the whole bird cooks in 90 minutes! Ask your butcher to split the turkey and flatten it for you. The brining ensures a tender and juicy bird.

Make gravy using the pan juices. Add a little water or unsalted stock to the pan and place over high heat. Let the liquid bubble for a few minutes as you scrape up all the browned bits from the bottom of the pan. Add more water or stock until a good balance between flavor and saltiness is achieved. You can now thicken the gravy using the Cauliflower Trick (page 191).

24 cups	(5.7 L)	water
1¼ cups	(300 ml)	kosher salt
1		whole garlic head, peeled
2		bay leaves, crushed
1		turkey, about 15 lb. (6.8 kg)
2 Tbsp.	(30 ml)	vegetable oil

◦§ Place the water in a very large container. Add the salt and stir to dissolve. Add the garlic and bay leaves.

◦§ Split the turkey down the backbone and pound on the breastbone to flatten it. Submerge in the brine, cover, and refrigerate for 8 hours. Remove from the brine, pat dry, and refrigerate uncovered for 8 to 12 hours. (This ensures that the skin will be crisp, so don't skip this step.)

◦§ Preheat the oven to 450°F (225°C).

◦§ Place the turkey on a large rimmed baking sheet or roasting pan and brush with the oil. Place on the bottom oven rack. Roast for 40 minutes. Rotate the pan from front to back. Roast for another 40 to 60 minutes, until an instant-read thermometer inserted into the thickest part of the thigh registers 175°F (80°C); the thickest part of the breast should register 165°F (74°C).

◦§ Remove the turkey from the pan and let sit for 20 minutes before carving.

Per serving. Effective carbohydrates: 0 g; Carbohydrates: 0 g; Fiber: 0 g; Protein: 58.4 g; Fat: 33.8 g; Calories: 554

TURKEY TENDERLOIN WITH PESTO AND SMOKED MOZZARELLA

Makes 6 servings

Leftovers are fabulous! If you want to dress this up a bit, serve it with Tomato Garlic Cream Sauce (page 244).

Other types of smoked cheese can be used, such as cheddar or provolone. If you don't have homemade pesto, commercially prepared is fine.

4		turkey tenderloins, about 2 lb. (908 g)
		Sea salt and freshly ground black pepper
½ cup	(120 ml)	Basil Pesto (page 240)
4 oz.	(112 g)	thinly sliced smoked mozzarella cheese, cut into ½-inch (1.2-cm) strips

◦§ Preheat the oven to 350°F (175°C).

◦§ Cut each tenderloin lengthwise almost in half and open like a book. Sprinkle inside and out with salt and pepper. Using half of the pesto, spread it evenly over the top side of the tenderloins. Place the cheese evenly on top of the pesto, positioning it on one side of each tenderloin.

◦§ With toothpicks, skewer the tenderloins closed. Brush each tenderloin with the remaining pesto. Transfer to a rimmed baking sheet.

◦§ Bake for 25 minutes, or until cooked through. Slice the tenderloins crosswise into 1-inch (2.5-cm) rounds and arrange on a serving platter. Serve with the pan juices poured on top.

Per serving. Effective carbohydrates: 1.4 g; Carbohydrates: 2.3 g; Fiber: 0.9 g; Protein: 44.6 g; Fat: 16.2 g; Calories: 342

TURKEY SNACKIN' CAKE

Makes 16 squares

This isn't the sugar and flour kind of cake but a tasty pairing of ground turkey with a cream cheese and shredded zucchini "frosting"! The combination of the turkey and sage will give a holiday aroma to your kitchen.

This cake is great to have around for snacks and lunch or breakfast on the go.

Note: *My favorite turkey for this dish is the leg meat. You could also use ground chicken instead of turkey.*

ZUCCHINI TOPPING

1 lb.	(454 g)	zucchini
8 oz.	(227 g)	cream cheese, at room temperature
2		large eggs
½ tsp.	(2.5 ml)	sea salt
2 Tbsp.	(30 ml)	minced green onion tops

TURKEY

2 lb.	(908 g)	ground turkey
2		large eggs
½ cup	(120 ml)	finely chopped onion
¾ tsp.	(3.7 ml)	sea salt
1 Tbsp.	(15 ml)	chopped fresh sage or 1 tsp. (5 ml) dried sage leaves
½ cup	(120 ml)	freshly grated Parmesan cheese
¼ tsp.	(1.2 ml)	freshly grated nutmeg
		Freshly ground black pepper

⁃ Preheat the oven to 350°F (175°C).

⁃ *To make the zucchini topping:* Trim the zucchini and shred finely. Place in a sieve to drain.

⁃ Place the cream cheese in a medium bowl and beat with an electric mixer until smooth. Beat in the eggs, one at a time. Beat in the salt and green onion. Squeeze any remaining water out of the zucchini with your hands and stir into the bowl.

⋙ *To make the turkey:* In a large bowl, mix the turkey, eggs, onion, salt, sage, cheese, nutmeg, and pepper to taste until well-blended. Pat into a 8 × 8-inch (20 × 20-cm) baking dish.

⋙ Bake for 15 minutes. Remove from the oven and let sit for 10 minutes. Hold a pot lid firmly on the meat and tip the pan to pour out any accumulated juices. The cake will have shrunk from the sides of the pan, and this is fine.

⋙ Spread with the zucchini mixture and bake for 30 minutes longer. Let sit for at least 15 minutes before cutting.

Per square. Effective carbohydrates: 1.5 g; Carbohydrates: 2 g; Fiber: 0.5 g; Protein: 14 g; Fat: 11.7 g; Calories: 170

THE CAULIFLOWER TRICK

While teaching the 90-Minute Miracle Turkey (page 188) in a cooking class—and contemplating my speech on thickening gravies—my eyes wandered over to the pot of cauliflower puree on the stove waiting to be seasoned. Potato purees can be used for thickening sauces, so why not cauliflower? I tried it in the pan juice from the turkey, and it worked like a charm. Just make sure the cauliflower is well-cooked and smoothly pureed. Add a little at a time until the gravy reaches the consistency you want. Then add a splash of whipping cream.

You can also use cream cheese or xanthan gum to thicken gravies. Add a little cream cheese at a time and stir until the cream cheese melts and the sauce thickens. With xanthan gum, sprinkle it over the top, whisking constantly—a hand-held blender works well for this—until the gravy is as thick as you like it.

BEEF, PORK, AND LAMB

When I was growing up, there was a 1-hour window where the occasional Sunday roast beef would be sitting—cooked, on the counter, and unattended—before it hit the table. I would take advantage of this opportunity to sneak into the kitchen and pick off bits of the crispy, salty fat. The beef itself never had the same allure, being well done and not as succulent.

Beef was a near-taboo subject for many years, almost eclipsed by the boneless, skinless chicken breast. Even through those—ahem—"lean times," I still enjoyed a big, fatty rib-eye steak. The accompaniments were all wrong, though!

For the right accompaniments, look to Roasted Mushrooms with Garlic and Thyme (page 126), Broiled Tomatoes with Goat Cheese, Pancetta, and Fennel (page 134), Basic Cauliflower Mash (page 112), or Broccoli Dijon (page 104)—and let them take their rightful place beside the beef.

Though there is nothing like a grilled medium-rare rib eye or strip steak, try these non-beef alternatives.

Donald's Deep-Dish Pizza Quiche (pages 212 and 213)
Slow-Roasted Spice-Cured Pork Shoulder (page 211)
Pork Loin Steaks with Lemon Thyme Cream (page 216)
Moroccan-Style Lamb Stew (page 221)
Unplugged Coriander Lamb Kebabs with Tomato Vinaigrette (pages 222 and 223)

GRILLED FLANK STEAK WITH CUMIN AIOLI

Makes 6 servings

You can use a sirloin steak in place of the flank steak. In fact, any steak is good with the cumin aioli. Flank steak is best served medium-rare or less, and leftovers are wonderful.

CUMIN AIOLI

1 Tbsp.	(15 ml)	cumin seeds
1		large egg
1 tsp.	(5 ml)	Dijon mustard
½ tsp.	(2.5 ml)	sea salt
1		garlic clove, minced
½ cup	(120 ml)	vegetable oil
4 tsp.	(20 ml)	freshly squeezed lemon juice
½ cup	(120 ml)	extra-virgin olive oil

STEAK

3 Tbsp.	(45 ml)	extra-virgin olive oil
½ tsp.	(2.5 ml)	sea salt
2		garlic cloves, minced
½ tsp.	(2.5 ml)	freshly ground black pepper
1 2½-lb.	(1.1 kg)	flank steak

To make the cumin aioli: Place the cumin seeds in a small frying pan and stir over medium heat for 2 minutes, or until they darken a shade. Remove from the heat. Finely grind half of the cumin seeds in a coffee grinder or with a mortar and pestle.

In a blender or food processor, combine the egg, mustard, salt, garlic, and the ground cumin seeds. Process briefly to blend. With the motor running, add the vegetable oil in a slow, steady stream. Pour in the lemon juice and then slowly add the olive oil until the aioli is emulsified. If the mixture seems too thick, add a spoonful or two of water. Scrape the aioli into a bowl and stir in the whole cumin seeds. Cover and refrigerate.

To make the steak: In a small bowl, mix the oil, salt, garlic, and pepper. Spread on both sides of the steak. Cover and refrigerate up to overnight.

→ Preheat the grill or broiler. Grill or broil the steak for 3 to 4 minutes on each side for medium-rare. Remove the steak from the heat and let it sit for a few minutes. Slice very thinly across the grain and serve with the aioli on the side.

Per serving. Effective carbohydrates: 1.2 g; Carbohydrates: 1.5 g; Fiber: 0.3 g; Protein: 42.7 g; Fat: 58 g; Calories: 701

SLOW-ROASTED PRIME RIB

Makes 8 large servings

I think I can safely say that any beef lover loves tender and juicy prime rib. This recipe simulates the long, slow roasting that restaurants use to achieve a juicy and evenly cooked roast. You'll never roast any other way when you try this method.

1	3-rib	**prime rib roast, about 7 lb. (3.2 kg), tied**
		Sea salt and freshly ground black pepper

→ Remove the roast from the fridge and let sit at room temperature for 3 hours before cooking. This step is important for the roast to cook to even, juicy perfection.

→ Adjust your oven rack to the lowest position and preheat the oven to 200°F (93°C).

→ Place the roast on a rack in a large roasting pan and season generously with salt and pepper. Stand the roast on its rounded end so it looks somewhat like a triangular shape (don't place it bone side down).

→ Roast for 3½ hours—about 30 minutes per pound—or until an instant-read thermometer registers 130°F (54°C) for medium-rare beef. At this point, you can turn on the broiler to crisp the fat if you like.

→ Remove from the oven and let rest for 10 to 15 minutes before slicing.

Per serving. Effective carbohydrates: 0 g; Carbohydrates: 0 g; Fiber: 0 g; Protein: 65.6 g; Fat: 118.9 g; Calories: 1,355

SHEPHERD'S PIE WITH MUSHROOMS, SMOKED CHEDDAR, BACON, AND SOUR CREAM

Makes 9 servings

The smoked cheddar is great, but regular cheddar will do. This is fabulous for breakfast!

BEEF

3 lb.	(1.3 kg)	lean ground beef
1 cup	(240 ml)	finely diced onion
1 cup	(240 ml)	finely diced celery
¼ tsp.	(1.2 ml)	dried thyme or ½ tsp. (2.5 ml) fresh thyme leaves
1 Tbsp.	(15 ml)	tomato paste
		Sea salt and freshly ground black pepper
2 Tbsp.	(30 ml)	unsalted butter
½ lb.	(227 g)	mushrooms, coarsely chopped

CAULIFLOWER PUREE

2 lb.	(908 g)	cauliflower, trimmed
2 cups	(480 ml)	shredded smoked cheddar cheese
¼ cup	(60 ml)	sour cream
2 Tbsp.	(30 ml)	unsalted butter
1		large egg
8		bacon slices, cooked until crisp and crumbled
		Paprika

To make the beef: Place the beef in a large pot and cook over high heat, crumbling the meat with a spoon until it loses its raw, red color. Stir in the onion, celery, thyme, and tomato paste. Season lightly with salt and pepper. Cover tightly, turn the heat to low, and cook for 20 minutes, stirring occasionally. Add a touch of water if the mixture looks too dry; it should look juicy but not wet.

🍂 Heat the butter in a large frying pan over high heat until the foam subsides. Add mushrooms and cook briskly until the water has evaporated and the mushrooms are soft. Add the mushrooms to the beef mixture and cook for 10 minutes longer.

🍂 *To make the cauliflower puree:* Chop the cauliflower, including the core, into chunks. Place in a large pot and add enough water to cover the pieces by 1 inch (2.5 cm). Bring to a boil over high heat and cook until extremely tender, about 20 minutes. Drain well. Transfer to a food processor and blend until smooth. Remove 1 cup of the puree and stir into the pot with the beef.

🍂 To the remaining cauliflower in the food processor, add the cheese, sour cream, and butter; blend well. Add the egg and blend until smooth. Add the bacon and pulse once or twice to combine.

🍂 Preheat the oven to 350°F (175°C).

🍂 Spread the beef mixture in a 9 × 9-inch (22.5 × 22.5-cm) deep baking dish. Cover with the cauliflower mixture and smooth the top. Sprinkle with the paprika or make criss-cross lines, dots, or whatever strikes your fancy. Place the baking dish on a large rimmed baking sheet to catch any drips.

🍂 Bake for 45 minutes, or until bubbly and browned. Let sit for 10 minutes before serving.

Per serving. Effective carbohydrates: 5.8 g; Carbohydrates: 9.1 g; Fiber: 3.3 g; Protein: 42.9 g; Fat: 29.5 g; Calories: 475

TAMARIAN'S UPSIDE-DOWN SHEPHERD'S PIE

Makes 8 servings

We all swooned when Tamarian, the Webmaster of lowcarber.org, brought this to a potluck. I've toned down the seasonings a bit to make it more "family friendly," but that hasn't changed the swoonability factor at all.

Note: *After opening a small can of tomato paste, put it in the freezer. When it's frozen, open the closed end with a can opener and leave the bottom lid on it. To use the tomato paste, push the paste out (using the lid) and slice off the amount you need. One-quarter inch (0.6 cm) is about 1 Tbsp. (15 ml) of tomato paste. Store the can in a plastic bag.*

CAULIFLOWER BASE

2 lb.	(908 g)	cauliflower, trimmed and grated, about 5 cups (1.2 L)
1 cup	(240 ml)	full-fat cottage cheese
1½ tsp.	(7.5 ml)	sea salt
1 Tbsp.	(15 ml)	unsalted butter

FILLING

1 cup	(240 ml)	finely diced red bell pepper
¾ cup	(180 ml)	finely diced onion
4		garlic cloves, minced
1 Tbsp.	(15 ml)	extra-virgin olive oil
2 lb.	(908 g)	lean ground beef
6 Tbsp.	(90 ml)	tomato paste
¼ cup	(60 ml)	malt vinegar
1 tsp.	(5 ml)	curry powder
		Sea salt and freshly ground black pepper
4 oz.	(112 g)	full-fat mozzarella cheese, shredded

⌘ *To make the cauliflower base:* In a large pot (preferably nonstick), combine the cauliflower, cottage cheese, and salt. Cook over medium-low heat, stirring frequently, until the cauliflower is tender but still has a bit of resistance, about 30 minutes.

◦§ Add the butter and mash by hand or puree in a food processor or with a hand-held blender. Spread in the bottom of an 11 × 8½-inch (27.5 cm × 21-cm) baking dish.

◦§ *To make the filling:* While the cauliflower is cooking, combine the red pepper, onion, garlic, and oil in a large pot. Sauté over medium heat until tender but not browned, about 5 minutes. Turn the heat to high and add the beef. Cook, crumbling the beef with a spoon, until completely browned.

◦§ Stir in the tomato paste, vinegar, curry powder, and salt and pepper to taste. Turn the heat to low and cook until thickened, about 15 minutes. Spread over the cauliflower and sprinkle with the cheese.

◦§ Preheat the oven to 350°F (175°C).

◦§ Bake for 20 to 25 minutes. Remove from the oven and let sit for 10 minutes before serving.

Per serving. Effective carbohydrates: 8.3 g; Carbohydrates: 12.3 g; Fiber: 4 g; Protein: 31 g; Fat: 31.5 g; Calories: 457

KEEMA (SPICED GROUND BEEF)

Makes 4 servings

I'm always looking for interesting things to go with salads—especially things that can be made ahead of time and reheated. Since I'm a huge fan of East Indian cooking, I often turn to that cuisine for inspiration.

You can prepare the keema entirely on the stovetop, as directed below. Or you can finish it in the oven: After adding the water and spices, cover the pot and bake at 300°F (150°C) for 1 hour, checking occasionally to make sure that the water has not evaporated.

This is great with a spinach salad, zucchini, or green beans. One of my favorite breakfasts is heating up the keema until sizzling and scrambling eggs into it.

Note: *One of the easiest ways I've found to crumble ground beef, pork, or sausages as they cook is to use a potato masher. The ones that have a grid of small squares work the best, but any kind will do. I have a wooden potato masher that I bought when I was 18, and it still serves me well.*

¼ cup	(60 ml)	vegetable oil
2		bay leaves
1 3-inch	(7.5-cm)	cinnamon stick
1½ cups	(360 ml)	finely chopped onion
1 Tbsp.	(15 ml)	grated fresh ginger
5		garlic cloves, minced
1 Tbsp.	(15 ml)	ground coriander
1 Tbsp.	(15 ml)	ground cumin
1 tsp.	(5 ml)	turmeric
1 Tbsp.	(15 ml)	tomato paste
2 lb.	(908 g)	lean ground beef
½ cup	(120 ml)	water
¼ tsp.	(1.2 ml)	freshly grated nutmeg
¼ tsp.	(1.2 ml)	ground mace
1 tsp.	(5 ml)	sea salt
¼ to ½ tsp.	(1.2 to 2.5 ml)	cayenne pepper

⁓ Heat the oil in a large pot over high heat. Add the bay leaves and cinnamon. Cook for a few moments until the bay leaves darken. Add the onion, ginger, and garlic. Cook, stirring occasionally, over medium heat until the onion turns dark brown. Add the coriander, cumin, and turmeric. Cook for 2 minutes. Stir in the tomato paste.

⁓ Add the beef and cook, breaking up the pieces, until browned. Add the water, nutmeg, mace, salt, and cayenne to taste. Turn the heat to low. Cover and simmer for 1 hour, stirring frequently and adding more water as needed to prevent the mixture from sticking. Remove the bay leaves.

Per serving. Effective carbohydrates: 6.6 g; Carbohydrates: 8.1 g; Fiber: 1.5 g; Protein: 43.7 g; Fat: 48.3 g; Calories: 648

MEAT-LOVER'S PIZZA

Makes 8 slices

I love having cold pizza for breakfast. It reminds me of my former life, when I used to sock away half a large pizza in one sitting and eat the leftovers for breakfast.

You can use ground chicken, turkey, pork, or lamb for the crust instead of beef. For true decadence, make the crust entirely out of Italian sausage.

Use the mushroom and pepper topping given here or whatever toppings are your favorites. Two of mine are prosciutto with black olives and onion and Italian sausage with green olives and mushrooms. I used to love the salty, hot, and sweet combination of anchovy, hot peppers, and pineapple, but there's no good substitute for pineapple. I don't think strawberries would cut it!

MEAT CRUST

2 lb.	(908 g)	extra-lean ground beef
¼ cup	(60 ml)	finely diced onion
1		garlic clove, minced
1		large egg
½ cup	(120 ml)	freshly grated Parmesan cheese
¾ tsp.	(3.7 ml)	sea salt
¼ tsp.	(1.2 ml)	freshly ground black pepper

MUSHROOM AND PEPPER TOPPING

2 Tbsp.	(30 ml)	extra-virgin olive oil
¾ lb.	(340 g)	mushrooms, sliced
		Sea salt and freshly ground black pepper
1 cup	(240 ml)	thinly sliced red bell pepper
1 cup	(240 ml)	Simple Tomato Sauce (page 242)
12 oz.	(340 g)	full-fat mozzarella cheese, grated
1 tsp.	(5 ml)	dried oregano (optional)

◦§ *To make the meat crust:* Preheat the oven to 450°F (225°C).

◦§ In a large bowl, mix the beef, onion, garlic, egg, cheese, salt, and pepper. Pat evenly in a 16-inch (40-cm) rimmed pizza pan.

◆§ Bake for 10 minutes. Remove from the oven and carefully pour out the juices that have accumulated in the pan. The meat will have shrunk to about 12 inches (30 cm), and this is fine.

◆§ *To make the mushroom and pepper topping:* Heat the oil in a large frying pan over high heat. Add the mushrooms, season with salt and black pepper, and fry for 5 to 10 minutes, or until the mushrooms are browned and the liquid has evaporated. Scoop the mushrooms out of the pan into a sieve to drain. Add the red pepper to the pan. Fry until the peppers are slightly limp. Add to the mushrooms.

◆§ Preheat the broiler. Spread the tomato sauce evenly over the meat crust and scatter the mushrooms and peppers over it. Cover evenly with the cheese and sprinkle with the oregano (if using).

◆§ Broil until bubbly and lightly browned. Cool on a rack for a few minutes before slicing and serving.

Per slice. Effective carbohydrates: 8.9 g; Carbohydrates: 11 g; Fiber: 2.1 g; Protein: 38.5 g; Fat: 40.1 g; Calories: 564

Per crust (8 servings). Effective carbohydrates: 5.8 g; Carbohydrates: 6.5 g; Fiber: 0.7 g; Protein: 209 g; Fat: 99 g; Calories: 1,812

JAPANESE PIZZA?

Believe it or not, mayonnaise is a very common pizza ingredient in Japan, and it's quite delicious. It's used in place of tomato sauce. If you're in the weight-loss phase of low-carbing, it's something to consider. You can also mix tomato sauce or pesto with mayonnaise to cut down on the carbohydrate count.

BOLOGNESE LASAGNA

Makes 8 servings

In my former life, Bolognese was the *lasagna. But it gave me bedtime indigestion so bad that I stopped eating it. Thank goodness for this recipe. No indigestion, is good cold, and reheats wonderfully!*

1½ lb.	(680 g)	ricotta cheese
2		large eggs
⅛ tsp.	(0.6 ml)	freshly grated nutmeg
½ tsp.	(2.5 ml)	sea salt
½ cup	(120 ml)	freshly grated Parmesan cheese
3 cups	(720 ml)	Bolognese Sauce (page 232) or meat sauce, warmed
		Digwig's Collaboration Lasagna Noodles (page 142)
1½ cups	(360 ml)	shredded full-fat mozzarella cheese

◄§ In a medium bowl, mix the ricotta, eggs, nutmeg, salt, and Parmesan. Cover and refrigerate for up to 1 day.

◄§ Spread one-quarter of the sauce in a 13 × 9-inch (32.5 × 22.5-cm) baking dish. Carefully transfer 1 lasagna noodle to the dish. Spread with another quarter of the sauce. Evenly spread the ricotta filling on top.

◄§ Add more sauce, the remaining lasagna noodle, and the rest of the sauce.

◄§ Bake for 35 minutes. Sprinkle with the mozzarella and bake for 10 minutes longer. Remove from the oven and let rest for 10 minutes before serving.

Per serving. Effective carbohydrates: 10.5 g; Carbohydrates: 11.5 g; Fiber: 1 g; Protein: 49.8 g; Fat: 75.7 g; Calories: 942

BOLOGNESE LASAGNA

Makes 8 servings

In my former life, Bolognese was the *lasagna. But it gave me bedtime indigestion so bad that I stopped eating it. Thank goodness for this recipe. No indigestion, is good cold, and reheats wonderfully!*

1½ lb.	(680 g)	ricotta cheese
2		large eggs
⅛ tsp.	(0.6 ml)	freshly grated nutmeg
½ tsp.	(2.5 ml)	sea salt
½ cup	(120 ml)	freshly grated Parmesan cheese
3 cups	(720 ml)	Bolognese Sauce (page 232) or meat sauce, warmed
		Digwig's Collaboration Lasagna Noodles (page 142)
1½ cups	(360 ml)	shredded full-fat mozzarella cheese

◦§ In a medium bowl, mix the ricotta, eggs, nutmeg, salt, and Parmesan. Cover and refrigerate for up to 1 day.

◦§ Spread one-quarter of the sauce in a 13 × 9-inch (32.5 × 22.5-cm) baking dish. Carefully transfer 1 lasagna noodle to the dish. Spread with another quarter of the sauce. Evenly spread the ricotta filling on top.

◦§ Add more sauce, the remaining lasagna noodle, and the rest of the sauce.

◦§ Bake for 35 minutes. Sprinkle with the mozzarella and bake for 10 minutes longer. Remove from the oven and let rest for 10 minutes before serving.

Per serving. Effective carbohydrates: 10.5 g; Carbohydrates: 11.5 g; Fiber: 1 g; Protein: 49.8 g; Fat: 75.7 g; Calories: 942

SLIGHTLY ITALIANO MEAT LOAF

Makes 12 servings

I like to have meat loaf around for breakfast, dinner, or a cold snack. I enjoy it fried and served with eggs for breakfast. Or heated under the broiler, then spread with mayonnaise and Dijon mustard, smothered with cheese and a few slices of tomato, and broiled again until the cheese is bubbly.

Note: *You can use bacon in place of the pancetta if you prefer.*

¼ lb.	(112 g)	pancetta, diced
3		large eggs
3 lb.	(1.3 kg)	lean ground beef
½ cup	(120 ml)	freshly grated Parmesan cheese
2 Tbsp.	(30 ml)	finely chopped fresh parsley
½ cup	(120 ml)	finely chopped onion
2		garlic cloves, minced
1 tsp.	(5 ml)	sea salt
½ tsp.	(2.5 ml)	freshly ground black pepper
2 Tbsp.	(30 ml)	finely diced sun-dried tomatoes

◦§ Preheat the oven to 350°F (175°C).

◦§ Place the pancetta in a food processor and process until finely ground. Add the eggs and pulse to combine. Place in a large bowl and add the beef, cheese, parsley, onion, garlic, salt, pepper, and tomatoes. Mix well with your hands and pack into a 12 × 4½-inch (30 × 11.5 cm) loaf pan.

◦§ Bake for 1¼ hours. Let cool for 15 minutes before slicing.

Per serving. Effective carbohydrates: 1 g; Carbohydrates: 1.2 g; Fiber: 0.2 g; Protein: 27.6 g; Fat: 12.7 g; Calories: 236

MORE ENTERTAINING LOW-CARB STYLE

In addition to the menus on pages 24 and 62, here are a few more to inspire you to serve sumptuous gourmet meals—all low carb.

My Big Fat Greek Low-Carb Dinner

Hummus, page 23

Broiled Spinach with Four Cheeses, page 129 (as a dip)

Moussaka, pages 226 to 227

Olive, Walnut, and Parsley Salad, page 81

Basic Cauli-flied "Rice" (with grated lemon rind), page 110

Pound Cake, pages 306 to 307, served with Lemon Curd, pages 284 to 285

Tex-Mex

Black Soybean Dip, page 32

Guacamole, page 27

Grilled Flank Steak with Cumin Aioli, pages 194 to 95

Warm Turkey, Bacon, and Mushroom Salad, page 85

Frozen Bourbon, Chocolate, and Burnt Almond Cheesecake, pages 266 to 267

Middle Eastern Mezze

Hummus, page 23

Lamb, Feta, and Olive Meatballs, pages 224 to 225

Pine Nut and Parsley Salad, page 68

Cinnamon-Spiced Lemon Chicken, page 171

Eggplant Salad with Sour Cream Dressing, page 118

Tofu-lafels, page 138

Coffee Jelly, page 290

PORK

Pork is one of my favorite meats. There is nothing more succulent or satisfying than a slow-cooked shoulder or tender ribs that fall off the bone.

Thinking of all the luscious preparations that are made with pork is enough to make me swoon. Prosciutto, salami, ham, bacon, sausages, pâté, pancetta, and—of course—the low-carbers' snack of choice, pork rinds!

Pork is a good source of potassium. There are 408 mg of potassium in 3 oz. (100 g) of cooked pork.

BASIC BACK RIBS WITH QUICK BARBECUE GLAZE

Makes 2 racks of ribs

This is an easy method for making very tender ribs. After an initial baking, glaze the ribs with sauce and then broil them until browned. Use the following quick glaze or Smoky Barbecue Sauce (page 234).

Note: *Liquid smoke is readily available in the spice aisle of grocery stores.*

RIBS

2		**racks pork back ribs**
		Sea salt

GLAZE

2 Tbsp.	(30 ml)	tomato paste
2 Tbsp.	(30 ml)	mayonnaise
1 tsp.	(5 ml)	Worcestershire sauce
1 Tbsp.	(15 ml)	soy sauce
⅛ tsp.	(0.6 ml)	liquid smoke
½ tsp.	(2.5 ml)	garlic powder
½ tsp.	(2.5 ml)	*each* Splenda and Canadian Sugar Twin or 2 tsp. (10 ml) Splenda

(continued on page 210)

PORK

Pork is one of my favorite meats. There is nothing more succulent or satisfying than a slow-cooked shoulder or tender ribs that fall off the bone.

Thinking of all the luscious preparations that are made with pork is enough to make me swoon. Prosciutto, salami, ham, bacon, sausages, pâté, pancetta, and—of course—the low-carbers' snack of choice, pork rinds!

Pork is a good source of potassium. There are 408 mg of potassium in 3 oz. (100 g) of cooked pork.

BASIC BACK RIBS WITH QUICK BARBECUE GLAZE

Makes 2 racks of ribs

This is an easy method for making very tender ribs. After an initial baking, glaze the ribs with sauce and then broil them until browned. Use the following quick glaze or Smoky Barbecue Sauce (page 234).

Note: *Liquid smoke is readily available in the spice aisle of grocery stores.*

RIBS

2		**racks pork back ribs**
		Sea salt

GLAZE

2 Tbsp.	**(30 ml)**	**tomato paste**
2 Tbsp.	**(30 ml)**	**mayonnaise**
1 tsp.	**(5 ml)**	**Worcestershire sauce**
1 Tbsp.	**(15 ml)**	**soy sauce**
⅛ tsp.	**(0.6 ml)**	**liquid smoke**
½ tsp.	**(2.5 ml)**	**garlic powder**
½ tsp.	**(2.5 ml)**	***each* Splenda and Canadian Sugar Twin or 2 tsp. (10 ml) Splenda**

(continued on page 210)

To make the ribs: Preheat the oven to 250°F (125°C).

Place the ribs on a piece of heavy-duty foil and sprinkle lightly with salt. Close the foil over the ribs, forming a loose tent, and crimp the edges securely. Place on a rimmed baking sheet.

Bake for 1½ to 2 hours. You can let the ribs cool at this point for finishing later or glaze them and broil immediately.

To make the glaze: In a small bowl, mix the tomato paste, mayonnaise, Worcestershire sauce, soy sauce, liquid smoke, garlic powder, and sweetener.

Preheat the broiler and position the rack 8 inches (20 cm) from the heat.

Open the foil and pour off the liquid. Using the back of a spoon, liberally apply the glaze to one side of the ribs. Place under the broiler and broil until bubbly with a few darkened spots. Turn the ribs over and apply the remaining glaze. Broil again until browned and bubbly.

Per serving. Effective carbohydrates: 4 g; Carbohydrates: 5 g; Fiber: 1 g; Protein: 76 g; Fat: 37 g; Calories: 670
Per serving (sauce only). Effective carbohydrates: 4.2 g; Carbohydrates: 4.6 g; Fiber: 0.4 g; Protein: 1.7 g; Fat: 11.2 g; Calories: 123

HOW DO I KNOW WHEN IT'S DONE?

Buy yourself an instant-read meat thermometer. It takes all the anxiety and guesswork out of cooking meat. To use it, insert it into the thickest part of the meat so the point is in the middle and give it a few seconds to adjust. Use these recommendations for beef, pork, lamb, and veal.

105° to 110°F (40° to 43°C): rare
115° to 125°F (46° to 51°C): medium-rare (I personally prefer 115°F)
130° to 140°F (54° to 60°C): medium
Over 150°F (65°C): well on the way to well-done!

Keep in mind that roasts and larger cuts of meat should sit for at least 15 to 30 minutes before slicing. As the meat rests, it continues to cook, so keep this in mind when checking the temperature. (It is recommended that poultry be cooked to 180°F or 82°C.)

SLOW-ROASTED SPICE-CURED PORK SHOULDER

Makes 10 servings

The slow-roasting and dry marinade make the pork very tender and succulent. It's just fantastic cold. I like to put this in the oven before I go to bed and cook it overnight. And yes, it does take 6 hours.

The carb count is negligible because the spices are washed off and not eaten.

Note: *For best results, make sure the pork shoulder is not rolled or tied.*

1 4- to 5-lb.	(1.8- to 2.2-kg)	boneless, skinless pork shoulder
2 Tbsp.	(30 ml)	coriander seeds
1 Tbsp.	(15 ml)	black peppercorns
12		cloves
1 Tbsp.	(15 ml)	sea salt
2		bay leaves, crumbled
2 Tbsp.	(30 ml)	fresh rosemary leaves, coarsely chopped
6		garlic cloves, thinly sliced

❧ With a sharp knife, score the pork fat in a crosshatch pattern. Combine the coriander, peppercorns, and cloves in a coffee grinder or mortar. Grind coarsely and combine with the salt, bay leaves, rosemary, and garlic.

❧ Spread half of the spice mixture in the bottom of a glass or other noncorrodible baking dish. Place the pork on top. Pat on the remaining mixture. Cover and refrigerate overnight.

❧ Preheat the oven to 250°F (125°C). Rinse the pork with cold water and pat dry. Place, fat side up, in a large baking dish.

❧ Bake for 6 hours (that's right, 6 hours). Let sit for 15 minutes before slicing.

Per serving. Effective carbohydrates: 0.9 g; Carbohydrates: 1.6 g; Fiber: 0.7 g; Protein: 38.2 g; Fat: 8.5 g; Calories: 243

DONALD'S DEEP-DISH PIZZA QUICHE

Makes 8 servings

Donald is a lowcarber.org success story. He's lost more than 100 pounds.

Donald cuts the quiche into pieces and then freezes them to take to work for lunch. Of course, you can use any pizza toppings that you prefer. The mushrooms and sausage are my preference. This is one of the most popular recipes ever from lowcarber.org.

4 oz.	(112 g)	cream cheese, at room temperature
4		large eggs
⅓ cup	(80 ml)	whipping cream
¼ cup	(60 ml)	freshly grated Parmesan cheese
1 Tbsp.	(15 ml)	minced fresh chives
½ tsp.	(2.5 ml)	minced garlic
½ tsp.	(2.5 ml)	dried oregano
1 cup	(240 ml)	shredded Asiago cheese
2 cups	(480 ml)	shredded full-fat mozzarella cheese
½ cup	(120 ml)	tomato sauce
2 cups	(480 ml)	sliced mushrooms, sautéed
2		Italian sausages, casing removed, crumbled, and cooked

◦§ Preheat the oven to 350°F (175°C). Butter a 13 × 9-inch (32.5 × 22.5-cm) baking dish.

◦§ In a food processor, blend together the cream cheese and eggs until smooth. Add the cream, Parmesan, chives, garlic, and oregano. Blend until smooth.

◦§ Scatter the Asiago and 1 cup of the mozzarella in the prepared baking dish. Pour the egg mixture over the cheese. Bake for 30 minutes.

◦§ Spread with the tomato sauce. Scatter the mushrooms and sausage over the top. Cover with the remaining 1 cup mozzarella.

◦§ Turn on the broiler and broil about 6 inches from the heat until brown and bubbly. Let sit for 5 minutes or so before cutting.

Per serving. Effective carbohydrates: 3.5 g; Carbohydrates: 4 g; Fiber: 0.5 g; Protein: 16.3 g; Fat: 25 g; Calories: 305

PORK AND SHIITAKE MUSHROOM MEATBALLS

Makes 24 meatballs

These taste a lot like the inside of a wonton. Like all meatballs, they are good cold and make a great appetizer. Serve with soy sauce mixed with vinegar and sweetener to taste or Thai Sweet-and-Sour Chile Dipping Sauce (page 241).

I like adding these meatballs to chicken broth with some finely shredded cabbage and ginger and eating as a soup.

10		medium dried shiitake mushrooms
2 lb.	(908 g)	ground pork
2 Tbsp.	(30 ml)	soy sauce
1 tsp.	(5 ml)	sea salt
¼ tsp.	(1.2 ml)	*each* Splenda and Canadian Sugar Twin or 1 tsp. (5 ml) Splenda
¼ cup	(60 ml)	finely chopped green onion
1 tsp.	(5 ml)	toasted sesame oil
2		large eggs

◦§ Place the mushrooms in a bowl and cover them with boiling water. Let stand until completely soft, about 30 minutes. Squeeze the water out of the mushrooms with your hands, remove the tough stems, and mince finely. Place in a large bowl.

◦§ Add the pork, soy sauce, salt, sweetener, green onion, oil, and eggs. Mix until everything is well-combined.

◦§ Bring a large pot of water to a boil. Shape the mixture into 24 meatballs, using 2 Tbsp. (30 ml) for each. Drop the meatballs gently into the water. When the water returns to a boil, cover the pot, turn down the heat to a simmer, and cook gently for 15 minutes. Remove with a slotted spoon.

Per meatball. Effective carbohydrates: 1.2 g; Carbohydrates: 1.4 g; Fiber: 0.2 g; Protein: 7 g; Fat: 10.6 g; Calories: 131

PORK LOIN STEAKS
WITH LEMON THYME CREAM

Makes 4 servings

This goes fast once you start cooking and is perfect for company.

3 Tbsp.	(45 ml)	freshly squeezed lemon juice
1 Tbsp.	(15 ml)	chopped fresh thyme or 1 tsp. (5 ml) dried thyme
2 tsp.	(10 ml)	grated lemon rind
2		garlic cloves, minced
¼ tsp.	(1.2 ml)	sea salt
8 ½-inch	(1.2-cm)	boneless pork loin slices, about 3 oz. (100 g) each
1 Tbsp.	(15 ml)	unsalted butter
1 cup	(240 ml)	whipping cream
		Freshly ground black pepper

◦§ In a large bowl, mix the lemon juice, thyme, lemon rind, garlic, and ¼ tsp. (1.2 ml) salt. Add the pork and toss to coat with the mixture. Cover and refrigerate for at least 1 hour or up to overnight.

Melt the butter in a large frying pan over medium-high heat. Remove the pork from the marinade and place the pieces flat in the pan. (Work in batches if necessary.) Fry on both sides, turning once, until browned.

◦§ Return the pork to the pan and add any marinade remaining in the bowl. Add the cream and bring to a boil. Turn down to a simmer and cook until the cream thickens. Season to taste with salt and pepper.

Per serving. Effective carbohydrates: 3.1 g; Carbohydrates: 3.3 g; Fiber: 0.2 g; Protein: 37 g; Fat: 29 g; Calories: 429

LION'S HEAD

Makes 4 servings

In this classic Chinese dish, the meatballs and cabbage are said to resemble the head and mane of a lion. It's generally served on special occasions to symbolize happiness.
   Note: *Chinese cabbage is also known as Napa cabbage.*

MEATBALLS

1½ lb.	(680 g)	lean ground pork
¼ cup	(60 ml)	finely diced water chestnuts
2		green onions, minced
1		large egg
2 Tbsp.	(30 ml)	soy sauce
½ tsp.	(2.5 ml)	sea salt
1½ Tbsp.	(22.5 ml)	shaohsing rice wine or dry sherry
½ tsp.	(2.5 ml)	Splenda
		Vegetable oil

CABBAGE

1 tsp.	(5 ml)	minced fresh ginger
1 tsp.	(5 ml)	finely chopped garlic
1½ cups	(360 ml)	chicken stock
1 tsp.	(5 ml)	Splenda
½ tsp.	(2.5 ml)	sea salt
8		large Chinese cabbage leaves
½ tsp.	(2.5 ml)	toasted sesame oil

◆§ *To make the meatballs:* In a large bowl, combine the pork, water chestnuts, green onions, egg, soy sauce, salt, wine or sherry, and sweetener. Mix thoroughly and form into 8 meatballs.

◆§ Heat 1 inch (2.5 cm) of vegetable oil in a large pot over high heat. Add the meatballs and cook until golden brown. Remove with a slotted spoon and drain on paper towels.

(continued on page 218)

To make the cabbage: Remove all but 2 Tbsp. (30 ml) oil from the pot and place over high heat until hot. Add the ginger and garlic and cook until fragrant. Add the meatballs, stock, sweetener, and salt. Bring to a boil and then reduce the heat to a simmer. Cover and simmer for 20 minutes.

Place the cabbage leaves over the meatballs. Cover and simmer for 15 minutes longer. Sprinkle with the sesame oil before serving.

Per serving. Effective carbohydrates: 1.7 g; Carbohydrates: 3.1 g; Fiber: 1.4 g; Protein: 32.2 g; Fat: 38.2 g; Calories: 499

LAMB

My first experience with lamb was a leg steak, cooked by my maternal grandmother. I was never a picky eater as a child, so my grandmother had me as a willing accomplice in enjoying with her all the foods my parents wouldn't eat. Along with the lamb, she fried slices of eggplant that had been marinated in bottled Italian dressing. My mother couldn't stand the smell of lamb, so we had to air out the house after it was cooked.

My next experience with lamb was as an adult. The phrase "rack of lamb" had a certain mystique about it. It was expensive, elegant, and in my mind, aloof. It was in the same league as caviar, lobster, and Baked Alaska.

I was in a fancy restaurant and decided to have this particular dish. I was even nervous saying it. I repeated "rack of lamb" to myself until I felt confident enough to say it out loud. Thankfully, I didn't stumble over the words and sound the way I felt, like a gourmet impostor.

"And how would you like that cooked?" inquired the server. This was part of the conversation that I had not anticipated. I immediately scrambled around in the food files of my brain. Medium-rare meat was what cool people ate. And I wanted desperately to be cool. "Medium-rare" rolled off my tongue. "Very good," replied the server. "Medium-rare." I passed the test and basked in my newfound coolness.

When the lamb arrived, it lived up to my anticipation. Perfectly pink, round nuggets of meat, attached to slender and elegant bones. And it was perfectly delicious!

Lamb is not as mysterious to me now, and I like exotic flavors with it. I still enjoy a rack every now and again. Lamb, Feta, and Olive Meatballs (pages 224 to 225) are one of my favorites, and I like them cold for breakfast.

If you want to add some oomph to your lamb, try it with Aioli (page 248) as a dip. Marinate it with Garam Masala (page 249). Or serve it with Grainy Mustard and Vermouth Sauce (page 237) or Basic Herb and Wine Pan Sauce (page 231)—using chopped mint as the herb beats mint jelly, hands down!

CUMIN AND CORIANDER-CRUSTED LEG OF LAMB

Makes 8 servings

The flavors of the Middle East are highlighted in this simple lamb dish. The lamb can be grilled on your barbecue, making it a good choice for cool summer eating. Serve it with Pine Nut and Parsley Salad (page 68).

1 Tbsp.	(15 ml)	coriander seeds, coarsely crushed
1 Tbsp.	(15 ml)	cumin seeds, coarsely crushed
1 tsp.	(5 ml)	coarsely ground black pepper
½ tsp.	(2.5 ml)	ground cinnamon
½ tsp.	(2.5 ml)	turmeric
1 tsp.	(5 ml)	sea salt
6		garlic cloves, minced
2 Tbsp.	(30 ml)	extra-virgin olive oil
¼ cup	(60 ml)	full-fat yogurt
1 4-lb.	(1.8-kg)	boneless lamb leg, trimmed and butterflied

◈ In a small bowl, mix the coriander, cumin, pepper, cinnamon, turmeric, salt, garlic, oil, and yogurt. Place the lamb in a large baking dish and coat with the mixture. Cover and refrigerate for at least 1 hour or up to 24 hours.

◈ Preheat the oven to 350°F (175°C).

◈ Place the lamb in a roasting pan and roast for 45 minutes to 1 hour, basting every 15 minutes, until an instant-read thermometer inserted in the thickest section reads 120°F (49°C) for medium-rare.

◈ Transfer the lamb to a platter and let sit for 10 to 15 minutes before slicing. Transfer the pan juices to a cup and skim off the fat. Slice the lamb and drizzle with the pan juices.

Per serving. Effective carbohydrates: 1.5 g; Carbohydrates: 1.7 g; Fiber: 0.2 g; Protein: 39.5 g; Fat: 50.9 g; Calories: 632

MOROCCAN-STYLE LAMB STEW

Makes 4 servings

This stew is great on a cold day, and leftovers are even better! I think lamb shoulder makes the best stewing meat. Serve with Basic Cauli-flied "Rice" (page 110).

2 Tbsp.	(30 ml)	extra-virgin olive oil
1 cup	(240 ml)	finely chopped onion
3		cloves garlic, minced
2 lb.	(908 g)	lamb stew meat
½ tsp.	(2.5 ml)	sea salt
½ tsp.	(2.5 ml)	ground ginger
½ tsp.	(2.5 ml)	freshly ground black pepper
½ tsp.	(2.5 ml)	ground cinnamon
¼ tsp.	(1.2 ml)	ground allspice
1½ cups	(360 ml)	water
¼ cup	(60 ml)	finely chopped fresh parsley
¼ cup	(60 ml)	finely chopped fresh cilantro
1 to 2 Tbsp.	(15 to 30 ml)	freshly squeezed lemon juice

Heat the oil in a large heavy pot over medium-heat. Add the onion and garlic and cook until the onion is lightly browned, about 5 minutes.

Stir in the lamb, salt, ginger, pepper, cinnamon, allspice, water, parsley, and cilantro. Bring to a boil. Turn down to a bare simmer, cover, and cook until the lamb is tender, about 1½ to 2 hours; replenish the water if necessary. Add the lemon juice and adjust the seasoning.

Per serving. Effective carbohydrates: 4.6 g; Carbohydrates: 5.8 g; Fiber: 1.2 g; Protein: 56.2 g; Fat: 63.1 g; Calories: 826

UNPLUGGED CORIANDER LAMB KEBABS WITH TOMATO VINAIGRETTE

Makes 4 servings

Why unplugged? The lamb is not threaded on skewers and grilled but is stir-fried instead.

VINAIGRETTE

2		medium ripe tomatoes, seeded and chopped
3 Tbsp.	(45 ml)	white wine vinegar
2		garlic cloves, minced
½ cup	(120 ml)	extra-virgin olive oil
⅓ cup	(80 ml)	cilantro leaves, coarsely chopped

KEBABS

2 lb.	(908 g)	boneless lamb leg
3 Tbsp.	(45 ml)	coriander seeds
2		garlic cloves, minced
6 Tbsp.	(90 ml)	extra-virgin olive oil
		Sea salt and freshly ground black pepper
1		small red onion, cut into 8 wedges

◆§ *To make the vinaigrette:* In a blender or food processor, combine the tomatoes, vinegar, and garlic. Process until smooth. With the motor running, slowly drizzle in the oil. Add the cilantro and pulse to combine. Cover and refrigerate.

◆§ *To make the kebabs:* Trim the fat and sinew from the lamb and cut into 1-inch (2.5-cm) cubes. Place in a large bowl.

◆§ Place the coriander in a small frying pan. Stir over medium-heat for a few minutes, until fragrant. Cool and grind coarsely in a coffee grinder or with a mortar and pestle. Transfer to a small bowl and stir in the garlic and 3 Tbsp. (45 ml) of the oil. Season to taste with salt and pepper. Add to the lamb and toss well to coat. Cover and refrigerate for at least 2 hours or up to overnight.

(continued on page 224)

◆§ Heat the remaining 3 Tbsp. (45 ml) oil in a large heavy frying pan over high heat until almost smoking. Add the lamb and onion. Toss and stir occasionally until browned on the outside and medium-rare on the inside, 4 to 5 minutes. Serve with the vinaigrette on the side.

Per serving. Effective carbohydrates: 5.8 g; Carbohydrates: 8.5 g; Fiber: 2.7 g; Protein: 40.6 g; Fat: 69.9 g; Calories: 821

LAMB, FETA, AND OLIVE MEATBALLS

Makes 16 meatballs

These Middle Eastern meatballs are flavor-packed. (And they're equally good made with ground beef.) If you don't have the Tunisian Spice Mixture on hand, you can replace it with ½ tsp. (2.5 ml) dried oregano in the meatballs and omit it altogether in the tomato sauce.

MEATBALLS

1 lb.	(454 g)	ground lamb
½ cup	(120 ml)	coarsely chopped fresh parsley
½ cup	(120 ml)	crumbled feta cheese
½ cup	(120 ml)	pitted green olives, coarsely chopped
2 Tbsp.	(30 ml)	finely chopped onion
1 Tbsp.	(15 ml)	Tunisian Spice Mixture (page 225)
2		large eggs

SAUCE

		Simple Tomato Sauce (page 242)
½ cup	(120 ml)	water
1		lemon wedge, seeds removed
1 tsp.	(5 ml)	Tunisian Spice Mixture (page 225)

- *To make the meatballs:* Preheat the broiler.

- In a large bowl, mix the lamb, parsley, cheese, olives, onion, spice mixture, and eggs. Shape into 16 meatballs. Place about 2 inches (5 cm) apart on a baking sheet.

- Broil the meatballs 3 inches (7.5 cm) from the heat until browned on top. Turn over and broil on the other side. Transfer to a baking dish large enough to hold them in a single layer.

- Turn the oven to 350°F (175°C).

- *To make the sauce:* In a medium saucepan, combine the tomato sauce and water. Bring to a boil and stir in the spice mixture. Pour over the meatballs and tuck the lemon wedge in the middle. Bake for 15 minutes.

Per meatball. Effective carbohydrates: 2.2 g; Carbohydrates: 2.9 g; Fiber: 0.7 g; Protein: 7.4 g; Fat: 12.1 g; Calories: 153

SPICY BITS

This fragrant mixture gives a flavor lift to everything from meat to vegetables. It's as wonderful on buttered cauliflower or other vegetables as it is in Lamb, Feta, and Olive Meatballs (opposite).

TUNISIAN SPICE MIXTURE
Makes about 2 Tbsp. (30 ml)

As with all spices, store this in a tightly covered container away from heat and light.

2 Tbsp.	(30 ml)	coriander seeds
2 tsp.	(10 ml)	caraway seeds
1		dried red chile pepper

- Place the coriander, caraway, and chile in a medium frying pan. Stir over medium heat for a few minutes, until fragrant. Cool and grind finely in a coffee grinder or with a mortar and pestle.

MOUSSAKA

Makes 10 servings

I love the flavor of lamb with tomatoes and cinnamon. And it makes the kitchen smell utterly delicious. Serve the moussaka with a Greek salad or fried zucchini with garlic, lemon, and oregano.

Moussaka is a great dish to feed a crowd, and the leftovers are perfect for breakfast! You can also try it with beef.

EGGPLANT

2 1-lb.	(454-g)	eggplants
½ cup	(120 ml)	extra-virgin olive oil

LAMB

2 Tbsp.	(30 ml)	extra-virgin olive oil
¾ cup	(180 ml)	finely chopped onion
2		garlic cloves, minced
3 lb.	(1.3 kg)	lean ground lamb
1 cup	(240 ml)	canned Italian plum tomatoes, well-drained and finely chopped
1 tsp.	(5 ml)	sea salt
1 tsp.	(5 ml)	ground cinnamon
1 tsp.	(5 ml)	dried oregano
3		large eggs
1 cup	(240 ml)	freshly grated Parmesan cheese

SAUCE

2 cups	(480 ml)	ricotta cheese
½ cup	(120 ml)	freshly grated Parmesan cheese
¼ cup	(60 ml)	finely grated Pecorino Romano cheese
¼ tsp.	(1.2 ml)	freshly grated nutmeg
¼ tsp.	(1.2 ml)	sea salt
		Freshly ground black pepper
3		large eggs

⋅§ *To make the eggplant:* Preheat the broiler.

⋅§ Trim the stem end from the eggplants and slice lengthwise into ⅓-inch (0.8-cm) slices. Brush both sides with the oil and place on rimmed baking sheets. Broil 4 inches (10 cm) from the heat until browned on one side. Turn over and brown the other side.

⋅§ *To make the lamb:* Heat the oil in a large pot over medium-high heat. Add the onion and garlic and sauté until the onion browns slightly. Add the lamb and cook over high heat, breaking up lumps with a spoon, until the meat loses its raw look. (I find a hand-held blender comes in handy to do this, after the meat is cooked.)

⋅§ Add the tomatoes, salt, cinnamon, and oregano. Cook at a simmer for 30 minutes. Remove from the heat and let cool. Beat in the eggs and cheese.

⋅§ *To make the sauce:* In a medium bowl, mix the ricotta, Parmesan, Pecorino Romano, nutmeg, salt, and pepper. Beat in the eggs.

⋅§ *To assemble:* Preheat the oven to 350°F (175°C).

⋅§ Place a layer of eggplant (without overlapping the slices) in a 13 × 9-inch (32.5 × 22.5-cm) glass baking dish. Spoon half of the meat in an even layer over the eggplant. Top with another layer of eggplant and then the remaining meat. Place the remaining eggplant on top and cover with the sauce, spreading it out evenly.

⋅§ Bake for 45 minutes to 1 hour, until the top is golden brown. Let sit for at least 10 minutes before cutting.

Per serving. Effective carbohydrates: 7.4 g; Carbohydrates: 10.2 g; Fiber: 2.8 g; Protein: 42.6 g; Fat: 46.6 g; Calories: 633

SAUCES AND CONDIMENTS

IN THE SAME WAY THAT VEGETABLES CAN MAKE A MEAL, SO CAN SAUCES. A plain piece of meat and a plain vegetable need never be boring if you have a few tricks up your sleeve. A simple pan sauce is a good basic to be comfortable with: After you have finished cooking meat or fish in a frying pan, place the food on a plate and keep warm. Drain off most of the fat and add a splash of wine, stock, or water to the pan. Bring to a boil, scraping the bottom of the pan to release the flavorful brown bits, then add a splash of whipping cream and boil until thickened. Believe it or not, you can also blend liquids like soy sauce or citrus juice into commercially prepared mayonnaise and heat it for a warm sauce. You can also melt cheese into mayo for a quickie cheese sauce or blend in a combination of water and cream for a more creamy sauce. Or try one of these recipes.

Grainy Mustard and Vermouth Sauce (page 237)

Roasted Almond and Parsley Pesto (page 238)

Thai Sweet-and-Sour Chile Dipping Sauce (page 241)

Tomato Garlic Cream Sauce (page 244)

Aioli (page 248)

FLAVORED BUTTERS

Flavored butters are a great way to give a little oomph to meats and vegetables. All you have to do is mix seasonings into softened butter. Fresh or dried herbs, garlic, shallots, green onions, citrus rind, chipotle chiles, sun-dried tomatoes, and even cheese or nuts can be used, but try not to use wet ingredients, as they don't mix well with the butter.

Roll the mixture into a cylinder, using plastic wrap to shape it, and then chill. Cut slices and let them melt on top of the meats or vegetables. Or you can just bypass this procedure and add large dollops of the softened mixture to your food. Here a few suggestions for flavor combinations.

- Blue cheese and walnut for steak or beef

- Shallot and tarragon for steak or beef (delicious if you simmer the shallots in a little red wine until it's evaporated before blending into the butter)

- Orange rind and basil for chicken, fish, or green vegetables such as broccoli and asparagus

- Pine nut, lemon rind, basil, and garlic for fish, vegetables, and chicken

- Sun-dried tomato, feta, and oregano for chicken, pork, or lamb

- Rosemary, lemon, and garlic for chicken, pork, or lamb

- Ginger, green onion, toasted sesame oil, and toasted sesame seeds for Asian flair on vegetables, chicken, lamb, fish, or pork

- Lime rind and chipotle chiles for chicken or pork

- Curry powder, toasted almonds, and green onion for vegetables, chicken, lamb, fish, or pork

- Prepared horseradish and chives for beef or fish

- Dijon mustard, sweetener, and lemon rind for chicken or pork

- Prepared wasabi and green onion for fish or asparagus

- Whole-grain mustard and sage or rosemary for chicken or pork

BASIC HERB AND WINE PAN SAUCE

Makes 4 servings

Rosemary, thyme, dill, and tarragon are all good in this sauce, but really any herb that complements the food will work. If using soft herbs like dill, basil, or parsley, increase the amount to 1 Tbsp. (15 ml).

Use white wine for a lighter sauce and red wine for a dark one. There's nothing wrong with a red wine sauce on fish!

3 Tbsp.	(45 ml)	minced shallot or green onion (white part only)
1 Tbsp.	(15 ml)	red wine or white wine
¾ cup	(180 ml)	chicken stock
1 tsp.	(5 ml)	minced fresh herbs
4 Tbsp.	(60 ml)	cold unsalted butter, cut into cubes
		Sea salt and freshly ground black pepper

◦§ Remove from the pan whatever meat or fish you cooked and place it on a plate. Cover with foil to keep warm.

◦§ Discard all but 1 Tbsp. (15 ml) of the fat in the pan. Turn the heat to medium. Add the shallot or green onion and sauté until softened, about 2 minutes. Add the wine and stock.

◦§ Use a spoon or metal spatula to scrape up any browned bits clinging to the bottom of the pan. Bring to a boil and cook until the liquid is reduced by half. Stir in the herbs.

◦§ Remove the pan from the heat. Stirring constantly, swirl in the butter until emulsified. Season to taste with salt and pepper.

Per serving. Effective carbohydrates: 1.8 g; Carbohydrates: 2 g; Fiber: 0.2 g; Protein: 0.4 g; Fat: 11.1 g; Calories: 111

BOLOGNESE SAUCE

Makes about 6 cups (1.4 L)

It's great to have your own meat sauce on hand for quick meals. It can be tossed with cooked cauliflower, cabbage, or spaghetti squash and cheese. You can even pour it on a salad or use it as a dip.

Since this sauce simmers for several hours, it's worth making in quantity.

2 Tbsp.	(30 ml)	unsalted butter
¼ cup	(60 ml)	finely chopped onion
¼ cup	(60 ml)	finely chopped celery
2 lb.	(908 g)	lean ground beef or beef and pork
1 cup	(240 ml)	dry white wine
2 28-oz.	(794-ml)	cans Italian plum tomatoes with juice, finely chopped
1½ tsp.	(7.5 ml)	sea salt
1 cup	(240 ml)	whipping cream

❧ Melt the butter in a large heavy pot over medium heat. Add the onion and celery and cook until soft but not brown, about 5 minutes. Add the meat and raise the heat. Cook, crumbling the meat into small pieces with a spoon, until browned.

❧ Add the wine and cook until it evaporates. Add the tomatoes and salt, bring to a boil, and turn down to a simmer. Cook for at least 3 hours, stirring from time to time. (Cooking for 4 to 5 hours is not out of line.) The sauce should be thick but not too thick to pour.

❧ Add the cream and simmer for 30 minutes longer. Adjust the seasoning.

Per ½ cup (120 ml). Effective carbohydrates: 4.8 g; Carbohydrates: 6.2 g; Fiber: 1.4 g; Protein: 15 g; Fat: 25 g; Calories: 333

KETCHUP

Makes 4 cups (960 ml)

This is for all you ketchup lovers out there. I've made this a little less sweet and sour than the standard sugar-filled version, so you may want to tweak it with more sweetener and vinegar.

You may want to use a splatter screen as you cook the ketchup, because this has a tendency to decorate the stove!

Note: *This makes a lot. Either freeze part of it or cut the recipe in half if it's more than you can handle.*

2 6-oz.	(170-g)	cans tomato paste
3 cups	(720 ml)	water
1/16 tsp.	(0.3 ml)	ground cloves
1/16 tsp.	(0.3 ml)	ground cinnamon
1/16 tsp.	(0.3 ml)	ground allspice
1/16 tsp.	(0.3 ml)	ground ginger
2 Tbsp.	(30 ml)	finely chopped celery
1/4 cup	(60 ml)	finely diced onion
2 tsp.	(10 ml)	*each* Splenda and Canadian Sugar Twin or 8 tsp. (40 ml) Splenda
5 tsp.	(25 ml)	white wine vinegar
1/2 tsp.	(2.5 ml)	sea salt

◦§ In a large pot, mix the tomato paste, water, cloves, cinnamon, allspice, ginger, celery, onion, sweetener, vinegar, and salt. Bring to a boil over medium-high heat. Boil hard for 3 minutes.

◦§ Remove from the heat and cool completely. Strain through a sieve, pressing on the solids. Discard the solids. Store in the refrigerator.

Per 1 Tbsp. (15 ml). Effective carbohydrates: 0.6 g; Carbohydrates: 0.7 g; Fiber: 0.1 g; Protein: 0.2 g; Fat: 0 g; Calories: 4
Made with Splenda only: Add 0.3 g carbohydrates

SMOKY BARBECUE SAUCE

Makes about 1 cup (240 ml)

This is fabulous. Feel free to add any spices you like.

1 cup	(240 ml)	Ketchup (page 233)
3 Tbsp.	(45 ml)	soy sauce
½ tsp.	(2.5 ml)	liquid smoke
¼ tsp.	(1.2 ml)	garlic powder
1 tsp.	(5 ml)	*each* Splenda and Canadian Sugar Twin or 4 tsp. (20 ml) Splenda

~§ In a small bowl, mix the ketchup, soy sauce, liquid smoke, garlic powder, and sweetener. Cover and store in the refrigerator.

Per 2 Tbsp. (30 ml). Effective carbohydrates: 2.1 g; Carbohydrates: 2.3 g; Fiber: 0.2 g; Protein: 0.7 g; Fat: 0.1 g; Calories: 12; Made with Splenda only: Add 0.2 g carbohydrates

VARIATIONS

Smokey Maple Barbecue Sauce: Add ½ tsp. (2.5 ml) maple extract to the barbecue sauce.

Per 2 Tbsp. (30 ml). Effective carbohydrates: 2.1 g; Carbohydrates: 2.3 g; Fiber: 0.2 g; Protein: 0.7 g; Fat: 0.1 g; Calories: 12; Made with Splenda only: Add 0.2 g carbohydrates

Chipotle Cilantro Barbecue Sauce: Add 2 chipotle chiles en adobo (finely chopped), 1 Tbsp. (15 ml) freshly squeezed lime juice, and 2 Tbsp. (30 ml) finely chopped cilantro to the barbecue sauce.

Per 2 Tbsp. (30 ml). Effective carbohydrates: 2.5 g; Carbohydrates: 2.8 g; Fiber: 0.3 g; Protein: 0.7 g; Fat: 0.1 g; Calories: 12; Made with Splenda only: Add 0.2 g carbohydrates

Coffee and Bourbon Barbecue Sauce: Add 1 tsp. (5 ml) instant coffee granules and 2 Tbsp. (30 ml) bourbon to the barbecue sauce. Stir until the granules dissolve.

Per 2 Tbsp. (30 ml). Effective carbohydrates: 2.1 g; Carbohydrates: 2.3 g; Fiber: 0.2 g; Protein: 0.7 g; Fat: 0.1 g; Calories: 12; Made with Splenda only: Add 0.2 g carbohydrates

TRADITIONAL COCKTAIL SAUCE

Makes 1¼ cups (300 ml)

Some people like cocktail sauce with eggs, hard-cooked or fried!

1 cup	**(240 ml)**	**Ketchup (page 233)**
3 Tbsp.	**(45 ml)**	**grated onion**
3 Tbsp.	**(45 ml)**	**prepared horseradish, or to taste**
2 Tbsp.	**(30 ml)**	**freshly squeezed lemon juice**
		Hot-pepper sauce
		Sea salt and freshly ground black pepper

◆§ In a medium bowl, mix the ketchup, onion, horseradish, lemon juice, and pepper sauce. Season to taste with salt and pepper. Cover and refrigerate for at least 1 hour to blend the flavors.

Per 1 Tbsp. (15 ml). Effective carbohydrates: 0.8 g; Carbohydrates: 0.9 g; Fiber: 0.1 g; Protein: 0.2 g; Fat: 0.5 g; Calories: 9

VARIATIONS

Hot Buttered Cocktail Sauce: Heat the cocktail sauce gently and stir in 4 Tbsp. (60 ml) unsalted butter until melted.

Per 1 Tbsp. (15 ml). Effective carbohydrates: 0.8 g; Carbohydrates: 0.9 g; Fiber: 0.1 g; Protein: 0.2 g; Fat: 5 g; Calories: 39

Creamy Cocktail Sauce: Add ½ cup (120 ml) mayonnaise to the cocktail sauce.

Per 1 Tbsp. (15 ml). Effective carbohydrates: 0.5 g; Carbohydrates: 0.6 g; Fiber: 0.1 g; Protein: 0.2 g; Fat: 8 g; Calories: 67

FONTINA AND PARMESAN CHEESE SAUCE

Makes about 1 cup (240 ml)

This sauce is a natural over vegetables. And, of course, you can use cheddar or any other type of hard cheese, depending on your taste.

Real Italian fontina is a deliciously smooth, creamy, and lightly tangy cheese. It melts beautifully, and you may want to try it in other dishes like pizza, quiche, or lasagna.

½ cup	(120 ml)	whipping cream
1 Tbsp.	(15 ml)	unsalted butter
½ cup	(120 ml)	freshly grated Parmesan cheese
½ cup	(120 ml)	shredded fontina cheese
		Sea salt

⋙ Bring the cream to a simmer in a small saucepan over medium-low heat. Stir in the butter and then whisk in the Parmesan until smooth. Add the fontina and whisk until the cheese is melted. Season to taste with salt. Serve immediately.

Per ¼ cup (60 ml). Effective carbohydrates: 1.4 g; Carbohydrates: 1.4 g; Fiber: 0 g; Protein: 8.4 g; Fat: 21.5 g; Calories: 230

THE PLOT THICKENS: LUXURIOUS SAUCES

You've made a lovely roast and want to thicken the pan juices. So how do you do it? My two favorite ways involve either cream cheese or cauliflower.

⋙ Whisk in softened cream cheese, bit by bit, until the sauce is lightly thickened.

⋙ Use the Cauliflower Trick (page 191).

Truth be told, using both techniques together doesn't hurt either! Also, whisking in a scant amount of xanthan gum at the end will help to keep the sauce together.

GRAINY MUSTARD AND VERMOUTH SAUCE

Makes about 1 cup (240 ml)

Good with pork, chicken, or salmon. A tip I learned from Julia Child is to keep a bottle of white vermouth handy for recipes calling for white wine. It keeps better than an opened bottle of wine, so you can always have it on hand.

4 Tbsp.	(60 ml)	unsalted butter, at room temperature
2 Tbsp.	(30 ml)	finely minced shallot
¾ cup	(180 ml)	dry white vermouth
1 cup	(240 ml)	chicken stock
¼ tsp.	(1.2 ml)	dried thyme or ¾ tsp. (3.7 ml) fresh thyme
¼ cup	(60 ml)	whole-grain mustard

⋟ Melt 2 Tbsp. (30 ml) of the butter in a small saucepan over medium heat. Add the shallot and cook until translucent, about 2 minutes. Add the vermouth and boil over high heat until reduced to a glaze.

⋟ Add the stock and thyme. Boil until reduced by one-third. Remove from the heat and stir in the mustard and the remaining 2 Tbsp. (30 ml) butter.

Per 1 Tbsp. (15 ml). Effective carbohydrates: 0.6 g; Carbohydrates: 0.6 g; Fiber: 0 g; Protein: 0.6 g; Fat: 3.4 g; Calories: 46

ROASTED ALMOND AND PARSLEY PESTO

Makes about 1 cup (240 ml)

For chicken, fish, and vegetables. It's even good on tomatoes. Use Italian parsley if you can.

½ cup	(120 ml)	whole unblanched almonds
1 cup	(240 ml)	packed fresh parsley leaves
1		garlic clove, minced
6 Tbsp.	(90 ml)	extra-virgin olive oil
¼ cup	(60 ml)	freshly grated Parmesan cheese
		Sea salt and freshly ground black pepper

⋑ Preheat the oven to 350°F (175°C). Spread the almonds on a baking sheet and bake for 8 to 10 minutes, until the nuts are lightly toasted. Cool.

⋑ Combine the almonds, parsley, garlic, and oil in a food processor and blend until pasty, scraping down the sides of the bowl as needed. Pulse in the cheese and season to taste with salt and pepper.

Per 1 Tbsp. (15 ml). Effective carbohydrates: 0.6 g; Carbohydrates: 1.2 g; Fiber: 0.6 g; Protein: 1.5 g; Fat: 7.6 g; Calories: 76

BASIL PESTO

Makes about 1½ cups (360 ml)

A spoonful of pesto goes well with almost anything. It's great on fish, in soup as a garnish, or stirred into cream cheese or mayonnaise as a dip or dressing. Just make sure that you don't pulverize it to death or the lovely flavor will be lost. You can make cilantro pesto by substituting cilantro for the basil.

Note: You can freeze the pesto in ice cube trays, transfer it to a plastic bag, and use just a cube as needed.

1		garlic clove, crushed
2 Tbsp.	(30 ml)	freshly grated Parmesan cheese
1½ cups	(360 ml)	firmly packed fresh basil leaves
½ tsp.	(2.5 ml)	sea salt
½ cup	(120 ml)	extra-virgin olive oil
¼ cup	(60 ml)	pine nuts (optional)

Place the garlic, cheese, basil, salt, and oil in a food processor. Pulse until the basil is finely chopped. Add the pine nuts (if using) and pulse again until the pine nuts are barely detectable.

Per 1 Tbsp. (15 ml). Effective carbohydrates: 0.2 g; Carbohydrates: 0.4 g; Fiber: 0.2 g; Protein: 0.7 g; Fat: 5.5 g; Calories: 52

THAI SWEET-AND-SOUR CHILE DIPPING SAUCE

Makes 1½ cups (360 ml)

The fans of this sauce are legion. It turns any plain meat into a Thai New Year celebration and is the very special guest of the Thai BBQ Chicken Bundles (pages 186 to 187). It's traditionally served with chopped roasted peanuts on top.

Note: *Look for xanthan gum in natural food or bulk stores.*

1 Tbsp.	(15 ml)	*each* Splenda and Canadian Sugar Twin or ¼ cup (60 ml) Splenda
1 cup	(240 ml)	water
½		red bell pepper, stem removed but seeds and core left in
1 to 3		fresh chile peppers
2		garlic cloves, smashed
1 tsp.	(5 ml)	sea salt
¼ cup	(60 ml)	freshly squeezed lemon juice or lime juice
3 Tbsp.	(45 ml)	fish sauce
1 tsp.	(5 ml)	xanthan gum

◦§ In a cup, mix the sweetener and water.

◦§ Roughly chop the bell pepper and chiles. Place in a food processor or blender and add the garlic, salt, and ¼ cup (60 ml) of the sweetened water. Blend until smooth. (The pepper seeds will remain whole.)

◦§ Add the lemon or lime juice, fish sauce, and the remaining ¾ cup (180 ml) water. Pulse a few times to combine. Sprinkle the xanthan gum evenly over the surface of the liquid and blend until thickened. Cover and refrigerate for up to 1 week.

Per 2 Tbsp. (30 ml). Effective carbohydrates: 1.6 g; Carbohydrates: 1.8 g; Fiber: 0.2 g; Protein: 0.5 g; Fat: 0 g; Calories: 8

SIMPLE TOMATO SAUCE

Makes 1½ cups (360 ml)

Although there are many good tomato sauces available that fit in with low-carb eating, it's great to know how to make your own.

2 Tbsp.	**(30 ml)**	**extra-virgin olive oil**
¼ cup	**(60 ml)**	**finely diced onion**
1 28-oz.	**(420-ml)**	**can Italian plum tomatoes, well-drained and finely chopped**
		Sea salt and freshly ground black pepper

Heat the oil in a heavy pot over medium heat. Add the onion and sauté until translucent. Add the tomatoes and cook at a lively simmer until the sauce has reduced and the oil starts to float to the top. Season to taste with salt and pepper.

Per ¼ cup (60 ml). Effective carbohydrates: 3.9 g; Carbohydrates: 5.2 g; Fiber: 1.3 g; Protein: 1.2 g; Fat: 4.5 g; Calories: 71

FRESH TOMATO SAUCE
WITH BALSAMIC VINEGAR

Makes about 1½ cups (360 ml)

This incredibly delicious sauce relies on two things: the sweet, ripe flavor of in-season tomatoes and an unbelievably simple technique. Do not use out-of-season or underripe tomatoes. You will be disappointed!

The sauce can be dressed up with garlic, fresh basil, or capers. Serve with simple grilled meats or Italian sausages.

1¼ lb.	(565 g)	**fresh ripe tomatoes**
½ tsp.	(2.5 ml)	**sea salt**
1 Tbsp.	(15 ml)	**extra-virgin olive oil**
1 tsp.	(5 ml)	**balsamic vinegar**

◆§ Cut the tomatoes in half crosswise and squeeze out the seeds. Holding each tomato half with the skin side against your palm, grate the tomato flesh into a bowl on the teardrop-shaped holes of a box grater; grate it right down to the skin. Discard the skin.

◆§ Place the pulp in a fine-meshed sieve over a bowl to drain for 30 minutes. Discard the water. Return the pulp to the bowl and stir in the salt, oil, and vinegar.

Per 2 Tbsp. (30 ml). Effective carbohydrates: 1.7 g; Carbohydrates: 2.2 g; Fiber: 0.5 g; Protein: 0.4 g; Fat: 1.2 g; Calories: 20

VARIATION

Caper and Basil Tomato Sauce: Add 1 Tbsp. (15 ml) small drained capers and 20 large fresh basil leaves torn into small pieces to the tomato sauce.

Per 2 Tbsp. (30 ml). Effective carbohydrates: 1.7 g; Carbohydrates: 2.3 g; Fiber: 0.6 g; Protein: 0.5 g; Fat: 1.3 g; Calories: 21

TOMATO GARLIC CREAM SAUCE

Makes about 1 cup (240 ml)

This sauce goes well with prawns, scallops, white fish, pork, or chicken.

1 Tbsp.	(15 ml)	unsalted butter
2		garlic cloves, minced
⅓ cup	(80 ml)	dry white wine or dry white vermouth
2 Tbsp.	(30 ml)	tomato paste
1 cup	(240 ml)	chicken stock
½ cup	(120 ml)	whipping cream
		Sea salt and freshly ground black pepper

⋅⋗ Melt the butter in a small saucepan over medium heat. Add the garlic and cook until it sizzles. Add the wine or vermouth and boil until it reduces to a glaze.

⋅⋗ Whisk in the tomato paste, stock, and cream. Boil until the sauce is reduced by about half and slightly thickened. Season to taste with salt and pepper.

Per 1 Tbsp. (15 ml). Effective carbohydrates: 0.7 g; Carbohydrates: 0.8 g; Fiber: 0.1 g; Protein: 0.6 g; Fat: 3.6 g; Calories: 41

BLENDER HOLLANDAISE SAUCE

Makes 1¼ cups (300 ml)

Wonderful with asparagus, broccoli, cauliflower, and steak! The butter needs to be very hot when it's added to the blender, so don't let it cool down at all.

16 Tbsp.	(227 g)	**unsalted butter (2 sticks)**
6		**egg yolks**
¼ tsp.	(1.2 ml)	**sea salt**
4 to 6 Tbsp.	(60 to 90 ml)	**freshly squeezed lemon juice**

◦§ Place the butter in a large saucepan and cook over high heat until it starts to foam and appears to be boiling.

◦§ As the butter melts, place the yolks, salt, and 4 Tbsp. (60 ml) of the lemon juice in a blender. Blend on high speed to combine. With the blender running, add the *hot* butter in a slow, steady stream through the hole in the blender lid; leave the milky residue behind in the pan. Adjust the seasoning with more lemon juice, if needed.

Per 1 Tbsp. (15 ml). Effective carbohydrates: 0.4 g; Carbohydrates: 0.4 g; Fiber: 0 g; Protein: 1 g; Fat: 10.7 g; Calories: 100

MAYONNAISE BY MACHINE

Makes about 1¼ cups (300 ml)

I remember the first time I made mayonnaise. I was all of 18 years old and following the recipe from The Joy of Cooking. *It was tense and joy-filled at the same time. After painstakingly whisking in the oil drop by drop, I had my reward. It seemed like a miracle that a few ingredients could combine to make something greater than the parts.*

One thing that seems to spook the new low-carber is reading the label on the trusty jar of mayo and finding that sugar is an ingredient. The amount is not enough to cause any harm.

While I am a big fan of commercially prepared mayonnaise, there is something about making your own that is fulfilling and comforting at the same time. A food processor or blender makes the job nearly foolproof. You can also use a hand-held blender and beat the ingredients in a bowl.

Your mayonnaise may curdle if the oil was added too quickly. If this happens, place 1 egg yolk in the food processor or blender and add 1 tsp. (5 ml) mustard. Very slowly, beat in the curdled mayonnaise. If it is too thick at any point, add a bit of warm water to thin it out. When you are halfway through, it is safe to add the curdled mixture more quickly.

1		large egg, at room temperature
1		large egg yolk, at room temperature
1 to 2 tsp.	(5 to 10 ml)	Dijon mustard
¼ tsp.	(1.2 ml)	sea salt
1 cup	(240 ml)	extra-virgin olive oil or vegetable oil
1 Tbsp.	(15 ml)	warm water
5 to 6 tsp.	(25 to 30 ml)	freshly squeezed lemon juice

◦§ In a food processor or blender, combine the egg, egg yolk, mustard, and salt. Blend to mix. With the motor running, blend in ⅓ cup (80 ml) of the oil *very* slowly—practically a drop at a time.

◦§ When the mixture starts to thicken, add the water. Then add the remaining ⅔ cup (160 ml) oil in a slow, steady stream. When all the oil is incorporated, blend in the lemon juice. Taste and adjust the seasoning with more lemon juice, mustard, and salt as needed.

Per 1 Tbsp. (15 ml). Effective carbohydrates: 0.2 g; Carbohydrates: 0.2 g; Fiber: 0 g; Protein: 0.1 g; Fat: 9.4 g; Calories: 85

MAYONNAISE WITH COOKED EGG YOLK

Makes about 1½ cups (360 ml)

If you're leery of raw eggs, this is the mayonnaise for you. (Another alternative is to use raw pasteurized eggs, available in some supermarkets and at www.safeeggs.com.)

2		**large egg yolks**
2 Tbsp.	**(30 ml)**	**freshly squeezed lemon juice**
2 Tbsp.	**(30 ml)**	**water**
1 tsp.	**(5 ml)**	**Dijon mustard**
¼ tsp.	**(1.2 ml)**	**sea salt**
1 cup	**(240 ml)**	**extra-virgin olive oil or vegetable oil**

⮞ Select a small heavy frying pan or saucepan to cook the egg mixture in. Then fill a larger baking dish (that will hold the pan) with water and ice and place in the sink.

⮞ Place the egg yolks, lemon juice, and water in the pan and mix with a heatproof rubber spatula. Place the pan over very low heat and stir constantly until the mixture begins to thicken. Remove from the heat immediately and rest the pan in the ice water; stir until the mixture is cool.

⮞ Scrape the mixture into a food processor or blender. Add the mustard and salt. Blend briefly. With the motor running, blend in ⅓ cup (80 ml) of the oil *very* slowly—practically a drop at a time. When the mixture starts to thicken, add the remaining ⅔ cup (160 ml) oil in a slow, steady stream.

Per 1 Tbsp. (15 ml). Effective carbohydrates: 0.2 g; Carbohydrates: 0.2 g; Fiber: 0 g; Protein: 0.3 g; Fat: 10.7 g; Calories: 100

AIOLI (GARLIC MAYONNAISE)

Makes 1¼ to 1½ cups (300 to 360 ml)

This French mayonnaise gives a lift to most any meat, fish, or vegetable.

	Mayonnaise by Machine (page 246) or Mayonnaise with Cooked Egg Yolk (page 247)
3	**garlic cloves, crushed to a paste**

◆ Prepare the mayonnaise as directed, adding the garlic at the end.

Per 1 Tbsp. (15 ml). Effective carbohydrates: 0.3 g; Carbohydrates: 0.3 g; Fiber: 0 g; Protein: 1 g; Fat: 10.7 g; Calories: 100

SPICE UP YOUR MAYONNAISE!

Mayonnaise makes an ideal sauce or accompaniment to all kinds of foods. It can be thinned down with water to make it easy to pour—think salad dressing. Or you can fold whipped cream into it to make it lighter and fluffier.

Adding a little spice to mayonnaise can turn a plain meal into a feast. Here are a few suggestions.

- ◆ Blended basil, garlic, and grated Parmesan cheese—or a spoonful of pesto
- ◆ Chopped cilantro, lime juice, and pureed avocado
- ◆ Curry powder
- ◆ Dijon mustard
- ◆ Grated ginger, toasted sesame seeds, and soy sauce
- ◆ Grated lemon, lime, or orange rind
- ◆ Grated or prepared horseradish
- ◆ Minced jalapeño chiles and cumin seeds
- ◆ Minced oil-packed sun-dried tomatoes
- ◆ Prepared wasabi paste and a touch of soy sauce
- ◆ Tarragon and minced shallots

GARAM MASALA

Makes about ½ cup (120 ml)

This is my favorite garam masala, which is a spice mixture from northern India.

It takes a little bit of work to remove the seeds from cardamom pods, but you will be rewarded with your own fresh and divinely aromatic blend. I put the whole pods, a few at a time, in a mortar and lightly pound them with a pestle to release the seeds. It's then easy to remove the seeds.

Black cardamom pods are much larger than the green, with a tantalizing smoked aroma. They're available at Indian markets or natural food stores.

3 Tbsp.	(45 ml)	cumin seeds
3 Tbsp.	(45 ml)	coriander seeds
2½ Tbsp.	(37.5 ml)	black peppercorns
2½ Tbsp.	(37.5 ml)	black cardamom seeds
1½ tsp.	(7.5 ml)	green cardamom seeds
1 2-inch	(5-cm)	cinnamon stick
5		cloves
⅙		nutmeg

◆§ Place the cumin and coriander seeds in a dry frying pan and stir over medium heat until lightly roasted and fragrant. Cool. Place in a coffee grinder and add the peppercorns, cardamom, cinnamon, cloves, and nutmeg. Grind to a fine powder.

Per 1 tsp. (5 ml). Effective carbohydrates: 0.7 g; Carbohydrates:1.7 g; Fiber: 0.8 g; Protein: 0.3 g; Fat: 0.3 g; Calories: 9

CRANBERRY SAUCE

Makes about 4 cups (960 ml)

Cranberries are rich in natural pectin and thicken just fine without sugar. The bourbon gives the sauce a wonderful fruity flavor. Add more to taste, if you like.

4½ cups	(1.1 L)	**fresh cranberries, about 1 lb. (454 g)**
1½ cups	(360 ml)	**water**
2		**orange rind strips**
2		**lime rind strips**
1		**cinnamon stick**
6		**cloves**
¼ cup	(60 ml)	***each* Splenda and Canadian Sugar Twin or 1 cup (240 ml) Splenda**
2 Tbsp.	(30 ml)	**bourbon (optional)**

◄§ In a large saucepan over medium-high heat, bring the cranberries, water, orange rind, lime rind, cinnamon, and cloves to a boil. Boil until the berry skins pop open (about 5 minutes). Remove from the heat. Add the sweeteners and bourbon (if using). Mix to thoroughly combine. Chill before serving.

Per 1 Tbsp. (15 ml). Effective carbohydrates: 0.7 g; Carbohydrates: 1 g; Fiber: 0.3 g; Protein: 0 g; Fat: 0 g; Calories: 5
Made with Splenda only: Add 0.3 g carbohydrates

DESSERTS

YES, YES, I KNOW THAT SOME PEOPLE CAN EAT SWEETS EVERY DAY AND STILL DO FINE WITH LOW-CARBING. As a former sugar junkie, I know all too well the perils of sugar and its seemingly benign counterpart, the artificial sweetener. For these recipes, you can use either a combination of granular—measures like sugar—Splenda (sucralose) and Canadian Sugar Twin (cyclamate) or Splenda alone. Sucralose and cyclamate work synergistically with each other. The taste is almost identical to real sugar, and you can use much less of each. That's why the Splenda-alone measurement is double in the recipes. (*Note:* Sugar Twin sold in the United States does not contain cyclamate, so it doesn't work the same way.)

My humble opinion is that sweets should be kept for an occasional treat. They're best saved for a special occasion, perhaps a dinner party where you want to impress your non-low-carb—or low-carb—friends. Making a daily habit of treats is a habit that you may have to break down the road, and that's no fun at all!

But when you do indulge, enjoy desserts to the hilt. Here are some of my favorites.

THE SWEET TRUTH

There aren't too many times when it's better to reject the real deal in favor of something fake. But if you want something sweet and you *don't* want sugar, you have a few options to consider.

Everyone has an opinion on artificial sweeteners—which are good for you, which are bad for you, and which should be avoided like the plague. No one can make up your mind for you, so a little research may be in order. It's up to you to make the choice.

Artificial sweeteners are classed as nonnutritive and are also known as *intense sweeteners,* since only a very tiny amount is required to give sweet taste. They provide a sweet sensation to the taste buds without raising blood sugar or insulin levels and may be useful for weight loss or blood sugar/insulin control. Here's what's out there.

Aspartame. The most common artificial sweetener is aspartame (sold as Equal and NutraSweet). It's calorie- and carb-free; however, it is far from being an ideal sweetener. It is not chemically stable, meaning that when exposed to heat and air, it breaks down into its chemical constituents: phenylalanine and aspartic acid. That makes it unsuitable for cooking.

Sucralose. Sold under the trade name Splenda, sucralose is spun from regular sucrose sugar in such a way that the body doesn't recognize it, so it's not absorbed. Thus it contributes no calories or carbohydrates in its pure form. (Fillers used to give the product bulk do contain carbohydrates; see Fillers on page 256.) It remains stable in heat, so it is ideal for cooking and baking. Splenda is available for home use as a bulk sweetener, which measures spoon for spoon exactly the same as sugar.

Acesulfame potassium. Many food and beverage manufacturers use a combination approach in their products—blending aspartame with another sweetener: acesulfame potassium (also known as acesulfame-K or ace-K; sold as Sunett and Sweet One). Ace-K tends to have a bitter aftertaste, but that's eliminated when it's combined with another sweetener. By combining sweeteners, an improved sweet taste is achieved and reduced amounts of each chemical are required.

Saccharin. Discovered over a century ago, saccharin has been used around the world as a noncaloric sweetener with a relatively high safety record. As a sweetener, saccharin is heat stable but may yield a metallic aftertaste. However, it exerts a synergistic effect when blended with other sweeteners, which minimizes the aftertaste. Saccharin is available as a tabletop sweetener in powder, liquid, or tablet form. Sugar Twin sold in the United States contains saccharin.

Cyclamate. This sweetener is available in Canada, the United Kingdom, Australia, and many other countries around the world. However, it has not been available in the United States since the 1970s. (Canadian Sugar Twin contains cyclamate; U.S. Sugar Twin does not.) Although it's expected to be approved and made available to U.S. consumers in the near future, at the present time the ban remains in effect. Cyclamate sweetener is sold for tabletop use and comes in powdered form, tablets, and liquid. There's also a brown sugar flavor, which some enjoy. Cyclamate is stable in heat, so it's fine to use in cooking and baking.

Fillers. Artificial sweeteners are very concentrated; only a tiny dot is needed to equal the sweetness of a teaspoon of sugar. Since it's not practical to measure a tiny dot, fillers are necessary to give the products bulk. The most common fillers are maltodextrin, dextrose, lactose, and water. Obviously, water has no carbohydrates, so liquid sweeteners contain zero calories, zero carbs. The other ingredients listed are carbohydrates and are digested as sugars. Read the label of your sweetener product carefully so you know what's in it. Fillers will be the source of any calories and carbohydrates listed on the nutrient panel.

Stevia. This is a noncaloric, zero-carb natural sweetener derived from a South American plant, *Stevia rebaudiana,* and has been in wide use in Asia for some years. It's becoming more readily available in North America; look for it in natural food stores. Some people find it has a slight anise/licorice flavor, which may or may not be objectionable. It's stable in heat,

so it's fine to use in cooking. Like artificial sweeteners, stevia does not have a direct effect on blood glucose or insulin levels, but just like any other sweetener, it can provoke cravings due to stimulating the sweet taste receptors.

Inulin. This is a natural soluble fiber extracted from chicory root and has been well-known in Europe for many years for its positive influence on digestive health. It's becoming more widely available in North America.

Inulin does have a sweet taste, and because it's a soluble fiber, it can bind with water to give bulk and texture. Thus it has many commercial uses as a fat and sugar replacement. It may also be used in powder form as a filler for artificial sweeteners, and many powdered stevia products use inulin or chicory root extract as a natural filler.

Sugar alcohols. In spite of the name, these sweeteners are neither sugars nor alcohols and are sometimes called polyols to avoid confusion. Some sugar alcohols that you may see on ingredient lists include: erythritol, HSH (hydrogenated starch hydrolysate, also called maltitol syrup), isomalt, lactitol, maltitol, mannitol, sorbitol, and xylitol.

Sugar alcohols provide the bulk and sweetness of sugar and corn syrup, but they're incompletely absorbed from the intestine. This yields fewer calories and carbs than sugar and results in a much slower and smaller rise in blood glucose and insulin.

Sugar alcohols do yield calories, however—although fewer than sugar, since they're not completely absorbed. Their average calorie content is 2.5 per gram, as opposed to sugar's 4 calories per gram. Be aware that sugar alcohols can cause gastric disturbances and can cause a slowdown in fat loss in certain people.

Glycerine. This is not a sugar alcohol, although it has similar properties. It's a sweet-tasting syrup. In nature, glycerine molecules are attached to fatty acid molecules to make triglycerides. By itself though, it's not a fat, and it's not technically a sugar or a carbohydrate either. Its most popular dietary use is in sports nutrition and protein bars because it is quickly absorbed and readily used as fuel by the muscles, without requiring insulin.

SPLENDA PACKET CONVERSION

Some people like to buy Splenda in individual packets, so here's a chart to remove the mystery. One packet is equal to the sweetening power of 2 tsp. (10 ml) of the measures-like-sugar Splenda—and also has the same amount of carbs.

Granular Splenda contains maltodextrin and sucralose. One tsp. (5 ml) contains 0.5 g carbohydrates, 2 calories, and 6 mg sucralose. Splenda packets contain dextrose, maltodextrin, and sucralose. One packet contains 1 g carbohydrates, 4 calories, and 12 mg sucralose.

1 cup (240 ml) = 24 packets

¾ cup (180 ml) = 18 packets

½ cup (120 ml) = 12 packets

⅓ cup (80 ml) = 8 packets

¼ cup (60 ml) = 6 packets

⅛ cup or 2 Tbsp. (30 ml) = 3 packets

1 Tbsp. (15 ml) = 1½ packets

1 tsp. (5 ml) = ½ packet

I like sweetness to be balanced in desserts, so none of these recipes is very sweet. If you like things sweeter, add more sweetener. Because artificial sweeteners don't add texture or bulk to baked goods, you can sweeten to taste. So if you taste a mixture and think it needs to be a little sweeter, go for it. The recipe will still turn out fine.

The bottom line with sugar alcohols and glycerine is that because of each person's unique individual chemistry, our bodies can react differently to these chemicals. The sweet taste may trigger emotions that will result in a "rush" of hormones and enzymes in the body—ultimately leading to an insulin spike and fat storage. Always remember that candy is *not* a meal substitute. There's little or no protein, vitamins, or essential fatty acids.

DARK CHOCOLATE BARS

Makes 4 bars

You can make a decent homemade chocolate that melts smoothly and richly in your mouth. The secret is cocoa butter. Buy the solid kind that comes in a block or chunks; look for it in natural food or baking supply stores.

Be sure to use a high-quality chocolate like Callebaut, Valrhona, or Scharffen Berger. Standard supermarket brands can be grainy, a fault that's accentuated in low-carb cooking. They also lack the depth of flavor and complexity of fine chocolate.

Note: *Both the dark bars and their two variations can be cut up and used as chocolate chips in cakes, breads, and chilled desserts. They tend to run if used in cookies.*

2 oz.	(56 g)	**pure cocoa butter**
2 oz.	(56 g)	**unsweetened chocolate**
½ cup	(120 ml)	**whipping cream**
5 tsp.	(25 ml)	***each* Splenda and Canadian Sugar Twin** *or* **6 Tbsp. (90 ml) Splenda**
⅛ tsp.	(0.6 ml)	**sea salt**
1 tsp.	(5 ml)	**pure vanilla extract**
6 Tbsp.	(90 ml)	**whey protein isolate**

◆§ Line 4 mini loaf pans, about 4 × 2 inches (10 × 5 cm), with parchment or wax paper.

◆§ Chop the cocoa butter and chocolate into small pieces. Place in a heatproof bowl and melt over hot—not boiling—water. Remove from the heat and stir to combine.

◆§ In a food processor or blender, combine the cream, sweetener, salt, and vanilla. Pulse to combine. Add the whey protein and pulse to combine. Let sit for a minute or two to dissolve the protein powder, then blend briefly until smooth.

◆§ With the motor running, slowly add the chocolate mixture. Pour into the prepared pans. Smooth and level the mixture. Refrigerate until firm. Store tightly wrapped in the refrigerator.

Per bar. Effective carbohydrates: 3.7 g; Carbohydrates: 5.8 g; Fiber: 2.1 g; Protein: 7.2 g; Fat: 19.8 g; Calories: 328; Made with Splenda only: Add 1.3 g carbohydrates

VARIATIONS

Milk Chocolate Bars: Decrease the unsweetened chocolate to ½ oz. (14 g). Decrease the sweetener to 1 Tbsp. (15 ml) *each* Splenda and Canadian Sugar Twin *or* ¼ cup (60 ml) Splenda.

Per bar. Effective carbohydrates: 2.3 g; Carbohydrates: 2.8 g; Fiber: 0.5 g; Protein: 6.2 g; Fat: 27 g; Calories: 273; Made with Splenda only: Add 1.3 g carbohydrates

White Chocolate Bars: Omit the unsweetened chocolate. Increase the cocoa butter to 3 oz. (84 g), the vanilla extract to 2 tsp. (10 ml), and the whey protein isolate to ½ cup (120 ml).

Per bar. Effective carbohydrates: 1.9 g; Carbohydrates: 1.9 g; Fiber: 0 g; Protein: 7.5 g; Fat: 25.2 g; Calories: 263 Made with Splenda only: Add 1.3 g carbohydrates

---

HEAVENLY TRUFFLES

Truffles are ultra fancy, yet they're easy to make. You can turn any of these chocolate bars into an impressive little batch. Just add ½ cup (120 ml) more whipping cream. If desired, drizzle in a bit of alcohol as a flavoring; try rum, bourbon, brandy, or cognac. The truffles can be further spiffed up by adding finely grated citrus rind; sugar-free dried cranberries, blueberries, or strawberries; finely grated ginger; chopped toasted nuts; or extracts such as maple or the wonderful fruit extracts from Boyajian.

When the mixture is cool and firm, roll it into small balls. You can then roll them in cocoa, cinnamon, ground nuts, or coconut.

A modern Indian restaurant that I frequent serves after-dinner truffles spiked with their own garam masala—a curry-type spice! If you're game, see Garam Masala on page 249.

WANDA'S VANILLA ICE CREAM

Makes 8 servings

Wanda arrived at my door in 2001 looking for an apprenticeship. There was something about her demeanor that let me know she would be great. Today, she is my cooking class assistant as well as one of the restaurant cooks. A dedicated low-carber, she has a knack for cooking that is rare and wonderful to see. This ice cream is only one of the brilliant recipes in her repertoire.

Note: You can find vanilla paste at gourmet food stores. If that's not available, vanilla extract is fine. Or try a whole vanilla bean: Split it lengthwise and heat with the cream. After beating the cream into the egg mixture, retrieve the bean and scrape the tiny black seeds into the custard. Discard the leftover bean or reserve it for another use.

2		**large eggs**
5		**large egg yolks**
3 cups	**(720 ml)**	**whipping cream**
¼ cup	**(60 ml)**	***each* Splenda and Canadian Sugar Twin *or* 1 cup (240 ml) Splenda**
		Large pinch of sea salt
1½ tsp.	**(7.5 ml)**	**vanilla paste or 1 Tbsp. (15 ml) pure vanilla extract**

◆ In a large bowl, beat the eggs and egg yolks together with a whisk.

◆ Combine the cream, sweetener, and salt in a very large pot. Bring the mixture to a full rolling boil that rises up in the pot (watch it carefully so it doesn't burn).

◆ Immediately start to dribble the cream into the eggs, whisking constantly. After you've added about a third, slowly pour in the remainder, still whisking. Add the vanilla.

◆ Place in the refrigerator and whisk occasionally until cold. Cover and refrigerate until completely chilled, preferably overnight.

◆ Transfer to an ice-cream maker. Churn according to the manufacturer's instructions. Scrape into a storage container and freeze.

Per serving. Effective carbohydrates: 4 g; Carbohydrates: 4 g; Fiber: 0 g; Protein: 5.1 g; Fat: 37.5 g; Calories: 372
Made with Splenda only: Add 1 g carbohydrates

CHOCOLATE SAUCE

Makes 1½ cups (360 ml)

Totally yummy! And it makes very good hot chocolate syrup. To make hot chocolate, place 2 to 3 Tbsp. (30 to 45 ml) of the syrup in a mug. Bring a combination of whipping cream and water to a boil and slowly stir into the syrup.

⅓ cup	(80 ml)	**Dutch-processed cocoa powder**
1¼ cups	(300 ml)	**water**
2		**large egg yolks**
1 oz.	(28 g)	**unsweetened chocolate, finely chopped**
4 Tbsp.	(60 ml)	**unsalted butter, at room temperature**
4 tsp.	(20 ml)	*each* **Splenda and Canadian Sugar Twin** *or* **⅓ cup (80 ml) Splenda**
		Pinch of sea salt
1 tsp.	(5 ml)	**pure vanilla extract**
1 tsp.	(5 ml)	**pure chocolate extract (optional)**

➝ Place the cocoa in a small saucepan and slowly whisk in the water to form a smooth paste. Stirring constantly, bring the mixture to a boil over high heat and stir for 1 minute. Remove from the heat.

➝ In a medium bowl, whisk the egg yolks until blended. Whisking constantly, very slowly pour the cocoa mixture into the yolks. Stir in the chocolate, butter, sweetener, salt, and extracts and continue stirring until the butter and chocolate have melted. Cool and refrigerate.

Per 1 Tbsp. (15 ml). Effective carbohydrates: 0.5 g; Carbohydrates: 1 g; Fiber: 0.5 g; Protein: 0.6 g; Fat: 3 g; Calories: 31
Made with Splenda only: Add 0.2 g carbohydrates

YOUR OWN ICE CREAM PARLOR

The variations on Wanda's Vanilla Ice Cream are almost limitless! You can add extracts, berries, nuts, and chunks of tasty morsels like chopped brownies (pages 310 and 312) or Banana Bread (page 307). Brandy, bourbon, and rum are all good in ice cream. (And alcohol will prevent the ice cream from freezing rock hard.)

One of the best ice creams I ever had was flavored with nutmeg, cinnamon, and fresh basil. Other herbs, like lavender and rosemary, are delicious, too. Here are more of my favorite variations.

Cappuccino and Cocoa Nib: Add 1 Tbsp. (15 ml) instant espresso granules to the warm custard and stir until dissolved; chill. Add 2 Tbsp. (30 ml) cocoa nibs to the ice cream when it's almost finished churning.

Per serving. Effective carbohydrates: 5 g; Carbohydrates: 5 g; Fiber: 0 g; Protein: 5.3 g; Fat: 38 g; Calories: 381; made with Splenda only: Add 1 g carbohydrates

Chocolate: Finely chop 4 oz. (112 g) unsweetened chocolate and stir into the warm custard until melted. A little bourbon is also fabulous!

Per serving. Effective carbohydrates: 5.9 g; Carbohydrates: 8 g; Fiber: 2.1 g; Protein: 6.6 g; Fat: 45.3 g; Calories: 446; made with Splenda only: Add 1 g carbohydrates

Chocolate Chunk: Make Dark Chocolate Bars (pages 258 to 259) and cut them into chunks. Add to the ice cream when it's almost finished churning. Turn this into Tin Roof by adding chopped roasted peanuts. For Almost Cherries Garcia, add ½ tsp. (2.5 ml) Boyajian cherry extract.

Per serving. Effective carbohydrates: 5.9 g; Carbohydrates: 6.9 g; Fiber: 1 g; Protein: 8.7 g; Fat: 54.6 g; Calories: 536; made with Splenda only: Add 1 g carbohydrates

German's Chocolate: Finely chop 2 oz. (56 g) unsweetened chocolate and stir into the warm custard until melted; chill. Prepare the topping from the German's Chocolate Cheesecake (pages 270 to 272), pour into a shallow container, and chill. Tear into small pieces and add to the ice cream mixture when it's almost finished churning.

Per serving. Effective carbohydrates: 5.1 g; Carbohydrates: 9.5 g; Fiber: 4.4 g; Protein: 11.5 g; Fat: 36.9 g; Calories: 395; made with Splenda only: Add 1 g carbohydrates

Gingerbread: Finely grate 2 Tbsp. (30 ml) fresh ginger. Squeeze out the juice and add the juice to the chilled custard along with 1 Tbsp. (15 ml) ground cinnamon, ½ tsp. (2.5 ml) freshly grated nutmeg, and ¼ tsp. (1.2 ml) ground allspice.

Per serving. Effective carbohydrates: 4.6 g; Carbohydrates: 5.1 g; Fiber: 0.5 g; Protein: 5.2 g; Fat: 37.6 g; Calories: 376; made with Splenda only: Add 1 g carbohydrates

Green Tea: Omit the vanilla. Dissolve 2 Tbsp. (30 ml) matcha in 2 Tbsp. (30 ml) boiling water and add to the chilled custard.

Per serving. Effective carbohydrates: 4.6 g; Carbohydrates: 5.1 g; Fiber: 0.5 g; Protein: 5.2 g; Fat: 37.6 g; Calories: 376; made with Splenda only: Add 1 g carbohydrates

Maple Walnut: Add 1 Tbsp. (15 ml) pure maple extract and 1 cup (240 ml) chopped walnuts to the ice cream when it's almost finished churning.

Per serving. Effective carbohydrates: 5.1 g; Carbohydrates: 6.1 g; Fiber: 1 g; Protein: 7.4 g; Fat: 47.3 g; Calories: 473; made with Splenda only: Add 1 g carbohydrates

Strawberry: Add 1 cup (240 ml) crushed strawberries to the ice cream when it's almost finished churning. Other berries can be used, too.

Per serving. Effective carbohydrates: 5 g; Carbohydrates: 5.4 g; Fiber: 0.4 g; Protein: 5.2 g; Fat: 37.6 g; Calories: 378; made with Splenda only: Add 1 g carbohydrates

RICOTTA SEMIFREDDO

Makes 6 servings

Semifreddo *means "half frozen" in Italian. It's similar to ice cream but grainier in texture. For best results, let it soften in the fridge for an hour before serving.*

You can also freeze the semifreddo in a loaf pan and slice it to serve. Line the pan with plastic wrap or parchment paper to make removal easier. Cut the loaf while still frozen.

This is great with warmed Rhubarb Compote (page 279) and can be served with fresh berries in the summer.

Note: This is excellent made with a real vanilla bean. Split it lengthwise and place in a small saucepan with the water and ¼ cup (60 ml) of the cream. Bring to a simmer, remove from the heat, and cool completely. Scrape the seeds from the bean and add them to the cream. You can discard the "spent" bean or you can rinse and dry the bean, then store it in your box of sweetener. It will scent the sweetener with vanilla.

8 oz.	(227 g)	**full-fat ricotta cheese**
2 tsp.	(10 ml)	**pure vanilla extract**
¼ cup	(60 ml)	**water**
¾ cup	(180 ml)	**whipping cream**
2		**large egg yolks**
1 Tbsp.	(15 ml)	***each* Splenda and Canadian Sugar Twin *or* ¼ cup (60 ml) Splenda**
		Pinch of sea salt

◦§ In a food processor, blend the ricotta and vanilla until smooth. With the motor running, pour in the water and ¼ cup (60 ml) of the cream. Transfer to a medium bowl.

◦§ In a small bowl, beat the egg yolks, sweetener, and salt until thick and lemon-colored. Fold into the ricotta mixture.

◦§ In another bowl, beat the remaining ½ cup (120 ml) cream until soft peaks form. Fold into the ricotta mixture. Pour into 6 attractive 6-oz. (90-ml) serving bowls or ramekins and freeze.

◦§ To serve, remove from the freezer 1 hour ahead of time and place in the refrigerator to soften.

Per serving. Effective carbohydrates: 2.8 g; Carbohydrates: 2.8 g; Fiber: 0 g; Protein: 6 g; Fat: 17.6 g; Calories: 195
Made with Splenda only: Add 0.5 g carbohydrates

HIDE-AND-SEEK: SUGAR IN DISGUISE

It's lurking where you least expect it, and sometimes you need to be a detective to spot sugar in its many forms.

In chemistry, the ending "ose" indicates sugar; so look out for "ose" ingredients on food labels. Table sugar—the white granulated type, as well as its brown cousins—is known as sucrose. Other sugars you might encounter include dextrose, fructose, glucose, lactose, and maltose. These sugars are pure carb; thus 1 gram of sugar = 1 gram of carbohydrate = 4 calories.

Check food labels for these other commonly used sugar ingredients: barley syrup, cane juice, confectioners' sugar, corn syrup, demerara sugar, fruit juice concentrate, honey, icing sugar, malt syrup, maple syrup, molasses, rice syrup, Sucanat, and turbinado sugar.

Beware of foods that boast "no added sugar" or "sugar free" on the label. Many foods such as "natural" jams and fruit drinks are sweetened with concentrated grape and apple juices, which are very sweet, high-fructose syrups and yield the same carb and calorie counts as table sugar.

Fructose occurs naturally in fruits and vegetables, but it's present in relatively small amounts. In addition, the fiber, pectin, vitamins, and minerals in these foods balance the fructose content. On the other hand, fructose that is added to commercially processed food is a highly refined, purified sugar created in a lab from corn syrup, other syrups, and chemically treated sucrose sugar.

FROZEN BOURBON, CHOCOLATE, AND BURNT ALMOND CHEESECAKE

Makes 9 servings

Fellow low-carber Rachel inspired this cheesecake by being so fond of a toasted nut crust on another cheesecake and by wanting something small, freezable, and cheesecake-like. This isn't small, but it can be cut into small pieces, individually wrapped, and stored in the freezer. The alcohol prevents it from freezing rock hard.

You can make it plain or experiment with other flavors, such as lemon, lime, or orange rind and different liquors. Or perk it up with a few fresh berries folded into the cheese mixture.

Note: *Quark is a light tangy cheese, similar to cream cheese. Grocery stores carry it in the dairy section in tubs. You can use cream cheese in place of the quark.*

ALMOND BITS

¼ cup	(60 ml)	almonds
1 oz.	(28 g)	unsweetened chocolate, chopped
3 Tbsp.	(45 ml)	unsalted butter, at room temperature
1½ tsp.	(7.5 ml)	*each* Splenda and Canadian Sugar Twin *or* 6 tsp. (30 ml) Splenda
		Pinch of sea salt

FILLING

8 oz.	(227 g)	cream cheese, at room temperature
8 oz.	(227 g)	quark, at room temperature
2 Tbsp.	(30 ml)	*each* Splenda and Canadian Sugar Twin *or* ½ cup (120 ml) Splenda
½ tsp.	(2.5 ml)	pure vanilla extract
3		large eggs, separated
3 Tbsp.	(45 ml)	bourbon
1 cup	(240 ml)	whipping cream

◆§ Line an 8 × 8-inch (20 × 20-cm) baking dish with foil or parchment paper. Place in the freezer.

◆§ *To make the almond bits:* Preheat the oven to 300°F (150°C). Spread the almonds on a baking sheet and bake for 15 minutes, or until well-browned and almost to the point of being burnt. Let cool and chop coarsely.

◦§ Place the chocolate in a small heatproof bowl and melt over simmering water or in the microwave. Let cool to room temperature. Cut 2 Tbsp. (30 ml) of the butter into small bits and stir into the chocolate until melted. Stir in 1 tsp. (5 ml) *each* of the Splenda and Sugar Twin—or 4 tsp. (20 ml) of the Splenda.

◦§ In a small frying pan, melt the remaining 1 Tbsp. (15 ml) butter over medium heat and continue cooking until it turns a rich and nutty-smelling brown. Add the almonds, salt, and the remaining ½ tsp. (2.5 ml) *each* of the Splenda and Sugar Twin—or 2 tsp. (10 ml) of the Splenda. Stir into the chocolate. Spread evenly in the frozen pan. Place in the freezer until hardened. Break into small pieces, place back in the pan, and return the pan to the freezer.

◦§ *To make the filling:* In a large bowl, combine the cream cheese or quark, sweetener, and vanilla. Beat until smooth and light. Beat in the egg yolks and bourbon. Stir in the frozen almond bits.

◦§ In another bowl, beat the cream until stiff. Fold into the cheese mixture.

◦§ In a clean bowl with clean beaters, beat the egg whites until firm peaks form. Fold into the cheese mixture. Spread evenly in the frozen pan. Freeze for at least 6 hours or overnight.

Per serving. Effective carbohydrates: 3.6 g; Carbohydrates: 4.5 g; Fiber: 0.9 g; Protein: 8 g; Fat: 37 g; Calories: 375
Made with Splenda only: Add 1.5 g carbohydrates

MELTING CHOCOLATE—CLEAN AND EASY

When I melt chocolate in a microwave, I put a wooden chopstick in the bowl and leave it there while the chocolate is microwaving. When I remove the chocolate to check its progress, I use the chopstick to stir it. This eliminates messy, chocolate-coated spoons and plates that they rest on.

NEW YORK CHEESECAKE

Makes 12 servings

This is my definitive baked cheesecake. So smooth, so rich, and so creamy. It can be baked without the crust, if you like.

Note: To cut cheesecakes cleanly, dip your knife into very hot water and wipe the blade dry. Repeat the procedure after each cut and you'll have beautifully smooth slices of cheesecake.

CRUST

1 cup	(240 ml)	almond meal (finely ground almonds)
1 tsp.	(5 ml)	ground cinnamon
1 tsp.	(5 ml)	*each* Splenda and Canadian Sugar Twin *or* 4 tsp. (20 ml) Splenda
		Pinch of sea salt
2 Tbsp.	(30 ml)	unsalted butter, melted
1		large egg white

FILLING

2½ lb.	(1.1 kg)	cream cheese, at room temperature
½ cup	(120 ml)	sour cream
5 Tbsp.	(75 ml)	*each* Splenda and Canadian Sugar Twin *or* 1¼ cups (300 ml) Splenda
2 tsp.	(10 ml)	freshly squeezed lemon juice
2 tsp.	(10 ml)	pure vanilla extract
		Pinch of sea salt
2		large egg yolks
6		large eggs

⊷ Preheat the oven to 350°F (175°C). Line the bottom of a 9-inch (22.5-cm) springform pan with parchment paper and coat the inside of the pan with butter.

⊷ *To make the crust:* In a medium bowl, mix the almond meal, cinnamon, sweetener, and salt. Add the butter and mix well.

⊷ In a small bowl, beat the egg white with a whisk until foamy and add to the almond mixture. Stir well and pat into the bottom of the prepared pan.

◦§ Bake for 10 to 12 minutes, or until lightly browned. (If the crust rises up, just poke it with a fork and press it down.) Let cool.

◦§ Increase the oven temperature to 500°F (260°C).

◦§ *To make the filling:* In a food processor or large bowl, beat the cream cheese until smooth. Add the sour cream, sweetener, lemon juice, vanilla, and salt. Mix well. Blend in the egg yolks. Add the eggs, 1 at a time, blending well after each addition. Scrape the bowl frequently while you are mixing.

◦§ Place the springform pan on a rimmed baking sheet. Carefully pour the filling over the crust. Bake for 5 minutes.

◦§ Reduce the oven temperature to 200°F (93°C). Continue baking for 1½ hours. (Do not open the door during this time!) The cheesecake should still look soft in the center.

◦§ Remove from the oven and run a knife around the outside of the cheesecake. Let cool on a wire rack to room temperature. Serve immediately or chill.

Per serving. Effective carbohydrates: 5 g; Carbohydrates: 5.8 g; Fiber: 0.8 g; Protein: 13.7 g; Fat: 44.7 g; Calories: 473
Made with Splenda only: Add 1.6 g carbohydrates

GERMAN'S CHOCOLATE CHEESECAKE

Makes 12 servings

When I was younger, German's Chocolate Cake was always my birthday cake. In the spirit of the original, the chocolate flavor in this cake is light.

CRUST

1 cup	(240 ml)	almond meal (finely ground almonds)
½ cup	(120 ml)	unsweetened shredded coconut
1½ tsp.	(7.5 ml)	*each* Splenda and Canadian Sugar Twin *or* 2 Tbsp. (30 ml) Splenda
2 Tbsp.	(30 ml)	Dutch-processed cocoa powder
		Large pinch of sea salt
2 Tbsp.	(30 ml)	unsalted butter, melted
1		large egg white

FILLING

5 oz.	(140 g)	unsweetened chocolate, chopped
3 oz.	(84 g)	cocoa butter, chopped
1½ lb.	(680 g)	cream cheese, at room temperature
¼ cup	(60 ml)	*each* Splenda and Canadian Sugar Twin *or* 1 cup (240 ml) Splenda
3		large eggs
2 tsp.	(10 ml)	pure vanilla extract
2 tsp.	(10 ml)	pure chocolate extract (optional)
⅛ tsp.	(0.6 ml)	sea salt
½ cup	(120 ml)	sour cream

TOPPING

4 Tbsp.	(60 ml)	unsalted butter
¾ cup	(180 ml)	whipping cream
1 cup	(240 ml)	whey protein isolate
1 Tbsp.	(15 ml)	*each* Splenda and Canadian Sugar Twin *or* ¼ cup (60 ml) Splenda
¼ tsp.	(1.2 ml)	sea salt
¼ cup	(60 ml)	roasted almond butter
1 tsp.	(5 ml)	pure vanilla extract
½ tsp.	(2.5 ml)	pure caramel extract
1½ cups	(360 ml)	unsweetened shredded coconut
1 cup	(240 ml)	pecan pieces

- Preheat the oven to 350°F (175°C). Line the bottom of a 9-inch (22.5-cm) springform pan with parchment paper and coat the inside of the pan with butter.

- *To make the crust:* In a medium bowl, mix the almond meal, coconut, sweetener, cocoa powder, and salt. Add the butter and mix well.

- In a small bowl, beat the egg white with a whisk until foamy and add to the almond mixture. Stir well and pat into the bottom of the prepared pan.

- Bake for 10 minutes. (If the crust rises up, just poke it with a fork and press it down.) Let cool.

- Reduce the oven temperature to 275°F (135°C).

- *To make the filling:* Combine the chocolate and cocoa butter in the top of a double boiler. Place over simmering water until melted. Remove from the heat, stir to mix well, and let cool.

- In a food processor or large bowl, beat the cream cheese until smooth. Add the sweetener. Add the eggs, 1 at a time, blending well after each addition. Scrape the bowl frequently while you are mixing. Add the extracts and salt. Blend in the chocolate mixture and then the sour cream.

- Place the springform pan on a rimmed baking sheet. Carefully pour the filling over the crust.

- Bake for 45 minutes. Remove from the oven and run a knife around the outside of the cheesecake. Let cool on a wire rack to room temperature, then make the topping.

- *To make the topping:* In a small frying pan, heat the butter over medium heat until it starts to turn a rich, golden brown. Remove from the heat.

- Warm the cream in a small saucepan over medium-low heat.

(continued on page 272)

In a food processor, combine the whey protein, sweetener, and salt. Pulse to combine. Add the cream and blend until smooth. Add the almond butter and blend again until smooth. Add the extracts and blend until smooth once more. Add the coconut and pecans; pulse once or twice to just combine. Pour over the cheesecake and spread out smoothly. Chill overnight.

Per serving. Effective carbohydrates: 8.8 g; Carbohydrates: 14.3 g; Fiber: 5.5 g; Protein: 16.7 g; Fat: 67 g; Calories: 697
Made with Splenda only: Add 1.7 g carbohydrate

WHAT'S IN A NAME?

Interestingly, German's Chocolate Cake—commonly known as simply German Chocolate Cake—has nothing to do with Germany. Here's the scoop: In 1957, a recipe for "German's Chocolate Cake" first appeared in a Dallas, Texas, newspaper. It was sent in by a Dallas homemaker and used a brand of chocolate bar called German's. (The chocolate had been developed in 1852 for Baker's Chocolate Company by a man named Sam German.) The cake got such an enthusiastic response that General Foods—which owned Baker's Chocolate—sent pictures of the cake to newspapers all over the country. The recipe received the same overwhelming response wherever it traveled, and sales of the chocolate exploded.

LIME ANGEL CUSTARD

Makes 8 servings

This custard is like a crème brûlée with a thin, soft, meringue-like top. You can use lemon juice and rind if you prefer or omit both and add 2 tsp. (10 ml) pure vanilla extract or another extract.

4 Tbsp.	(60 ml)	unsalted butter, at room temperature
3 Tbsp.	(45 ml)	*each* Splenda and Canadian Sugar Twin *or* ¾ cup (180 ml) Splenda
		Grated rind of 3 limes
4		large eggs, separated
2 Tbsp.	(30 ml)	almond meal (finely ground almonds)
2 Tbsp.	(30 ml)	vital wheat gluten
½ cup	(120 ml)	freshly squeezed lime juice
1 cup	(240 ml)	whipping cream
½ cup	(120 ml)	water

◆§ Preheat the oven to 375°F (180°C). Place eight 5-oz. (75-ml) ramekins or custard cups in a roasting pan or baking dish.

◆§ In a medium bowl, beat the butter, sweetener, and lime zest until smooth. Beat in the egg yolks, almond meal, and wheat gluten. Stir in the lime juice, cream, and water. It's okay if the mixture looks curdled.

◆§ In a clean bowl with clean beaters, beat the egg whites until stiff peaks form. Fold into the lime mixture. Divide among the ramekins. Pour hot water into the larger pan to come halfway up the sides of the ramekins.

◆§ Bake for 30 to 35 minutes, or until puffed and golden brown but still jiggly in the middle. Serve warm, at room temperature, or chilled.

Per serving. Effective carbohydrates: 3.4 g; Carbohydrates: 3.8 g; Fiber: 0.4 g; Protein: 6.1 g; Fat: 20.6 g; Calories: 219
Made with Splenda only: Add 1 g carbohydrates

STOCKING UP:
ESSENTIALS FOR LOW-CARB BAKING

Low-carb baking is strange territory to the uninitiated. All these odd potions and powders! Without flour and sugar, the low-carb baker must mimic their action and results. There is no straight-across-the-board substitute for flour, but once you start using low-carb ingredients and gain an understanding of how they work—experimentation is a great teacher—you'll start fitting it all together and using existing low-carb recipes as a springboard for your own wild and wonderful creations.

Almond meal. This is also called almond flour or ground almonds. But it all amounts to the same thing: almonds that have been finely ground. You can do this yourself by pulsing small amounts of the nut in a canister-type coffee grinder. Although you could use a food processor, it's too easy to turn the nuts into almond butter, so you must proceed carefully. Other nuts can also be made into meal. I think you get the best flavor results by combining them with equal parts almond meal rather than using them full strength.

Butter, unsalted. I've been using unsalted butter for so long that I find regular butter to taste overly salty. There are a few reasons why I like to use unsalted butter. First, it's fresher. Salt is a preservative, so you don't know how long salted butter has been hanging around. Salt attracts water, so there is less pure fat and more water in salted butter. And most important, I like to control the salt I'm putting into food.

Cocoa nibs. These are the low-carb chocolate chips! Cocoa nibs are roasted cocoa beans separated from their husks and broken into small bits. They add crunchiness and subtle chocolate flavor to baked goods and can even be used in savory dishes. I add them to chocolate desserts for an extra chocolate boost. One tablespoon goes a long way.

Chocolate, unsweetened. Like good-quality extracts, good-quality chocolate can make all the difference in your desserts. It's deeper and richer in flavor and smoother in texture than regular grocery store unsweetened chocolate. Good brands are Scharffen Berger, Valrhona, and Callebaut.

Cocoa butter. Cocoa butter is pure fat, expressed from cocoa beans during the chocolate- and cocoa-making process. Sadly, it doesn't taste like chocolate! I use it to provide a better mouthfeel in chocolate desserts. Because there is no sugar, chocolate desserts lack the smoothness that sugar provides, and cocoa butter does an admirable job of replacing the smoothness.

Cocoa powder. There are two types of cocoa powder: Dutch-processed and natural unsweetened. Because of their differences, do not substitute one for the other in recipes.

The Dutch version has undergone a technique that alkalizes the cocoa powder to neutralize its acids. Because it is neutral and does not react with baking soda (which needs an acid), it

must be used in recipes calling for baking powder—unless there are other acidic ingredients used in sufficient quantities such as buttermilk or sour cream. It has a reddish-brown color and mild flavor, and it's easy to dissolve in liquids. Droste, Fry's, Lindt, and Valrhona are all examples of Dutch-process cocoa.

Natural unsweetened cocoa powder tastes bitter and gives a deep chocolate flavor to baked goods. Its intense flavor is suited for use in brownies, cookies, and some chocolate cakes.

Extracts. Good-quality extracts make a huge difference to the flavor of low-carb baked goods and sweets. Buy extracts that are labeled pure, not imitation. Larger natural food stores will have a good selection as will gourmet food stores.

I can't hide the fact that low-carb desserts and sweets are an expensive endeavor, so why not carry through with the best-tasting extracts?

There's nothing like a pure vanilla extract. Mexican, Madagascar, and Tahitian all have different but equal qualities. You can also get whole vanilla beans, as well as vanilla paste.

Boyajian makes excellent extracts. The fruit ones and citrus oils are brilliant. Another company that makes excellent extracts is Star Kay White. Their chocolate extract is superb.

Soy protein isolate. This begins as soy flakes, which are washed to remove most of the carbohydrate content. The protein that's left from the process is then dried, producing an ingredient that is 90 percent protein based on dry weight. It's much higher in protein than soy flour or soy protein concentrate. Because of its low-carbohydrate content, it's an excellent baking ingredient.

Vital wheat gluten. This is the protein of wheat. It makes dough strong and gives it the ability to rise. When you knead bread or beat a batter, you're activating the gluten. Vital wheat gluten cannot be used as a substitute for flour but is great used in conjunction with other ingredients such as soy protein isolate, whey protein isolate, almond meal, oat flour, and flaxseed meal.

The wheat gluten you use should be 80 percent gluten. It weighs in at 24 g of carbohydrates per cup (240 ml), with no fiber. A widely available and reliable brand is Bob's Red Mill Vital Wheat Gluten.

Xanthan gum and guar gum. You've probably seen the names on ice cream, yogurt, and salad dressing. They're commonly used in the food industry as an emulsifier and stabilizer to thicken gravies, sauces, and stir-fries.

Xanthan gum is made by fermenting corn sugar with a microbe. It contains no carbohydrates. A popular low-carb thickener contains a combination of xanthan and guar gums. Unlike guar gum, xanthan gum does not require heat to thicken, and I find the texture to be less waxy than guar gum used alone. You can find it in natural food and bulk stores. These thickeners are best used by combining them with liquids in a blender or with a hand-held blender. In general, ¼ tsp. (1.2 ml) is usually enough to thicken 1 cup (240 ml) of liquid.

NO-BAKE VANCOUVER CHEESECAKE

Makes 16 servings

I like really light cheesecakes and was very pleased with the way this turned out. This was made to celebrate the first potluck of the Vancouver lowcarber.org group in 1992, hence the name. The nutty crust was compared to the middle of Almond Roca. Browning the almonds well and cooking the butter until browned really add an extra dimension of taste.

CRUST

1¼ cups	(300 ml)	almonds, toasted
3 Tbsp.	(45 ml)	unsalted butter
1½ tsp.	(7.5 ml)	*each* Splenda and Canadian Sugar Twin *or* 2 Tbsp. (30 ml) Splenda
		Large pinch of ground cinnamon

FILLING

2 cups	(480 ml)	whipping cream
5 tsp.	(25 ml)	unflavored gelatin
3		large eggs, separated
2 lb.	(908 g)	cream cheese, at room temperature
¼ cup	(60 ml)	*each* Splenda and Canadian Sugar Twin *or* 1 cup (240 ml) Splenda
2 tsp.	(10 ml)	pure vanilla extract

•§ Line the bottom of a 10-inch (25-cm) springform pan with parchment paper and coat the inside of the pan with butter.

•§ *To make the crust:* Place the almonds in a food processor and pulse until half of them are finely chopped and half remain coarse.

•§ Melt the butter in a medium heavy saucepan over medium heat and cook until it turns a rich, nutty-smelling brown. Add the almonds, sweetener, and cinnamon. Stir well and press into the bottom of the prepared pan. Refrigerate.

•§ *To make the filling:* Place 1 cup (240 ml) of the cream in a heatproof bowl and sprinkle with the gelatin. Let sit for 2 minutes to soften. Beat in the egg yolks. Place the bowl over

a pan of simmering water and beat the mixture with a whisk until it thickens and increases slightly in volume. Do not let the water touch the bottom of the pan. Remove from the heat and let cool slightly.

◦§ In a large bowl, beat the cream cheese until smooth. Beat in the sweetener and vanilla. Beat in the gelatin mixture.

◦§ In another bowl, beat the remaining 1 cup (240 ml) cream until stiff. Fold into the cream cheese mixture.

◦§ In a clean bowl with clean beaters, beat the egg whites until medium-firm peaks form. Fold into the cream cheese mixture.

◦§ Pour into the prepared crust and chill overnight. To remove cleanly from the pan, rinse a cloth in very hot water and wrap it around the outside of the pan. Let sit until the cloth gets cold; repeat. You now should be able to remove the ring easily from the cheesecake.

Per serving. Effective carbohydrates: 4.5 g; Carbohydrates: 5.8 g; Fiber: 1.3 g; Protein: 8.7 g; Fat: 39.6 g; Calories: 408 Made with Splenda only: Add 1 g carbohydrates

VARIATIONS:

Strawberry or Raspberry Cheesecake: Use 1½ lb. (680 g) cream cheese. Add 1 cup (240 ml) pureed strawberries or raspberries after you have added the gelatin mixture to the cream cheese. If you have it, use ½ tsp. (2.5 ml) Boyajian strawberry or raspberry extract.

Per serving (strawberry). Effective carbohydrates: 4.6 g; Carbohydrates: 6.3 g; Fiber: 1.7 g; Protein: 7.8 g; Fat: 34.7 g; Calories: 362; Made with Splenda only: Add 1 g carbohydrates

Per serving (raspberry). Effective carbohydrates: 4.4 g; Carbohydrates: 6.4 g; Fiber: 2 g; Protein: 7.8 g; Fat: 34.7 g; Calories: 362; Made with Splenda only: Add 1 g carbohydrates

Maple Walnut Cheesecake: Use 1¼ cups (300 ml) walnut pieces for the crust. Add 2 tsp. (10 ml) pure maple extract to the filling.

Per serving. Effective carbohydrates: 4.2 g; Carbohydrates: 4.8 g; Fiber: 0.6 g; Protein: 7.8 g; Fat: 40.1 g; Calories: 403 Made with Splenda only: Add 1 g carbohydrates

(continued on page 278)

Peanut Butter Cheesecake: Use 1½ lb. (680 g) cream cheese; add 1 cup (240 ml) natural peanut butter to it, beating until smooth. Replace the almonds in the crust with 1¼ cups (300 ml) roasted peanuts.

Per serving. Effective carbohydrates: 6.7 g, Carbohydrates: 8.7 g; Fiber: 2 g; Protein: 11.8 g; Fat: 42.6 g; Calories: 457
Made with Splenda only: Add 1 g carbohydrates

Lime and Coconut Cheesecake: Replace the cream for softening the gelatin with 1 cup (240 ml) unsweetened coconut milk. Add 2 tsp. (10 ml) finely grated lime rind to the filling and replace the vanilla with 1 tsp. pure coconut extract. Replace the almonds in the crust with 1¼ cups (300 ml) unsweetened shredded coconut.

Per serving. Effective carbohydrates: 5.8 g; Carbohydrates: 6.7 g; Fiber: 0.9 g; Protein: 6.7 g; Fat: 34.6 g; Calories: 349
Made with Splenda only: Add 1 g carbohydrates

RHUBARB COMPOTE

Makes 8 servings

Rhubarb is a nice dessert with a bit of cream. You can spice it up with cinnamon, if you like. I like it on the tangy side, so you may want to add more sweetener to this recipe.

1 lb.	**(454 g)**	**fresh young rhubarb with pink stems**
2 Tbsp.	**(30 ml)**	**water**
2 Tbsp.	**(30 ml)**	*each* **Splenda and Canadian Sugar Twin** *or* **½ cup (120 ml) Splenda**

◦§ Trim the leaves and the lower end of the stalks from the rhubarb. Cut the stalks into 1-inch (2.5-cm) pieces. Place in a noncorrodible saucepan with the water. Cover and set over low heat. Stew gently for 30 to 45 minutes, until soft. Stir in the sweetener. Cool and refrigerate.

Per serving. Effective carbohydrates: 2.3 g; Carbohydrates: 3.3 g; Fiber: 1 g; Protein: 0.5 g; Fat: 0.1 g; Calories: 15
Made with Splenda only: Add 1.3 g carbohydrates

BE FOOL-ISH!

Fools are old-fashioned desserts made by folding together fruit puree and whipped cream. They have a tangy balance of creamy, sweet, and sour. You can make lovely fools with drained Rhubarb Compote or sweetened pureed strawberries, raspberries, blueberries, blackberries, or gooseberries.

STRAWBERRY SHORTCAKES WITH MASCARPONE BALSAMIC CREAM

Makes 8 servings

The mascarpone cream is out of this world, but you can use sweetened whipped cream with the shortcakes if you like. Feel free to use any berry that's in season.

6 Tbsp.	(90 ml)	unsalted butter, at room temperature
4 oz.	(112 g)	cream cheese, at room temperature
4		large eggs
1 Tbsp.	(15 ml)	*each* Splenda and Canadian Sugar Twin *or* ¼ cup (60 ml) Splenda
1½ tsp.	(7.5 ml)	pure vanilla extract
¼ cup	(60 ml)	sour cream
1½ cups	(360 ml)	almond meal (finely ground almonds)
⅓ cup	(80 ml)	soy protein isolate
⅓ cup	(80 ml)	vital wheat gluten
1 tsp.	(5 ml)	baking powder
½ tsp.	(2.5 ml)	baking soda
⅛ tsp.	(0.6 ml)	sea salt
		Mascarpone Balsamic Cream (page 281)
3 cups	(720 ml)	sliced strawberries

◦§ Preheat the oven to 350°F (175°C). Line a baking sheet with parchment paper.

◦§ In a large bowl, beat the butter and cream cheese until smooth. Beat in the eggs, 1 at a time. Beat in the sweetener, vanilla, and sour cream.

◦§ In a medium bowl, mix the almond meal, soy protein, wheat gluten, baking powder, baking soda, and salt. Add to the cream cheese mixture and beat to mix well.

-◈ Place scant ¼-cup (60-ml) scoops of the mixture on the prepared baking sheet; you should have 16. With a wet fork, flatten the mounds out into 2½-inch (7.5-cm) rounds.

-◈ Bake for 10 to 12 minutes, or until browned.

-◈ For each serving, place 1 shortcake on a plate and top with cream and berries. Cover with a second shortcake, more cream, and then more berries.

Per serving. Effective carbohydrates: 9.3 g; Carbohydrates: 12.4 g; Fiber: 3.1 g; Protein: 19.2 g; Fat: 55.2 g; Calories: 608
Made with Splenda only: Add 1 g carbohydrates

MASCARPONE BALSAMIC CREAM

Makes 8 servings

This is so much more interesting than plain whipped cream. The only trick to making this is to beat the mixture until light and fluffy, but not to the point where it will curdle. This is wonderful on fresh berries and fruit.

1½ cups	(360 ml)	**mascarpone**
1 Tbsp.	(15 ml)	*each* **Splenda and Canadian Sugar Twin** *or* **¼ cup (60 ml) Splenda**
1 cup	(240 ml)	**whipping cream**
1 Tbsp.	(15 ml)	**balsamic vinegar**
2 tsp.	(10 ml)	**pure vanilla extract**

-◈ In a medium bowl, beat the mascarpone and sweetener until smooth. Slowly beat in the cream, stopping to scrape down the bowl occasionally, and beat until the mixture turns light and fluffy. Do not overbeat. Stir in the vinegar and vanilla.

Per serving. Effective carbohydrates: 1.2 g; Carbohydrates: 1.2 g; Fiber: 0 g; Protein: 1.6 g; Fat: 10.4 g; Calories: 104
Made with Splenda only: Add 1 g carbohydrates

BASIC ALMOND CRUST

Makes 1 crust

This is a perfect crust for cheesecakes or pies! I like to use almond meal (finely ground almonds) because of its neutral flavor. But depending on what you are making, you can replace half of the almonds with another nut. Hazelnut, pecan, walnut, and even coconut are all good meals to use.

2 cups	(480 ml)	almond meal (finely ground almonds)
1½ tsp.	(7.5 ml)	*each* Splenda and Canadian Sugar Twin *or* 2 Tbsp. (30 ml) Splenda
¼ tsp.	(1.2 ml)	sea salt
2 Tbsp.	(30 ml)	unsalted butter, melted
1		large egg white

◦§ Preheat the oven to 350°F (175°C). Line the bottom of a 9-inch (22.5-cm) springform pan or 8-inch (20-cm) pie pan with parchment paper. This will prevent the crust from sticking.

◦§ In a medium bowl, mix the almond meal, sweetener, and salt. Add the butter and mix well.

◦§ In a small bowl, beat the egg white with a whisk until foamy and add to the almond mixture. Stir well and pat into the prepared pan.

◦§ Bake for 10 to 15 minutes, or until a light golden brown. (If the crust rises up, just poke it with a fork and press it down.) Let cool.

Per crust. Effective carbohydrates: 17.9 g; Carbohydrates: 37 g; Fiber: 19.1 g; Protein: 42.8 g; Fat: 117.8 g; Calories: 1,356 Made with Splenda only: Add 1.9 g carbohydrates

VARIATIONS

Graham Wafer-y Crust: Add ½ tsp. (2.5 ml) cinnamon to the dry ingredients.

Chocolate Crust: Add 2 Tbsp. (30 ml) cocoa powder to the dry ingredients.

Crunchy Crust: Replace half of the almond meal with sliced almonds.

AVOCADO AND ESPRESSO MOUSSE

Makes 6 servings

I know what you're thinking: This is a bizarre combination. But it really is very tasty. The avocado becomes a background note and texture, and it takes the edge off the espresso.

Cocoa nibs are roasted and coarsely cracked cocoa beans that can be purchased at gourmet food stores.

2		**ripe Haas avocados, pitted and peeled**
1 Tbsp.	**(15 ml)**	**instant espresso granules**
4 tsp.	**(20 ml)**	***each* Splenda and Canadian Sugar Twin** *or* **⅓ cup (80 ml) Splenda**
2 tsp.	**(10 ml)**	**pure vanilla extract**
¼ cup	**(60 ml)**	**mascarpone**
1½ cups	**(360 ml)**	**whipping cream**
1 Tbsp.	**(15 ml)**	**cocoa nibs (optional)**

•§ In a food processor or with a hand-held blender, puree the avocados, espresso, sweetener, and vanilla until smooth. Add the mascarpone and process until blended.

•§ In a large bowl, beat the cream until medium-firm peaks form. Fold into the avocado mixture and add the cocoa nibs (if using). Spoon into 6 dessert glasses and chill.

Per serving. Effective carbohydrates: 4.3 g; Carbohydrates: 7.1 g; Fiber: 2.8 g; Protein: 3.7 g; Fat: 35.4 g; Calories: 351
Made with Splenda only: Add 1 g carbohydrates

BERRY LEMON PIE

Makes 8 servings

You can use whatever berry—or combination of berries—strikes your fancy. The almond crust variation using sliced almonds is especially nice with this.

		Lemon Curd (see below), cooled
		Basic Almond Crust (page 282), baked and cooled
1 cup	(240 ml)	sliced strawberries
1½ cups	(360 ml)	whipping cream
1½ tsp.	(7.5 ml)	*each* Splenda and Canadian Sugar Twin *or* 2 Tbsp. (30 ml) Splenda

⋖ Preheat the oven to 350°F (175°C).

⋖ Spread the lemon curd in the crust and smooth the top. Bake for 30 minutes. Cool completely. Refrigerate for at least 4 hours or overnight.

⋖ When ready to serve, spread the strawberries over the top of the pie. Whip the cream and sweetener to firm peaks and pour over the strawberries. Serve immediately.

Per serving. Effective carbohydrates: 7.7 g; Carbohydrates: 10.8 g; Fiber: 3.1 g; Protein: 9.6 g; Fat: 50.4 g; Calories: 529
Made with Splenda only: Add 2.1 g carbohydrates

LEMON CURD

Makes about 2 cups (480 g)

4		large eggs
¼ cup	(60 ml)	*each* Splenda and Canadian Sugar Twin *or* 1 cup (240 ml) Splenda
⅔ cup	(160 ml)	freshly squeezed lemon juice
		Grated rind of 2 lemons
12 Tbsp.	(180 ml)	unsalted butter, cut into small pieces (1½ sticks)

◦ In a large bowl, beat the eggs and sweetener until doubled in volume and light in color. Stir in the lemon juice and rind. Transfer to the top of a double boiler.

◦ Whisking constantly, cook over simmering water until thickened, about 5 minutes; periodically, use a heatproof rubber spatula to scrape the curd from around the sides of the pan. Remove from the heat and stir in the butter until melted. Cool and refrigerate.

Per 2 cups (480 g). Effective carbohydrates: 25.3 g; Carbohydrates: 27.2 g; Fiber: 1.9 g; Protein: 25.9 g; Fat: 153.2 g; Calories: 1,592; made with Splenda only: Add 15 g carbohydrates

GOING TO THE DOGS

If Lassie is losing her lassie-ish figure, maybe some low-carb treats are in order. (You can eat them too, but you probably won't find them as tasty as your canine counterpart does.)

PEANUT BUTTER DOGGY BITES
Makes about 15 bites

Make sure that you get the green stevia powder made from the leaf, not the white powder. The stevia adds a pleasant amount of sweetness that dogs love. You can omit the stevia with no change to the recipe.

½ cup	(120 ml)	natural peanut butter
1		large egg
1 tsp.	(5 ml)	powdered stevia leaf
1 cup	(240 ml)	old-fashioned rolled oats
2 Tbsp.	(30 ml)	flaxseed meal

◦ Preheat the oven to 300°F (150°C).

◦ In a medium bowl, mix the peanut butter, egg, and stevia until smooth. Stir in the oats and flaxseed meal to form a stiff dough. Knead with your hands to combine well. Roll into 1-inch (2.5-cm) balls and place on a baking sheet. They won't spread, so you can place them fairly close. Press down with a fork to flatten. Bake for 15 minutes, until firm.

Per bite. Effective carbohydrates: 4.5 g; Carbohydrates: 6 g; Fiber: 1.5 g; Protein: 3.7 g; Fat: 5 g; Calories: 80

VANILLA PANNA COTTA

Makes 6 servings

Think of ice cream on the verge of melting—that's what panna cotta is. This creamy Italian dessert is one of the most adaptable, because the flavors can be changed to suit your fancy or to complement the rest of the meal. It can be molded in ramekins and turned out onto plates for a fancy presentation or served in wine or champagne glasses.

Serve with fresh berries—for a real treat, make them strawberries splashed with balsamic vinegar. Go whole hog and serve with Lemon Curd (pages 284 to 285) plus fresh berries. The recipe can easily be halved or doubled and can be made the day before.

Note: The vanilla bean gives this dessert exceptional flavor, but you can use 2 tsp. (10 ml) pure vanilla extract instead.

¼ cup	**(60 ml)**	**water**
2½ tsp.	**(12.5 ml)**	**unflavored gelatin**
3 cups	**(720 ml)**	**whipping cream**
½		**vanilla bean**
2 Tbsp.	**(30 ml)**	***each* Splenda and Canadian Sugar Twin *or* ½ cup (120 ml) Splenda**

◦ᔥ Place the water in a small bowl and sprinkle with the gelatin. Let sit for 2 minutes to soften.

◦ᔥ Place 1½ cups (360 ml) of the cream in a medium saucepan. Slit the vanilla bean lengthwise and add to the pan. Bring to a boil, add the gelatin, and remove from the heat. Stir until the gelatin dissolves.

◦ᔥ Remove the vanilla bean and scrape the seeds into the mixture with the tip of a small knife. Stir in the sweetener and the remaining 1½ cups (360 ml) cream.

◦ᔥ Pour into 6 ramekins, dessert dishes, or wine glasses. Refrigerate until set, about 4 hours.

◦ᔥ If using ramekins, unmold them: Dip each ramekin in hot water nearly to its rim for 30 seconds. Run a very thin knife around the inside edge and place a dessert plate over the

top. Turn upside down and vigorously shake the ramekin while holding the plate securely. The panna cotta will fall out onto the plate.

Per serving. Effective carbohydrates: 4.5 g; Carbohydrates: 4.5 g; Fiber: 0 g; Protein: 3.3 g; Fat: 44.4 g; Calories: 423
Made with Splenda only: Add 1.3 g carbohydrates

VARIATIONS

Pumpkin Panna Cotta: In the "olden days," one of my favorite combinations was Baskin-Robbins pumpkin ice cream with chocolate brownie ice cream! I can relive the experience by pairing this with Chocolate Sauce (page 261). Reduce the whipping cream to 2 cups (480 ml). Whisk the heated mixture into 1 cup (240 ml) canned unsweetened pumpkin puree. Stir in 1 tsp. (5 ml) ground cinnamon, ½ tsp. (2.5 ml) ground ginger, and ¼ tsp. (1.2 ml) freshly grated nutmeg.

Per serving. Effective carbohydrates: 5.7 g; Carbohydrates: 7.1 g; Fiber: 1.4 g; Protein: 2.9 g; Fat: 29.7 g; Calories: 301
Made with Splenda only: Add 1.3 g carbohydrates

Chai Panna Cotta: Using brewed tea in place of some of the cream makes the panna cotta lighter and less rich. Replace 1½ cups (360 ml) of the whipping cream with an equal amount of strongly brewed chai tea. Perfect after an Indian meal! You can use other types of tea—a super-fragrant Earl Grey paired with Chocolate Sauce (page 261) has a taste reminiscent of chocolate-covered cherries. Panna cotta made with tea is best eaten the day it's made as it tends to get watery if it sits overnight.

Per serving. Effective carbohydrates: 2.3 g; Carbohydrates: 2.3 g; Fiber: 0 g; Protein: 3.3 g; Fat: 22.2 g; Calories: 212
Made with Splenda only: Add 1.3 g carbohydrates

Espresso Panna Cotta with Chocolate Sauce: Add 2 tsp. (10 ml) instant espresso or coffee granules to the cream. Serve with Chocolate Sauce (page 261).

Per serving. Effective carbohydrates: 7.4 g; Carbohydrates: 9.8 g; Fiber: 2.4 g; Protein: 6 g; Fat: 57 g; Calories: 555
Made with Splenda only: Add 1.3 g carbohydrates

CREAM CHEESE, COCONUT, AND LEMON MOUNDS

Makes 20 mounds

Nice little coconutty bites. If you use coconut milk instead of the whipping cream, they will be even more coconutty. Keep the mounds refrigerated or frozen to prevent spoilage—assuming they would last that long!

1 cup	(240 ml)	unsweetened finely shredded coconut
1½ tsp.	(7.5 ml)	*each* Splenda and Canadian Sugar Twin *or* 2 Tbsp. (30 ml) Splenda
½ cup	(120 ml)	whipping cream
½ tsp.	(2.5 ml)	pure vanilla extract
¼ cup	(60 ml)	cream cheese, at room temperature
1		large egg
½ tsp.	(2.5 ml)	finely grated lemon rind

◦§ In a medium bowl, mix the coconut, sweetener, cream, and vanilla. Let sit for 1 hour.

◦§ Preheat the oven to 350°F (175°C). Line a baking sheet with parchment paper.

◦§ Stir the cream cheese into the coconut mixture until blended. Add the egg and mix well. Stir in the lemon rind.

◦§ Drop by level tablespoons (making macaroon-shaped mounds) 2 inches (5 cm) apart on the prepared baking sheet. Bake for about 15 minutes, until the tops are lightly speckled with brown.

Per mound. Effective carbohydrates: 0.6 g; Carbohydrates: 1 g; Fiber: 0.4 g; Protein: 0.8 g; Fat: 5.4 g; Calories: 54
Made with Splenda only: Add 0.1 g carbohydrates

COFFEE JELLY

Makes 4 servings

This is a very popular dessert that I came to know in Japan. My version has cream in it, which makes it taste more like a latte. In Japan, it was served with whipped cream on top. If you don't have access to brewed espresso, dissolve 2 tsp. (10 ml) instant coffee or instant espresso granules in ½ cup (120 ml) boiling water.

2 Tbsp.	(30 ml)	plus 1½ cups (360 ml) water
2½ tsp.	(12.5 ml)	unflavored gelatin
1 Tbsp.	(15 ml)	*each* Splenda and Canadian Sugar Twin *or* ¼ cup (60 ml) Splenda
½ cup	(120 ml)	brewed espresso
½ cup	(120 ml)	whipping cream
		Whipped cream and whole coffee beans (optional)

◦§ Place 2 Tbsp. (30 ml) of the water in a small bowl and sprinkle with the gelatin. Let sit for 2 minutes to soften.

◦§ Heat ½ cup (120 ml) water in a small saucepan until hot but not boiling. Add the gelatin and remove from the heat. Stir until the gelatin dissolves. Add the sweetener, espresso, and the remaining 1 cup (240 ml) water. Stir well.

◦§ Transfer ¾ cup (180 ml) of the espresso mixture to a small bowl. Cover and refrigerate.

◦§ Stir the cream into the remaining espresso mixture. Pour into 4 small dessert dishes. Cover and refrigerate for at least 4 hours.

◦§ Remove the plain jelly from the bowl and cut into ½-inch (1.2-cm) cubes. Pile onto the jelly in the dessert dishes. If desired, garnish with whipped cream and a coffee bean or two.

Per serving. Effective carbohydrates: 1.7 g; Carbohydrates: 1.7 g; Fiber: 0 g; Protein: 1.9 g; Fat: 11.1 g; Calories: 112
Made with Splenda only: Add 0.2 g carbohydrates

FRESH BERRIES
WITH COOL CHAMPAGNE SABAYON

Makes 6 servings

A wonderfully festive way of serving fresh berries. Use any combination of summer berries that you like. Sabayon is a French relative of the Italian zabaglione, a warm dessert of whipped egg yolks and Marsala.

Don't let a lack of champagne prevent you from making this. White wine or sparkling wine is quite acceptable as well!

4		**large egg yolks**
2 Tbsp.	**(30 ml)**	*each* **Splenda and Canadian Sugar Twin** *or* **½ cup (120 ml) Splenda**
½ cup	**(120 ml)**	**dry champagne**
1 cup	**(240 ml)**	**whipping cream**
1 pint	**(475 ml)**	**raspberries**
1 pint	**(475 ml)**	**strawberries, quartered**

◆ In a large heatproof bowl, whisk the egg yolks, sweetener, and champagne until smooth. Place over a pan of gently simmering water without letting the bottom of the bowl touch the water. Whisk until thick and increased in volume.

◆ Place the bowl in a larger bowl of ice and let stand until cool, whisking occasionally. Cover and refrigerate.

◆ When you are ready to serve, whip the cream into soft peaks and fold into the champagne mixture. Divide the berries among 6 wine glasses and top with the sabayon.

Per serving. Effective carbohydrates: 6.6 g; Carbohydrates: 10.5 g; Fiber: 3.9 g; Protein: 4 g; Fat: 18.5 g; Calories: 229
Made with Splenda only: Add 1.3 g carbohydrates

SILKEN CHOCOLATE PUDDING

Makes 8 servings

Soft tofu makes wonderful desserts and is virtually undetectable in the finished product. If you like a lighter chocolate flavor, decrease the chocolate to 2 oz. (56 g).

Note: *The chocolate extract made by Star Kay White is an excellent product that will give all your chocolate desserts a real boost in flavor—but the pudding will be just fine if you don't use it.*

½ cup	(120 ml)	whipping cream
½ cup	(120 ml)	water
		Pinch of sea salt
2		large egg yolks
3 oz.	(84 g)	unsweetened chocolate, finely chopped
5⅓ Tbsp.	(80 ml)	unsalted butter, at room temperature
1 10-oz.	(285-g)	package soft tofu, drained
2 Tbsp.	(30 ml)	*each* Splenda and Canadian Sugar Twin *or* ½ cup (120 ml) Splenda
1 Tbsp.	(15 ml)	pure chocolate extract (optional)
1 tsp.	(5 ml)	pure vanilla extract

◦§ Bring the cream, water, and salt to a boil in a small saucepan.

◦§ In a small bowl, whisk the egg yolks to blend well. Remove the cream from the heat and slowly whisk a few big spoonfuls into the yolks to warm them. Then whisk in the remaining cream. Pour into the saucepan.

◦§ Place over low heat and stir constantly with a heatproof rubber spatula until the cream thickens. Immediately add the chocolate and butter. Remove from the heat and stir constantly until the chocolate and butter are melted. It will look curdled and that's fine.

◦§ In a food processor, combine the tofu, sweetener, and extracts; blend until smooth. Add the chocolate mixture and blend again until well-combined. Transfer to a bowl and chill for at least 4 hours.

Per serving. Effective carbohydrates: 3.5 g; Carbohydrates: 5.5 g; Fiber: 2 g; Protein: 4.6 g; Fat: 21.5 g; Calories: 220
Made with Splenda only: Add 1 g carbohydrates

STAINED GLASS WINDOW CAKE

Makes 12 servings

While this is in no way a new dessert, it's certainly a time-tested standard. My mother used to make it in the late 1960s with a graham cracker crust. If you would like a crust, see Basic Almond Crust (page 282).

Use whatever colors and flavors of Jell-O that strike your fancy.

1		package (4-serving size) sugar-free raspberry Jell-O
1		package (4-serving size) sugar-free orange Jell-O
1		package (4-serving size) sugar-free lime Jell-O
4½ cups	(1.1 L)	plus ¼ cup (60 ml) water
1 Tbsp.	(15 ml)	unflavored gelatin
2 cups	(480 ml)	whipping cream
1 tsp.	(5 ml)	*each* Splenda and Canadian Sugar Twin *or* 4 tsp. (20 ml) Splenda

◆§ Pour each flavor of Jell-O into a separate bowl and stir ½ cup (120 ml) cold water into each. Bring 3 cups (720 ml) water to a boil. Add 1 cup (240 ml) to each bowl and stir until the Jell-O dissolves.

◆§ Place the bowls in the refrigerator and chill until set, about 2 hours. Remove the Jell-O from the bowls and cut roughly into ½-inch (1.2-cm) cubes.

◆§ Place the remaining ¼ cup (60 ml) water in a small bowl and sprinkle with the unflavored gelatin. Let sit for 2 minutes to soften. Melt the softened gelatin over simmering water or in the microwave.

◆§ In a medium bowl, beat the cream and sweetener until soft peaks form. Add the gelatin and whip until stiff peaks form.

◆§ Fold the Jell-O cubes into this mixture. Pour into a 10-inch (25-cm) springform pan or a 13 × 9-inch (32.5 × 22.5-cm) baking dish. Chill until firm, about 2 hours.

Per serving. Effective carbohydrates: 1.2 g; Carbohydrates: 1.2 g; Fiber: 0 g; Protein: 2.3 g; Fat: 1.2 g; Calories: 150
Made with Splenda only: Add 0.1 g carbohydrates

TIRAMISU

Makes 8 generous servings

The dessert that makes strong men and women weep! A delicious end to any meal.
    Choose a large straight-sided dish, such as a soufflé dish, to assemble the tiramisu.
A straight-sided glass bowl will really show it off!

5		large eggs, separated
2 Tbsp.	(30 ml)	*each* Splenda and Canadian Sugar Twin *or* ½ cup (120 ml) Splenda
2½ cups	(600 ml)	mascarpone
		Basic Almond Sponge Cake (page 295), cooled
½ cup	(120 ml)	strong brewed coffee or espresso
3 Tbsp.	(45 ml)	rum
½ cup	(120 ml)	Dutch-processed cocoa

◦§ Place the egg yolks and sweetener in a large bowl and beat with an electric mixer until thick and lemon-colored. Add the mascarpone and beat on low speed, scraping down the bowl as needed, until incorporated. Do not overbeat or the mixture will curdle.

◦§ In a clean bowl with clean beaters, beat the egg whites until soft peaks form. Stir one-quarter of the whites into the mascarpone mixture, then fold in the remaining whites.

◦§ Cut the cake into 16 fingers (cut it in half crosswise, then lengthwise into 8 slices per half). Combine the coffee and rum in a shallow dish. Place the cocoa in a sieve over a bowl.

◦§ Sprinkle the bottom of a straight-sided serving dish lightly with cocoa. Quickly dip a few of the cake fingers into the coffee mixture and line the bottom of the dish. Do not get them too wet or your tiramisu will be runny. Spread on one-quarter of the mascarpone mixture and dust the top with cocoa.

◦§ Repeat the process two or three times so you have three or four layers. End with a sprinkling of cocoa. Cover and refrigerate overnight.

Per serving. Effective carbohydrates: 4.7 g; Carbohydrates: 7.9 g; Fiber: 3.2 g; Protein: 13.8 g; Fat: 40.8 g; Calories: 452
Made with Splenda only: Add 1 g carbohydrates

BASIC ALMOND SPONGE CAKE

Makes 1 cake

This sponge can be the base for all kinds of delectable treats. Layer it with whipped cream and strawberries for a shortcake. Or layer it with Lemon Curd (pages 284 to 285) and frost with whipped cream.

1¼ cups	(300 ml)	almond meal (finely ground almonds)
1 tsp.	(5 ml)	baking powder
¼ tsp.	(1.2 ml)	sea salt
6		large eggs, at room temperature
2 Tbsp.	(30 ml)	*each* Splenda and Canadian Sugar Twin *or* ½ cup (120 ml) Splenda
1 tsp.	(5 ml)	pure vanilla extract

◦§ Preheat the oven to 350°F (175°C). Butter a 15 × 10-inch (37.5 × 25-cm) jelly roll pan. Line with parchment paper and butter again.

◦§ In a small bowl, mix the almond meal, baking powder, and salt.

◦§ Place the eggs and sweetener in a large bowl. With an electric mixer, beat until thick, light, and tripled in volume, 8 to 10 minutes. Beat in the vanilla. Fold in the almond mixture. Spread evenly in the prepared pan.

◦§ Bake for 20 to 25 minutes, until the top springs back when pressed lightly. Cool in the pan on a wire rack.

Per cake. Effective carbohydrates: 19.7 g; Carbohydrates: 29.5 g; Fiber: 9.8 g; Protein: 62.6 g; Fat: 93.4 g; Calories: 1,176
Made with Splenda only: Add 7.5 g carbohydrates

PUMPKIN CHIFFON PIE

Makes 8 generous servings

I grew up with pumpkin chiffon pie that my mother made with Jell-O Instant Vanilla Pudding and Dream Whip. So for me, a chiffon-style pumpkin pie is the ultimate.

To toast the nuts, spread them on a baking sheet and bake at 350°F (175°C) for 8 minutes.

CRUST

4 Tbsp.	(60 ml)	unsalted butter
¾ cup	(180 ml)	almonds, toasted
¾ cup	(180 ml)	hazelnuts, toasted
6 Tbsp.	(90 ml)	plain whey protein isolate
1 tsp.	(5 ml)	*each* Splenda and Canadian Sugar Twin *or* 4 tsp. (20 ml) Splenda
		Pinch of sea salt
¾ tsp.	(3.7 ml)	ground ginger
½ tsp.	(2.5 ml)	pure vanilla extract

FILLING

¼ cup	(60 ml)	water
2½ tsp.	(12.5 ml)	unflavored gelatin
3 Tbsp.	(45 ml)	each Splenda and Canadian Sugar Twin or ¾ cup (180 ml) Splenda
1½ cups	(360 ml)	canned unsweetened pumpkin puree
¾ tsp.	(3.7 ml)	ground cinnamon
½ tsp.	(2.5 ml)	ground ginger
½ tsp.	(2.5 ml)	freshly grated nutmeg
¼ tsp.	(1.2 ml)	sea salt
1 tsp.	(5 ml)	pure vanilla extract
3		large eggs, separated
2 cups	(480 ml)	whipping cream
¼ tsp.	(1.2 ml)	cream of tartar

◦§ Line the bottom of a 9-inch (22.5-cm) pie pan with parchment paper.

◦§ *To make the crust:* Melt the butter in a small saucepan over medium-heat and cook until colored a deep brown. Remove from the heat.

(continued on page 298)

• In a food processor, coarsely grind the almonds and transfer to a large bowl. Coarsely grind the hazelnuts and add to the bowl. Mix in the whey protein, sweetener, salt, ginger, and vanilla. Add the butter and mix well. Press evenly into the prepared pie pan. Chill.

• *To make the filling:* Place the water in a small heatproof bowl and sprinkle with the gelatin. Let sit for 2 minutes to soften. Melt the softened gelatin over simmering water or in the microwave.

• If using Splenda and Sugar Twin, mix them in a cup.

• In a food processor, combine the pumpkin, cinnamon, ginger, nutmeg, salt, vanilla, egg yolks, softened gelatin, ½ cup (120 ml) of the cream, and ¼ cup (60 ml) of the mixed sweeteners or ½ cup (120 ml) of the Splenda. Blend until smooth. Transfer to a medium saucepan and cook, stirring constantly, over medium-high heat until the mixture just starts to splutter.

• Return the pumpkin mixture to the food processor and blend again until smooth. Transfer to a bowl and let stand at room temperature, stirring frequently, until cool.

• In a medium bowl, beat the egg whites until foamy. Add the cream of tartar and the remaining 2 Tbsp. (30 ml) mixed sweeteners or ¼ cup (60 ml) Splenda. Beat until stiff peaks form. Stir one-quarter of the whites into the pumpkin mixture, then fold in the remaining whites. Spread in the prepared crust and refrigerate for at least 2 hours.

• Up to 3 hours before serving, beat the remaining 1½ cups (360 ml) whipping cream to firm peaks and pile on top of the pie.

Per serving. Effective carbohydrates: 9.7 g; Carbohydrates: 14.3 g; Fiber: 4.6 g; Protein: 11.8 g; Fat: 45.3 g; Calories: 495
Made with Splenda only: Add 1 g carbohydrates

ORANGE CREAMSICLE WHIP

Makes 6 servings

It doesn't get much easier than this! You can use other flavors of Jell-O.

3 oz.	(84 g)	cream cheese, at room temperature
1		package (4-serving size) sugar-free orange Jell-O
½ cup	(120 ml)	boiling water
1½ cups	(360 ml)	whipping cream

◦§ In a medium bowl, beat the cream cheese until smooth.

◦§ Place the Jell-O in a small bowl and add the boiling water. Stir until dissolved and cool slightly. Slowly beat the Jell-O into the cream cheese until smooth.

◦§ In another medium bowl, beat the cream until medium-soft peaks form. Fold into the Jell-O mixture. Divide among individual dishes or leave in a big bowl. Refrigerate for at least 1 hour before serving.

Per serving. Effective carbohydrates: 2 g; Carbohydrates: 2 g; Fiber: 0 g; Protein: 2.9 g; Fat: 26.9 g; Calories: 260

WHIPPED CREAM THAT STANDS TALL

There's nothing more disappointing than weepy, soupy whipped cream. Here's how to stabilize that whipped cream so it won't "fall" as it sits in the fridge—and you'll have real whipped cream when you want it.

For each 1 cup (240 ml) of cream, use ½ tsp. (2.5 ml) unflavored gelatin and 1 Tbsp. (15 ml) cold water. Soften the gelatin by sprinkling it over the water and letting it sit for about 2 minutes. Place the container over a small pot of simmering water until the gelatin is melted (or microwave it in 5-second increments).

Whip the cream until it thickens, adding sweetener and vanilla if you like. Add the melted gelatin all at once and continue whipping until the cream forms soft peaks. Cover and refrigerate.

CHOCOLATE BOURBON BREAD PUDDING

Makes 8 slices

A killer. And even yummier with a large dollop of whipped cream.

		Basic Almond Sponge Cake (page 295), cooled
1 cup	(240 ml)	**whipping cream**
6 oz.	(170 g)	**unsweetened chocolate, chopped**
1 cup	(240 ml)	**water**
3 Tbsp.	(45 ml)	*each* **Splenda and Canadian Sugar Twin** *or* **¾ cup (180 ml) Splenda**
¼ cup	(60 ml)	**bourbon**
1 Tbsp.	(15 ml)	**pure vanilla extract**
4		**large eggs**

•§ Cut the cake into 1-inch (2.5-cm) squares. Place in a large bowl.

•§ Preheat the oven to 350°F (175°C). Butter an 8 × 4-inch (20 × 10-cm) loaf pan and line with parchment paper. Butter the parchment.

•§ Bring the cream to a boil in a large saucepan. Remove from the heat and stir in the chocolate until melted. Whisk in the water, sweetener, bourbon, and vanilla. Beat in the eggs, 1 at a time.

•§ Pour the mixture over the cake. Stir well and pour into the prepared loaf pan. Place the loaf pan in a larger pan and pour in hot water to come halfway up the sides of the loaf pan.

•§ Bake for 45 minutes. The center will be slightly soft. Remove the loaf pan from the water bath. Cool completely on a wire rack. To unmold, run a knife around the edges and turn out onto a plate. Slice and serve at room temperature or chilled.

Per slice. Effective carbohydrates: 7.5 g; Carbohydrates: 12 g; Fiber: 4.5 g; Protein: 15 g; Fat: 36.4 g; Calories: 411
Made with Splenda only: Add 1 g carbohydrates

CHILLED LEMON MERINGUE SOUFFLÉ

Makes 6 servings

Named by my friend Adrian because it is light as a feather and oh so good!

½ cup	(120 ml)	**freshly squeezed lemon juice**
2½ tsp.	(12.5 ml)	**unflavored gelatin**
⅔ cup	(160 ml)	**water**
⅓ cup	(80 ml)	**plus ¾ cup (180 ml) whipping cream**
2		**large egg yolks**
2 Tbsp.	(30 ml)	*each* **Splenda and Canadian Sugar Twin** *or* **½ cup (120 ml) Splenda**
2 tsp.	(10 ml)	**grated lemon rind**
5		**large egg whites, at room temperature**

◄§ Place the lemon juice in a small bowl and sprinkle with the gelatin. Let sit for about 2 minutes to soften.

◄§ In a small saucepan, combine the water and ⅓ cup (80 ml) of the cream. Bring to a boil.

◄§ Place the egg yolks and sweetener in a medium bowl and whisk well. Very slowly, dribble in the hot cream, beating constantly. Transfer the mixture back to the pan and cook over medium heat, stirring constantly with a heatproof rubber spatula, until the mixture thickens to the consistency of whipping cream, 4 to 5 minutes.

◄§ Strain through a sieve into a large bowl. Add the gelatin mixture and stir until dissolved. Place in a larger bowl of ice water and stir frequently until cool. Stir in the lemon rind.

◄§ In a clean bowl with clean beaters, beat the egg whites until soft peaks form. Stir one-third of the whites into the custard, then fold in the remaining whites.

◄§ Whip the remaining ¾ cup (180 ml) cream to soft peaks. Fold into the mixture. Transfer to a bowl—glass looks good—or soufflé dish and chill for at least 2 hours.

Per serving. Effective carbohydrates: 4.4 g; Carbohydrates: 4.5 g; Fiber: 0.1 g; Protein: 5.6 g; Fat: 17.6 g; Calories: 195
Made with Splenda only: Add 1 g carbohydrates

ZUCCHINI CAKE

Makes 12 servings

Oh joy! This baby tastes exactly like a carrot cake! It's a big cake that's moist and rich. Bring it to the table to cut it so everyone can ooh and aah over how good it looks.

10 oz.	(285 g)	cream cheese, at room temperature
12 Tbsp.	(180 ml)	unsalted butter, at room temperature (1½ sticks)
5 Tbsp.	(75 ml)	*each* Splenda and Canadian Sugar Twin *or* 1¼ cups (300 ml) Splenda
7		large eggs
1 lb.	(454 g)	zucchini, shredded and squeezed dry
1 Tbsp.	(15 ml)	pure vanilla extract
3 cups	(720 ml)	almond meal (finely ground almonds)
½ cup	(120 ml)	finely chopped walnuts
½ cup	(120 ml)	unsweetened shredded coconut
5 Tbsp.	(75 ml)	ground cinnamon
1 Tbsp.	(15 ml)	Dutch-processed cocoa powder
1½ tsp.	(7.5 ml)	baking powder
½ tsp.	(2.5 ml)	sea salt
		Orange Cream Cheese Frosting (page 304)

⋙ Preheat the oven to 350°F (175°C). Butter two 8-inch (20-cm) cake pans and line the bottoms with parchment paper.

⋙ In a large bowl, beat the cream cheese and butter until smooth. Add the sweetener and beat until combined. Beat in the eggs, 1 at a time, blending well after each addition. Stir in the zucchini and vanilla.

⋙ In a medium bowl, mix the almond meal, walnuts, coconut, cinnamon, cocoa, baking powder, and salt. Stir into the zucchini mixture. Divide the batter evenly between the prepared pans.

(continued on page 304)

⋅⋅⋅ Bake for 35 minutes, or until the layers are firm to the touch. Cool on a wire rack for 5 minutes. Turn the layers out onto the rack to cool completely.

⋅⋅⋅ Place 1 layer on a cake stand or serving platter. Spread the top with frosting. Top with the second layer and frost the top and sides. Refrigerate until the frosting is set. Store, covered, in the refrigerator.

Per serving. Effective carbohydrates: 10.1 g; Carbohydrates: 14.7 g; Fiber: 4.6 g; Protein: 16.9 g; Fat: 71.5 g; Calories: 748 Made with Splenda only: Add 1.4 g carbohydrates

ORANGE CREAM CHEESE FROSTING

Makes about 3 cups

Instead of orange rind as a flavoring, you could use lemon rind, freshly grated ginger, or maple extract to complement whatever cake you're using it on.

18 oz.	(510 g)	cream cheese, at room temperature
16 Tbsp.	(240 ml)	unsalted butter, at room temperature (2 sticks)
3 Tbsp.	(45 ml)	*each* Splenda and Canadian Sugar Twin *or* ¾ cup (180 ml) Splenda
1 Tbsp.	(15 ml)	pure vanilla extract
2 tsp.	(10 ml)	finely grated orange rind

⋅⋅⋅ In a medium bowl, beat the cream cheese and butter until smooth. Beat in the sweetener, vanilla, and orange rind. Continue beating until fluffy.

Per ¼ cup (60 ml). Effective carbohydrates: 2.4 g; Carbohydrates: 2.4 g; Fiber: 0 g; Protein: 3.2 g; Fat: 30.1 g; Calories: 289; made with Splenda only: Add 0.8 g carbohydrates

FERN'S PEANUT BUTTER CUPS

Makes 16 peanut butter cups

Fern, a long-standing lowcarber.org member, keeps these in the freezer because they melt quickly at room temperature. You won't have any problem eating them in the frozen state!

8 Tbsp.	(120 ml)	**unsalted butter (1 stick)**
1 oz.	(28 g)	**unsweetened chocolate**
4 tsp.	(20 ml)	***each* Splenda and Canadian Sugar Twin *or* ⅓ cup (80 ml) Splenda**
1 Tbsp.	(15 ml)	**whipping cream**
¼ cup	(60 ml)	**natural peanut butter**
2 Tbsp.	(30 ml)	**coarsely chopped peanuts**

•ᔓ Place 16 mini paper muffin liners in a mini-muffin tin, plate, or small tray.

•ᔓ Melt the butter and chocolate in a bowl over simmering water or in the microwave. Stir in the sweetener, cream, and peanut butter until smooth. Stir in the peanuts. Divide the mixture evenly between the cups. Freeze until firm.

Per peanut butter cup. Effective carbohydrates: 1 g; Carbohydrates: 1.6 g; Fiber: 0.6 g; Protein: 1.6 g; Fat: 9.6 g; Calories: 94; made with Splenda only: Add 0.3 g carbohydrates

CHOCOLATE: QUALITY RULES!

I can't stress this enough: Use high-quality chocolate. Callebaut, Valrhona, and Scharffen Berger are among the best. The graininess of grocery store brands really becomes apparent when they're used in low-carb cooking. And they just can't compare in depth of flavor with first-rate chocolate.

QUICK BREAD

Makes 16 slices

This basic quick bread can be the springboard for many different loaves, such as the variations given below. Other ideas: blueberry, lemon and poppy seed, maple walnut, cocoa nib, orange, cranberry, and so on. You can also replace half of the almond meal with ground hazelnuts or pecans.

7 oz.	(195 g)	cream cheese, at room temperature
6 Tbsp.	(90 ml)	unsalted butter, at room temperature
3 Tbsp.	(45 ml)	*each* Splenda and Canadian Sugar Twin *or* ¾ cup (180 ml) Splenda
4		large eggs
¼ cup	(60 ml)	sour cream
2 tsp.	(10 ml)	pure vanilla extract
1½ cups	(360 ml)	almond meal (finely ground almonds)
⅓ cup	(80 ml)	soy protein isolate
⅓ cup	(80 ml)	vital wheat gluten
1 tsp.	(5 ml)	baking powder
½ tsp.	(2.5 ml)	sea salt
½ tsp.	(2.5 ml)	baking soda
2 Tbsp.	(30 ml)	sliced almonds

◆§ Preheat the oven to 350°F (175°C). Line an 8 × 4-inch (20 × 10-cm) loaf pan with a length of parchment paper that will cover the bottom and sides. Don't worry about the ends. Coat with nonstick spray.

◆§ In a large bowl, beat the cream cheese and butter until smooth. Beat in the sweetener and eggs, 1 at a time, scraping down the bowl as necessary. Beat in the sour cream and vanilla.

◆§ In a medium bowl, mix the almond meal, soy protein, wheat gluten, baking powder, salt, and baking soda. Add to the cream cheese mixture and beat until smooth.

~§ Scrape into the prepared pan and smooth the top. Sprinkle with the sliced almonds. With a paring knife, cut a slash—go right down to the bottom of the pan—down the middle of the batter lengthwise. This will give the cake a nice mounded top.

~§ Bake for 1 hour, or until a cake tester comes out clean. Cool on a wire rack for 5 minutes, then loosen the sides carefully with a knife. Unmold onto the rack and cool before slicing. Store in the refrigerator.

Per slice. Effective carbohydrates: 2.2 g; Carbohydrates: 3.1 g; Fiber: 0.9 g; Protein: 8 g; Fat: 16.2 g; Calories: 185
Made with Splenda only: Add 0.8 g carbohydrates

VARIATIONS

Banana Bread: Reduce the amount of cream cheese to 4 oz. (112 g). Add ½ cup (120 ml) pureed overripe banana along with the sour cream. Replace the vanilla with 1½ tsp. (7.5 ml) pure banana extract. Omit the sliced almonds.

Per slice. Effective carbohydrates: 5 g; Carbohydrates: 6.2 g; Fiber: 1.2 g; Protein: 7.7 g; Fat: 14.5 g; Calories: 179
Made with Splenda only: Add 0.8 g carbohydrates

Pumpkin Pecan Maple Bread: Reduce the amount of cream cheese to 4 oz. (112 g). Add 1 cup (240 ml) canned unsweetened pumpkin puree along with the sour cream. Replace the vanilla with 2 tsp. (10 ml) pure maple extract. Add 2 tsp. (10 ml) ground cinnamon and ½ tsp. (2.5 ml) freshly grated nutmeg to the almond mixture. Fold in ½ cup (120 ml) coarsely chopped pecans at the end. Omit the sliced almonds.

Per slice. Effective carbohydrates: 3.3 g; Carbohydrates: 5 g; Fiber: 1.7 g; Protein: 8 g; Fat: 16.9 g; Calories: 197
Made with Splenda only: Add 0.8 g carbohydrates

JUDI'S BLUEBERRY ALMOND FLAX BREAD

Makes 12 slices

Judi, a longtime lowcarber.org alumna, says that you can use any berry. If they're large—like strawberries or even cranberries—a rough chop before stirring them in is appropriate. If Judi wants to make this bread really special, she doubles the blueberries. If you use frozen berries, don't thaw them before adding to the batter.

Serve with butter, cream cheese, or aged goat cheddar. This can be toasted, too.

3		large eggs
6 Tbsp.	(90 ml)	vegetable oil
¼ cup	(60 ml)	whipping cream
1 tsp.	(5 ml)	pure almond extract
1 cup	(240 ml)	almond meal (finely ground almonds)
1 cup	(240 ml)	whey protein isolate
¾ cup	(180 ml)	flaxseed meal
2½ tsp.	(12.5 ml)	baking powder
1½ tsp.	(7.5 ml)	ground cinnamon
¼ tsp.	(1.2 ml)	sea salt
2 Tbsp.	(30 ml)	*each* Splenda and Canadian Sugar Twin *or* ½ cup (120 ml) Splenda
1 cup	(240 ml)	fresh or frozen blueberries

◦§ Preheat the oven to 325°F (165°C). Line an 8 × 4-inch (20 × 10-cm) loaf pan with a length of parchment paper that will cover the bottom and sides. Don't worry about the ends. Coat with nonstick spray.

◦§ In a medium bowl, beat the eggs, oil, cream, and almond extract until smooth.

◦§ In a large bowl, mix the almond meal, whey protein, flaxseed meal, baking powder, cinnamon, salt, and sweetener. Gently stir in the egg mixture until the dry ingredients are thoroughly moistened but still lumpy. Fold in the blueberries just until evenly distributed. The batter will be quite wet.

◦§ Scrape the batter into the prepared pan and smooth the top. With a paring knife, cut a slash—go right down to the bottom of the pan—down the middle of the batter lengthwise. This will give the bread a nice mounded top.

◦§ Bake for 45 minutes, or until golden brown and the top springs back when pressed lightly. Cool on a wire rack for 5 minutes, then loosen the sides carefully with a knife. Unmold onto the rack and cool before slicing. Store in the refrigerator.

Per slice. Effective carbohydrates: 3.5 g; Carbohydrates: 7 g; Fiber: 3.5 g; Protein: 6.5 g; Fat: 17 g; Calories: 199
Made with Splenda only: Add 0.5 g carbohydrates

VARIATION

Blueberry Almond Flax Muffins: Butter or oil a 12-cup nonstick muffin pan. Evenly divide the batter among the cups, filling them three-quarters full. Bake at 325°F (165°C) for 15 to 20 minutes, or until golden brown and the tops spring back when pressed lightly.

Per muffin. Effective carbohydrates: 3.5 g; Carbohydrates: 7 g; Fiber: 3.5 g; Protein: 6.5 g; Fat: 17 g; Calories: 199
Made with Splenda only: Add 0.5 g carbohydrates

TAMARIAN'S PEANUT BUTTER–FROSTED BROWNIES

Makes 24 brownies

These cake-type brownies get raves. You can use almond or hazelnut butter in place of the peanut butter. Roasted almond butter is my favorite for a sophisticated chocolate icing.

Tamarian is the founder and Webmaster of lowcarber.org and a wonderfully intuitive cook. Be sure to try his Upside-Down Shepherd's Pie (pages 198 to 199).

BROWNIES

3		large eggs
8 Tbsp.	(120 ml)	unsalted butter, melted (1 stick)
¼ cup	(60 ml)	water
3 Tbsp.	(45 ml)	sour cream
2 Tbsp.	(30 ml)	*each* Splenda and Canadian Sugar Twin *or* ½ cup (120 ml) Splenda
1 tsp.	(5 ml)	pure vanilla extract
½ cup	(120 ml)	almond meal (finely ground almonds)
½ cup	(120 ml)	oat flour
¼ cup	(60 ml)	Dutch-processed cocoa powder
1½ tsp.	(7.5 ml)	baking powder

FROSTING

1 oz.	(28 g)	unsweetened chocolate
1 Tbsp.	(15 ml)	natural peanut butter
¼ cup	(60 ml)	whipping cream
1 Tbsp.	(15 ml)	*each* Splenda and Canadian Sugar Twin *or* ¼ cup (60 ml) Splenda

◈ Preheat the oven to 350°F (175°C). Butter a 9 × 9-inch (22.5 × 22.5-cm) baking pan.

◈ *To make the brownies:* In a large bowl, beat the eggs for a few minutes until light and fluffy. Add the butter, water, sour cream, sweetener, and vanilla. Beat until combined.

◈ In a small bowl, mix the almond meal, oat flour, cocoa, and baking powder. Add to the egg mixture and beat until well-blended. Pour the batter into the prepared baking pan.

◈ Bake for 25 minutes, until the top is firm. Let cool on a wire rack.

◈ *To make the frosting:* Melt the chocolate in a heatproof bowl over simmering water or in the microwave. Stir in the peanut butter until melted, then stir in the cream and sweetener. Pour over the cooled brownies and spread evenly. Let the frosting set before cutting.

Per brownie. Effective carbohydrates: 2.5 g; Carbohydrates: 3.1 g; Fiber: 0.6 g; Protein: 2.3 g; Fat: 8.3 g; Calories: 93
Made with Splenda only: Add 0.3 g carbohydrates

MY BROWNIES

Makes 48 brownies

These are decadently dense, rich, and moist.

10 oz.	(285 g)	cream cheese, at room temperature
16 Tbsp.	(240 ml)	unsalted butter, at room temperature (2 sticks)
4 oz.	(112 g)	unsweetened chocolate, melted and cooled
¼ cup	(60 ml)	*each* Splenda and Canadian Sugar Twin *or* 1 cup (240 ml) Splenda
4		large eggs
2 tsp.	(10 ml)	instant coffee granules
1½ tsp.	(7.5 ml)	pure vanilla extract
1½ tsp.	(7.5 ml)	pure chocolate extract (optional)
1½ cups	(360 ml)	almond meal (finely ground almonds)
6 Tbsp.	(90 ml)	Dutch-processed cocoa powder
¼ tsp.	(1.2 ml)	sea salt
1½ tsp.	(7.5 ml)	baking powder

⋅§ Preheat the oven to 350°F (175°C). Butter a 13 × 9-inch (32.5 × 22.5-cm) baking pan and line the bottom with parchment paper.

⋅§ In a large bowl, beat the cream cheese and butter until smooth. Beat in the chocolate and sweetener. Beat in the eggs, 1 at a time, scraping the bowl well after each addition. Add the coffee and extracts. Beat until combined.

⋅§ In a medium bowl, mix the almond meal, cocoa, salt, and baking powder. Add to the chocolate mixture and beat well. Scrape into the prepared pan and smooth the top.

⋅§ Bake for 35 to 40 minutes, until the top is firm. Cool on a wire rack before cutting. Store, covered, in the refrigerator.

Per brownie. Effective carbohydrates: 1.5 g; Carbohydrates: 2.1 g; Fiber: 0.6 g; Protein: 2.1 g; Fat: 9.7 g; Calories: 99
Made with Splenda only: Add 0.3 g carbohydrates

RECIPE NUTRIENTS AT A GLANCE

This table provides a summary of the nutrient information on all the recipes from the lowest carbohydrate counts to the highest.

NIBBLES AND DIPS

Recipe	Page #	ECC	Carb	Fiber	Pro	Fat	Cal
Buttery Tuna and Caper Mousse	32	0.1	0.2	0.1	4.3	8.4	93
Tuna-Stuffed Eggs	42	0.3	0.3	0.0	7.4	6.9	93
Black Soybean Dip	32	0.4	0.7	0.3	1.3	2.3	27
Guacamole	27	0.4	1.1	0.7	0.3	2.3	24
Shrimp and Nori Rolls	34	0.5	1.5	1.0	6.8	4.0	71
Mushroom Tapenade	22	0.6	0.9	0.3	0.8	6.9	66
Parmesan-Stuffed Eggs with Toasted Almonds	41	0.7	1.0	0.3	4.8	14.5	153
Warm Spinach Dip	30	0.9	1.3	0.4	2.2	3.6	45
Hummus	23	1.0	1.4	0.4	1.4	2.3	30
Nori and Sesame Crisps with Miso Cream Cheese	36	1.1	2.9	1.8	3.0	8.9	100
French Onion Dip	31	1.8	2.3	0.5	0.6	4.4	49
Prawns with Peppery Garlic Vinaigrette	26	2.2	2.3	0.1	27.8	13.2	244
Caponata	44	2.6	3.8	1.1	0.7	4.0	53
Antipasto Skewers	33	3.4	5.1	1.7	6.0	9.5	129
Five-Spice Sesame Walnuts	28	3.4	5.5	2.1	6.6	23.7	243
Edamame	38	5.0	9.0	4.0	8.0	3.0	100
Stir-Fried Edamame with Garlic, Chiles, and Soy	39	5.5	9.7	4.2	9.2	7.7	149

WHAT'S FOR BREAKFAST?

Recipe	Page #	ECC	Carb	Fiber	Pro	Fat	Cals
Almond Puff Pancakes	2	0.9	1.6	0.7	2.9	0.9	84
Egg and Sausage Muffins	4	1.0	1.0	0.0	15.0	20.7	256
Cheesecake Pancakes	4	1.5	2.1	0.6	5.5	13.3	149
Just the Flax Muffins	8	2.5	10.6	8.1	9.2	7.4	183
Flax Porridge	9	2.8	13.6	10.8	11.8	7.4	147
Colin's Omega Waffles	7	3.2	8.7	5.5	8.5	16.7	207
Roasted Red Pepper and Sausage Frittata	16	3.5	4.9	1.4	27.1	35.8	455
Kristine's Asparagus and Brie Frittata	15	3.6	5.4	1.8	20.5	32.1	389
Nat's Cottage Cakes	5	3.9	5.1	1.2	9.4	7.0	120
Gra(no)la	11	4.1	9.3	5.2	14.4	14.5	206
Norma June's Spaghetti Squash Breakfast Casserole	13	5.6	6.7	1.1	5.4	19.1	216
Curried Tofu, Mushroom, and Pepper Scramble	18	6.4	11.9	5.5	28.2	22.0	329
Flax and Yogurt	10	6.7	11.2	4.5	7.4	9.5	154
Upside-Down Goat Cheese Souffle	3	6.8	5.9	0.9	18.8	32.1	387
Strawberry Cheesecake Shake	12	7.3	8.8	1.5	26.6	20.0	326

SOUPS

Recipe	Page #	ECC	Carb	Fiber	Pro	Fat	Cals
Chicken Stock	48	1.0	2.0	1.0	1.0	0.5	20
Chawan Mushi	60	1.0	1.0	0.0	6.2	4.0	68
Italian Egg Drop and Parmesan Soup	49	1.5	1.5	0.0	10.5	5.7	104
Quick Korean-Style Beef and Spinach Soup	65	2.1	3.9	1.8	19.1	19.8	274
Cream of Broccoli Soup	52	2.9	5.6	2.8	6.6	3.9	100
Escarole Soup with Turkey Meatballs	54	4.3	10.1	5.8	34.0	18.5	346
Lisa N.'s Double Italian Sausage Soup	64	4.9	6.4	1.5	26.9	47.0	559
Thai Prawn Soup	61	4.3	0.5	0.7	18.3	1.5	109
Chilled Cucumber and Avocado Soup	51	6.1	11.0	4.9	4.1	25.2	270
Daikon Radish, Chinese Cabbage, and Tofu Soup	58	6.4	9.5	3.1	13.0	4.3	129
Winter Vegetable Soup	56	8.1	11.5	3.4	9.0	5.6	135
Dottie's Cream of Mushroom Soup	53	10.3	12.0	1.6	6.6	94.9	914

SALADS AND DRESSINGS

Recipe	Page #	ECC	Carb	Fiber	Pro	Fat	Cals
Basic Vinaigrette	91	0.3	0.3	0.0	0.0	9.0	81
Thousand Island Dressing	94	0.4	0.4	0.1	0.4	7.2	67
Green Goddess Dressing	93	0.4	0.4	0.1	0.4	4.8	45
Ranch Dressing	95	0.45	0.45	0.0	0.25	7.43	67
Japanese-Style Sesame Ginger Dressing	96	0.5	0.8	0.3	0.8	4.9	48
Caesar Dressing	92	0.5	0.5	0.0	0.7	6.2	59
Creamy Sesame Miso Dressing	97	0.9	1.1	0.2	1.2	1.2	21
Blue Cheese Dressing	94	0.6	0.6	0.0	1.3	5.2	54
Cucumber Salad with Umeboshi and Bonito Flakes	77	1.4	1.9	0.5	1.4	0.2	17
Tomato, Olive, and Goat Cheese Salad with Capers	80	3.3	4.5	1.2	2.0	14.9	155
Pine Nut and Parsley Salad	68	3.6	5.6	2.0	4.3	18.3	192
Spinach Salad with Bacon, Tomato, Avocado, and Ranch Dressing	75	4.0	7.5	3.5	7.3	32.0	334
Roasted Red Pepper and Preserved Lemon Salad	79	4.5	5.7	1.2	1.3	14.3	152
Warm Cauliflower, Bacon, and Egg Salad with Spinach	71	4.6	8.6	4.0	12.6	28.0	327
Cucumber Salad with Peanuts, Coconut, and Lime	76	5.2	7.1	1.9	4.7	13.6	159
Classic Celery Root Rémoulade	82	6.0	7.1	1.1	1.8	17.3	184
Mom's Cauliflower Salad	70	5.2	8.9	3.7	6.8	15.0	191
Sesame, Snow Pea, and Daikon Radish Salad	84	5.5	8.6	3.1	3.6	10.2	137
Olive, Walnut, and Parsley Salad	81	5.8	8.8	3.0	4.5	29.2	301
Cole Slaw with Bacon Buttermilk Dressing	72	6.1	9.0	2.9	6.4	24.6	277
Warm Steak Salad with Creamy Salsa Dressing	86	7.0	10.6	3.6	42.9	17.7	375
Michelle's Broccoli and Chicken Salad	90	7.4	13.1	5.6	58.0	59.0	807
Warm Turkey, Bacon, and Mushroom Salad	85	8.6	11.5	29.0	43.8	26.5	450
Beef Salad with Creamy Horseradish Dressing	88	15.4	18.9	3.5	56.6	71.8	941

VEGETABLES

Recipe	Page #	ECC	Carb	Fiber	Pro	Fat	Cals
Tofu-lafels	138	1.1	2.1	1.1	4.3	2.9	48
To-frites	140	1.5	2.8	1.3	36.0	26.9	401
Stir-Fried Celery with Sesame	100	1.5	2.8	1.3	1.8	5.9	74

Recipe	Page #	ECC	Carb	Fiber	Pro	Fat	Cals
Buttered Sesame Kale	121	1.6	5.9	4.3	3.7	4.3	76
Broiled Spinach with Four Cheeses	129	2.0	4.5	2.5	10.5	8.2	171
Broiled Tomatoes with Goat Cheese, Pancetta, and Fennel	134	2.3	3.1	0.8	3.1	21.5	239
Chayote with Tomatoes and Mint	114	2.7	4.0	1.3	0.7	6.9	77
Broccoli Italianissimo	105	3.1	6.4	3.3	6.1	12.2	150
Green Greens Puree	122	3.1	7.8	4.7	5.0	6.4	98
Daikon Cakes	116	3.2	5.0	1.8	2.8	3.6	63
Digwig's Collaboration Lasagna Noodles	142	3.3	3.5	0.2	17.7	36.0	408
Kohlrabi with Tarragon and Dijon	125	3.5	8.0	4.5	2.3	6.0	87
Kohlrabi with Butter and Parmesan	125	3.5	7.9	4.4	4.2	7.3	106
Broccoli Dijon	104	3.8	7.2	3.4	4.0	13.1	151
Kohlrabi with Cream and Thyme	124	4.0	8.5	4.5	2.7	11.0	136
Butter-Wrinkled Beans	101	4.0	10.0	6.0	2.0	7.0	115
Korean-Style Tofu	139	4.0	7.1	3.1	26.1	27.3	363
Basic Cauli-flied "Rice"	110	4.3	7.8	3.5	3.1	8.4	109
Basic Cauliflower Mash	112	4.6	8.0	3.4	5.4	16.6	193
Zucchini, Sour Cream, and Jack Cheese Bake	135	4.7	6.3	1.6	11.3	28.8	320
Tofu "Egg" Salad	141	4.8	5.7	0.9	14.2	30.0	333
Basic Spaghetti Squash	130	5.2	6.6	1.4	0.6	0.5	29
Roasted Mushrooms with Garlic and Thyme	126	5.4	2.4	6.8	1.4	7.2	98
Kohlrabi and Celery Gratin	123	5.4	10.1	4.7	5.8	16.8	209
Spaghetti Squash, Carbonara-Style	131	5.5	6.7	1.2	6.1	13.7	170
Green Beans with Eggs and Nutmeg	103	5.9	9.7	3.8	7.0	14.5	189
Twice-Baked Cauliflower	113	5.9	9.5	3.6	13.8	26.3	320
Spaghetti Squash Arrabbiata	132	6.2	7.8	1.6	4.8	6.3	102
Scalloped Savoy Cabbage	108	6.2	8.7	2.5	6.4	38.8	398
Chayote Stuffed with Spicy Sausage	115	6.3	8.5	2.3	21.0	24.5	339
Braised Fennel with White Wine and Parmesan	120	6.7	11.3	4.6	4.6	11.8	175
Brussels Sprouts Sautéed with Garlic, Pine Nuts, and Balsamic Vinegar	106	6.8	11.8	5.0	5.0	9.6	140
Mary's Brussels Sprouts with Cream Cheese, Toasted Almonds, and Nutmeg	107	7.0	12.6	5.6	7.7	20.9	253
Tofu-roni and Cheese	136	7.5	11.4	3.9	43.6	67.7	799
Parmesan-Crusted Cauliflower	109	7.6	12.9	5.2	22.8	21.9	329
Rutabaga with Balsamic Vinegar and Browned Butter	128	7.8	12.3	4.5	1.8	13.1	161
Soy, Sake, and Butter-Glazed Mushrooms	127	8.0	9.4	1.4	4.2	7.0	144
Spicy Roasted and Mashed Eggplant	119	8.5	13.5	5.0	2.4	12.7	168
Eggplant with Sour Cream Dressing	118	8.9	13.5	4.6	3.0	6.4	116
Spinach, Ricotta, and Pesto Lasagna	143	14.5	18.0	3.5	43.3	66.6	836

FISH

Recipe	Page #	ECC	Carb	Fiber	Pro	Fat	Cals
Fresh Salmon Cakes	154	0.3	0.3	0.1	18.5	15.0	209
Doreen's Incredibly Easy Salmon or Tuna Patties (salmon)	153	0.5	0.6	0.1	10.4	10.8	142
Doreen's Incredibly Easy Salmon or Tuna Patties (tuna)	153	0.5	0.6	0.1	11.6	7.7	120
Basic Steamed Fish	146	0.8	1.5	0.7	38.0	3.9	205

FISH

Recipe	Page #	ECC	Carb	Fiber	Pro	Fat	Cal
Salmon Steaks with Ginger Butter	155	1.0	1.3	0.3	46	37.1	530
Pancetta-Wrapped Salmon with Red Wine Butter	152	1.2	1.3	0.1	38.2	39.4	315
Salmon with Bacon, Tomato, and Caper Vinaigrette	158	1.3	1.6	10.0	37.2	22.4	367
Sole with Horseradish Cream Sauce	151	1.6	1.7	0.1	31.5	23.2	345
Quick Prawns, Scampi Style	166	1.9	2.0	0.1	19.3	20.5	273
Baked Halibut with Lemon Basil Vinaigrette	148	2.1	2.5	0.4	35.7	10.7	256
Halibut with Pine Nut and Parmesan Crust	150	2.4	3.3	0.9	42.3	21.0	364
Seared Tuna with Soy Wasabi Glaze	162	2.9	3.0	0.1	40.8	32.7	475
Mussels, Pizzeria-Style	167	3.6	4.2	0.6	5.3	15.2	195
Tuna Melt	161	4.3	5.0	0.7	45.9	26.6	452
Rosebud's Tuna and Spinach Bake	160	4.6	8.7	4.1	38.7	37.0	515
Salmon with Miso Glaze	157	4.7	5.3	0.6	35.5	19.3	336
Clams Steamed with Bacon, Green Olives, and Tomatoes	164	4.7	5.2	0.5	13.4	20.7	268
Stir-Fried Prawns with Tomato Coconut Cream	165	5.6	6.1	0.5	31.5	29.3	421

CHICKEN AND TURKEY

Recipe	Page #	ECC	Carb	Fiber	Pro	Fat	Cals
90-Minute Miracle Turkey	188	0.0	0.0	0.0	58.4	33.8	554
Flat-Roasted Chicken with Prosciutto and Green Olives	172	0.4	1.2	0.8	52.4	31.2	523
Oven-Fried Chicken	178	0.9	1.3	0.4	52.8	46.9	650
Buffalo-Style Wings	176	1.3	1.3	0.0	58.3	42.3	635
Doreen's Thighs with Lime, Garlic, Sesame, and Ginger	174	1.3	1.7	0.4	27.4	21.7	317
Turkey Tenderloin with Pesto and Smoked Mozzarella	189	1.4	2.3	0.9	44.6	16.2	342
Turkey Snackin' Cake	190	1.5	2.0	0.5	14.0	11.7	170
Cinnamon-Spiced Lemon Chicken	171	1.7	2.3	0.6	31.3	32.3	429
Simple Chicken and Coconut Milk Curry	175	1.7	2.8	1.1	19.0	38.7	425
Ruth's Easy Herbed Lemon Chicken	185	1.9	2.1	0.3	39.4	2.2	194
Lemongrass Chicken	180	2.0	2.5	0.5	51.2	16.8	379
Chicken with Bacon, Cream, and Thyme	181	2.1	2.1	0.0	43.7	41.7	565
Chicken Wings in Peanut Sauce	177	2.2	3.1	0.9	63.9	53.4	760
Rosebud's Butter Chicken	179	2.7	3.8	1.1	37.7	43.1	558
One-Pot Chicken with Mushrooms and Sour Cream	170	2.7	3.2	5.1	57.0	40.5	618
Thai BBQ Chicken Bundles	186	4.6	7.2	2.6	40.4	20.2	372
Donald's Awesome Chicken and Broccoli Casserole	184	5.9	8.2	2.3	63.7	45.9	703

BEEF, PORK, AND LAMB

Recipe	Page #	ECC	Carb	Fiber	Pro	Fat	Cals
Slow-Roasted Prime Rib	195	0.0	0.0	0.0	65.7	118.9	701
Slow-Roasted Spice-Cured Pork Shoulder	211	0.0	0.0	0.0	40.0	14.6	304
Slightly Italiano Meat Loaf	206	1.0	1.2	0.2	27.6	12.7	236
Lion's Head	217	1.2	1.4	0.2	32.2	38.2	499
Pork and Shiitake Mushroom Meatballs	214	1.2	1.4	0.2	7.0	10.6	131
Grilled Flank Steak with Cumin Aioli	194	1.2	1.5	0.3	42.7	42.7	701
Cumin and Coriander-Crusted Leg of Lamb	220	1.6	2.1	0.5	42.0	36.2	512
Lamb, Feta, and Olive Meatballs	224	2.2	2.9	0.7	7.4	12.1	153
Tunisian Spice Mix	225	2.2	8.4	6.2	2.2	2.5	48

Recipe	Page #	ECC	Carb	Fiber	Pro	Fat	Cals
Pork Loin Steaks with Lemon Thyme Cream	216	3.2	3.4	0.2	37.1	29.3	429
Donald's Deep Dish Pizza Quiche	213	3.5	4.0	0.5	16.3	25.0	305
Basic Back Ribs with Quick Barbecue Glaze	208	4.0	5.0	0.0	76.0	37.0	670
Moroccan-Style Lamb Stew	221	4.3	5.4	1.1	46.6	18.8	387
Unplugged Coriander Lamb Kebabs with Tomato Vinaigrette	222	5.0	7.6	2.6	47.0	60.0	758
Meat-Lover's Pizza Crust	202	5.8	6.5	0.7	209.0	99.0	1812
Shepherd's Pie with Mushrooms, Smoked Cheddar, Bacon, and Sour Cream	196	5.8	9.1	3.3	42.9	29.5	475
Keema (Spiced Ground Beef)	200	6.6	8.1	4.5	43.7	48.3	648
Moussaka	226	7.1	10.2	2.8	42.6	46.6	633
Meat-Lover's Pizza	202	8.9	11.0	2.1	38.5	40.1	564
Tamarian's Upside-Down Shepherd's Pie	198	11.0	16.4	5.4	41.4	42.1	610
Bolognese Lasagna	205	10.5	11.5	1.0	49.8	75.7	942

SAUCES AND CONDIMENTS

Recipe	Page #	ECC	Carb	Fiber	Pro	Fat	Cals
Mayonnaise with Cooked Egg Yolk	247	0.2	0.2	0.0	0.3	10.7	100
Mayonnaise by Machine	246	0.2	0.2	0.0	0.1	9.4	85
Basil Pesto	240	0.2	0.4	0.2	0.7	5.5	52
Aioli (Garlic Mayonnaise)	248	0.3	0.3	0.0	1.0	10.7	100
Blender Hollandaise Sauce	245	0.4	0.4	0.0	1.0	10.7	100
Grainy Mustard and Vermouth Sauce	237	0.6	0.6	0.0	0.6	3.4	46
Ketchup	233	0.6	0.7	0.1	0.2	0.0	4
Roasted Almond and Parsley Pesto	238	0.6	1.2	0.6	1.5	7.6	76
Tomato Garlic Cream Sauce	244	0.7	0.8	0.1	0.6	3.6	41
Cranberry Sauce	250	0.7	1.0	0.3	0.0	0.0	5
Garam Masala	249	0.7	1.7	0.8	0.3	0.3	9
Traditional Cocktail Sauce	235	0.8	0.9	0.1	0.2	0.5	9
Fontina and Parmesan Cheese Sauce	236	1.4	1.4	0.0	8.4	21.5	230
Thai Sweet-and-Sour Chile Dipping Sauce	241	1.6	1.8	0.2	0.5	0.0	8
Fresh Tomato Sauce with Balsamic Vinegar	243	1.7	2.2	0.5	0.4	1.2	20
Basic Herb and Wine Pan Sauce	231	1.8	2.0	0.2	0.4	11.1	111
Smokey Barbecue Sauce	234	2.0	2.3	0.2	0.7	0.1	12
Simple Tomato Sauce	242	3.9	5.2	1.3	1.2	4.5	71
Quick Barbecue Glaze	210	4.1	4.6	0.4	1.7	11.2	123
Bolognese Sauce	232	4.8	6.2	1.4	15.1	25.0	333

DESSERTS

Recipe	Page #	ECC	Carb	Fiber	Pro	Fat	Cals
Chocolate Sauce	261	0.5	1.0	0.5	0.6	3.0	31
Cream Cheese, Coconut, and Lemon Mounds	288	0.6	1.0	0.4	0.8	5.4	54
Fern's Peanut Butter Cups	305	1.0	1.6	0.6	1.6	9.6	94
Stained Glass Window Cake	293	1.2	1.2	0.0	2.3	14.8	150
Mascarpone Balsamic Cream	281	1.2	1.2	0.0	1.6	10.4	104
My Brownies	312	1.5	2.1	0.6	2.1	9.7	99
Coffee Jelly	290	1.7	1.7	0.0	1.9	11.1	112
Orange Creamsicle Whip	299	2.0	2.0	0.0	2.9	26.9	260

DESSERTS

Recipe	Page #	ECC	Carb	Fiber	Pro	Fat	Cal
Quick Bread	306	2.2	3.1	1.2	8.0	14.5	185
Rhubarb Compote	279	2.3	3.3	1.0	0.5	0.1	15
Tamarian's Peanut Butter-Frosted Brownies	310	2.5	3.1	0.6	2.3	8.3	93
Ricotta Semifreddo	264	2.8	2.8	0.0	6.0	17.6	195
Chai Panna Cotta	287	2.3	2.3	0.0	6.0	22.2	212
Pumpkin Pecan Maple Bread	307	3.3	5.0	1.7	8.0	16.9	197
Lime Angel Custard	273	3.4	3.8	0.4	6.1	20.6	219
Silken Chocolate Pudding	292	3.5	5.5	2.0	4.6	21.5	220
Judi's Blueberry Almond Flax Bread	308	3.5	7.0	3.5	6.5	17.0	199
Blueberry Almond Flax Muffins	309	3.5	7.0	3.5	6.5	17.0	199
Frozen Bourbon, Chocolate, and Burnt Almond Cheesecake	266	3.6	4.5	0.9	8.0	37.0	375
Wanda's Vanilla Ice Cream	260	4.0	4.0	0.0	5.1	37.5	372
Maple Walnut Cheesecake	277	4.2	7.8	0.6	4.8	40.1	403
Dark Chocolate Bars	258	4.3	6.3	2.0	8.6	32.6	332
Avocado and Espresso Mousse	283	4.3	7.1	2.8	3.7	35.4	351
Chilled Lemon Meringue Soufflé	301	4.4	4.5	0.1	5.6	17.6	195
Raspberry Cheesecake	277	4.4	6.4	2.0	7.8	34.7	362
Vanilla Panna Cotta	286	4.5	4.5	0.0	3.3	44.4	423
Peanut Butter Doggy Bites	285	4.5	6.0	1.5	3.7	5.0	80
Gingerbread Ice Cream	263	4.6	5.1	0.5	5.2	37.6	376
No-Bake Vancouver Cheesecake	276	4.5	5.8	1.3	8.7	39.6	408
Green Tea Ice Cream	263	4.6	5.1	0.5	5.2	37.6	376
Strawberry Cheesecake	277	4.6	6.3	1.7	7.8	34.7	362
Tiramisu	294	4.7	7.9	3.2	13.8	40.8	452
Cappucino and Cocoa Nib Ice Cream	262	5.0	5.0	0.0	6.6	38.0	381
New York Cheesecake	268	5.0	5.8	0.8	13.7	44.7	473
Strawberry Ice Cream	263	5.0	5.4	0.4	5.2	37.6	378
Banana Bread	307	5.0	6.3	1.3	7.8	14.5	180
German's Chocolate Ice Cream	263	5.2	9.6	4.4	11.5	36.9	395
Maple Walnut Ice Cream	263	5.1	6.1	1.0	7.4	47.3	473
Pumpkin Panna Cotta	287	5.7	7.1	1.4	2.9	29.7	301
Lime and Coconut Cheesecake	278	5.8	6.7	0.9	6.7	34.6	349
Chocolate Ice Cream	262	5.9	6.9	2.1	8.7	45.3	446
Chocolate Chunk Ice Cream	262	5.9	6.9	1.0	8.7	54.6	536
Fresh Berries with Cool Champagne Sabayon	291	6.6	10.5	3.9	4.0	18.5	229
Peanut Butter Cheesecake	278	6.7	8.7	2.0	11.8	42.6	457
Espresso Panna Cotta with Chocolate Sauce	287	7.4	9.8	2.4	6.0	57.0	555
Chocolate Bourbon Bread Pudding	300	7.5	12.0	4.5	15.0	36.4	411
Berry Lemon Pie	284	7.7	10.8	3.1	9.6	50.4	529
German's Chocolate Cheesecake	270	8.8	14.3	5.5	16.7	67.0	697
Strawberry Shortcakes with Mascarpone Balsamic Cream	280	9.3	12.4	3.1	19.2	55.2	608
Pumpkin Chiffon Pie	296	9.7	14.3	4.6	11.8	45.3	495
Zucchini Cake	303	10.1	14.7	4.6	16.9	71.5	748
Orange Cream Cheese Frosting	304	10.1	14.7	4.7	16.9	71.6	748
Basic Almond Crust	282	17.9	37.0	19.1	42.8	117.8	1356
Basic Almond Sponge Cake	295	19.7	29.5	9.8	62.6	93.4	1176
Lemon Curd	284	25.3	27.2	1.9	25.9	153.2	1592

INDEX